IMAGES
of America

NORTON

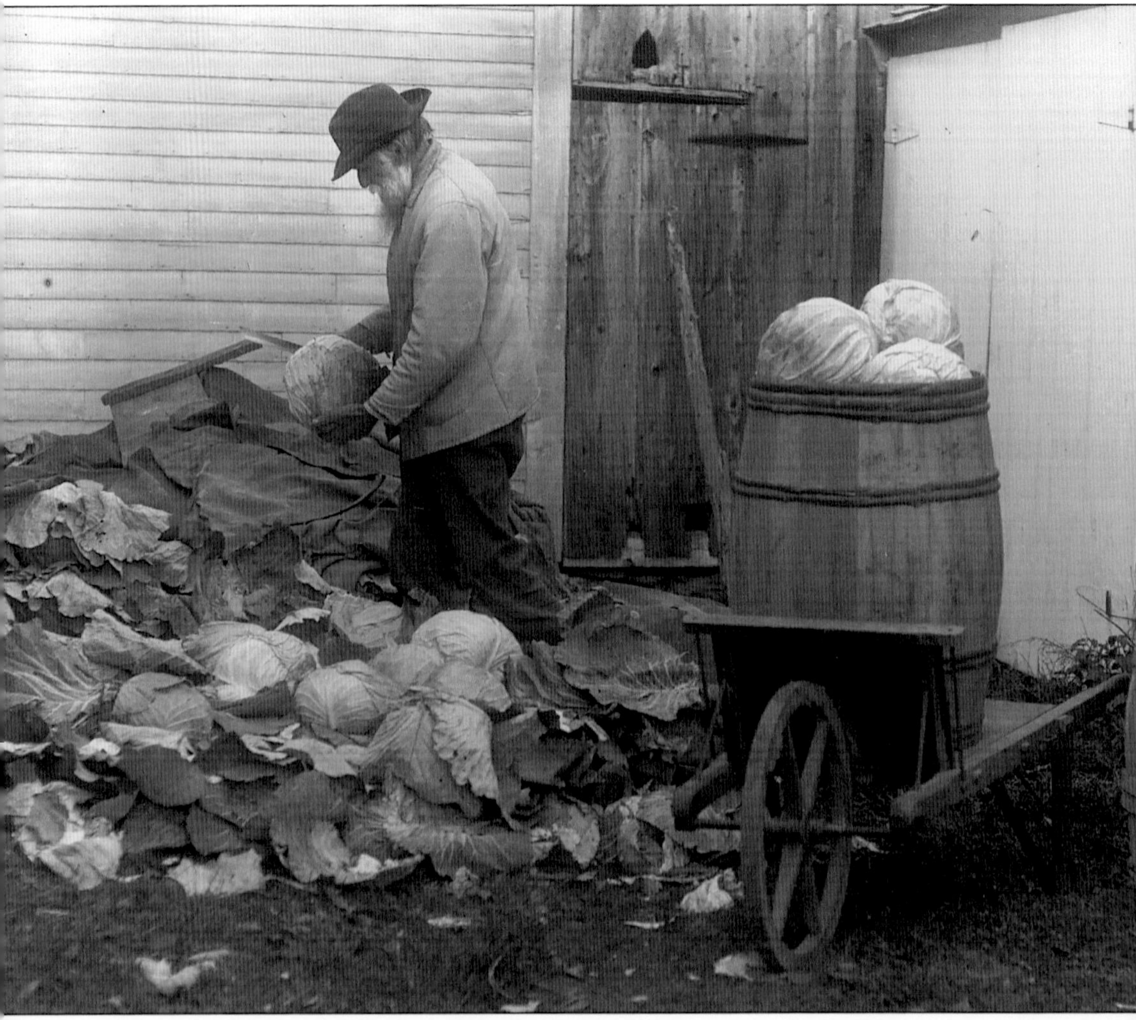

This photograph made from an Elmer Bruce glass negative depicts the harvesting of cabbages at the Bruce Farm in East Norton for the local markets.

On the cover: Elmer Bruce was a basket maker. His father, George, began the basket-making industry in a shop across the street from the family farm on North Washington Street.

IMAGES
of America

NORTON

George A. Yelle and Ruth E. Goold

ARCADIA
PUBLISHING

ISBN 978-0-7385-0264-9

Published by Arcadia Publishing
Charleston, South Carolina

Printed in the United States of America

Library of Congress Catalog Card Number: 99-069228

For all general information contact Arcadia Publishing at:
Telephone 843-853-2070
Fax 843-853-0044
E-mail sales@arcadiapublishing.com
For customer service and orders:
Toll-Free 1-888-313-2665

Visit us on the Internet at www.arcadiapublishing.com

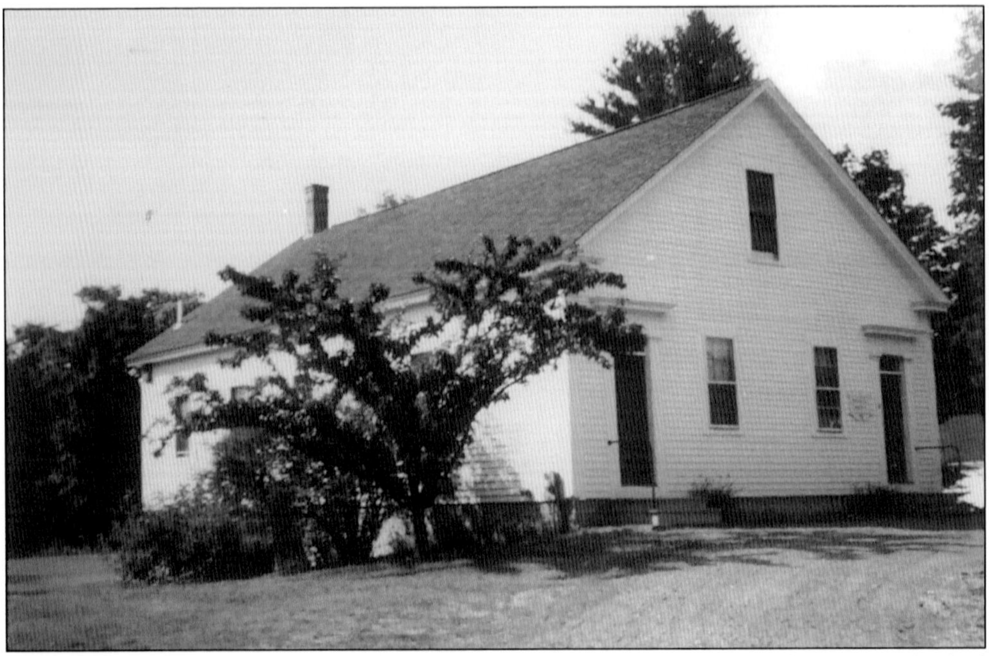

This book is dedicated to the founding members of the Norton Historical Society, who had the vision to preserve the history of our town. The members purchased the District No. 3 Schoolhouse and moved it to Norton Center for their headquarters and the town museum.

Contents

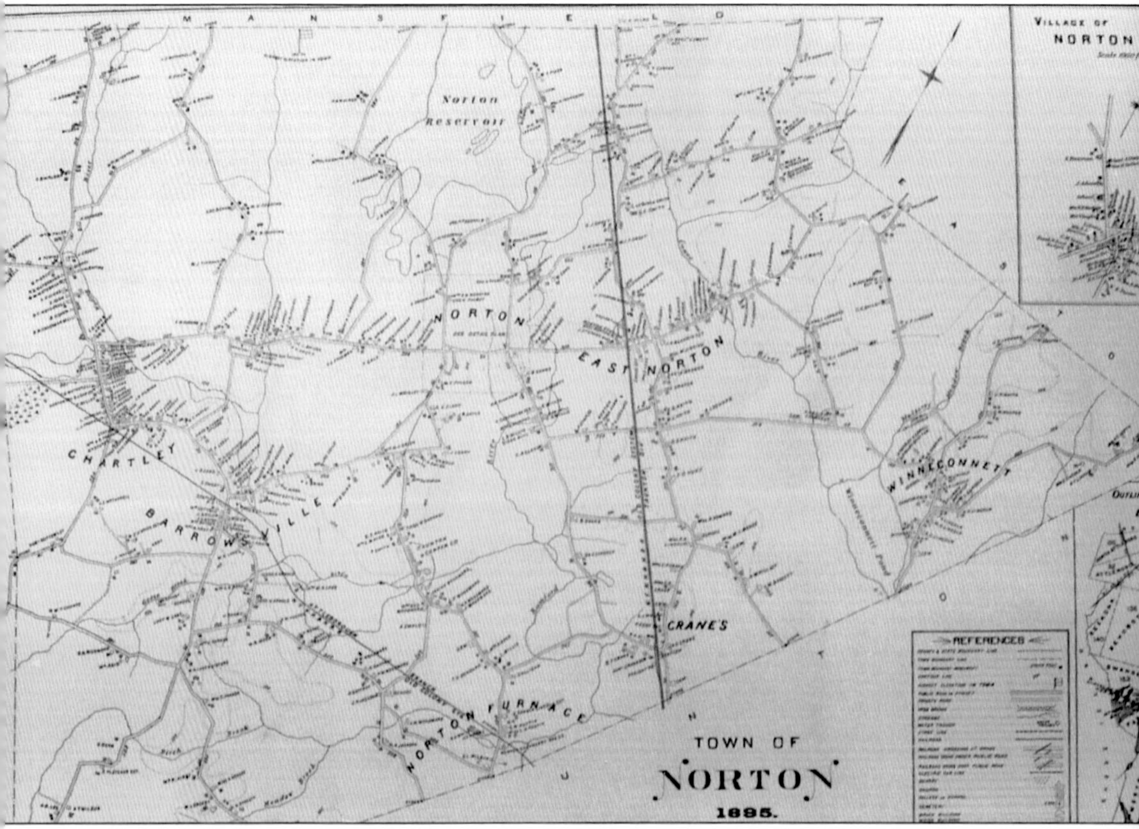

This 1895 map shows the location of the villages in the town of Norton. Note the spelling used for the village currently known as Winnecunnet; this map spells the town name as Winneconnett. Maps from 1830 to 1855 used the spelling Winnicunnet. A map from 1871 wrote the name as Winnicunnett.

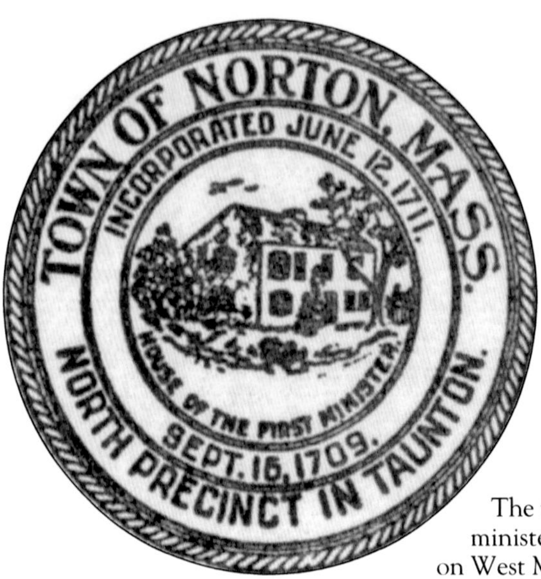

The town seal depicts the house of Norton's first minister, Rev. Joseph Avery; the house is located on West Main Street in Norton Center.

Introduction

The area known today as the town of Norton was originally part of the Taunton North Purchase. As more families settled in this area, the people wanted to form either their own town or a separate precinct. The main reasons were the distance and the poor roads that made it most inconvenient to attend church services in Taunton. The settlers petitioned for a minister, church, and the right to become a precinct. Thus, in 1709, this area became known as the North Precinct of Taunton.

On June 12, 1711, the said North Precinct was incorporated as the Town of Norton. The town built its first church on Norton Common. Rev. Joseph Avery was ordained as the first minister of the First Church of Christ in Norton. In later years, Mansfield and Easton were formed from the north and east sections of Norton.

Norton's composition is unique, as it developed by villages. Each village formed with its own characteristics and heritage. Some villages had their own post offices, railroad stations, fire stations, and schools. Some of the villages were composed of immigrant groups depending on the industries that situated in the area.

The chapters of this book depict with photographs an overall view of these villages during a period of time from 1870 to 1970. This book conveys a pictorial exhibit of the families, activities, buildings, and industries found in each of these villages. By viewing these villages through images, the reader can better visualize Norton slowly transforming from a rural, agricultural community into a town of small mills, industries, and businesses.

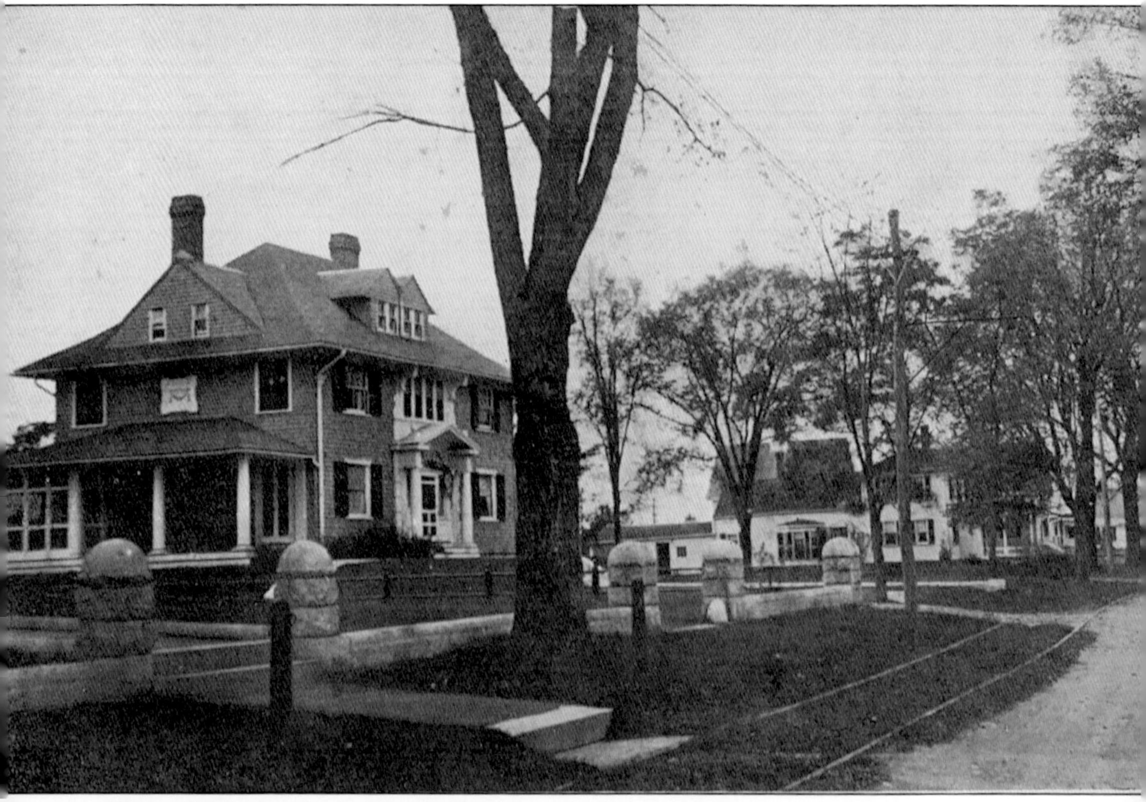

This *c.* 1915 view shows Mansfield Avenue at Norton Center.

ACKNOWLEDGMENTS

The authors are grateful to the following, who provided information, photographs, and encouragement: Robert Lanpher; Zephorene Stickney, Wheaton College archivist; permission to publish Wheaton photographs from the Gebbie Archives of the Wallace Library at Wheaton College in Norton, Massachusetts; and the Norton Historical Society photograph collection and archives.

One
NORTON CENTER

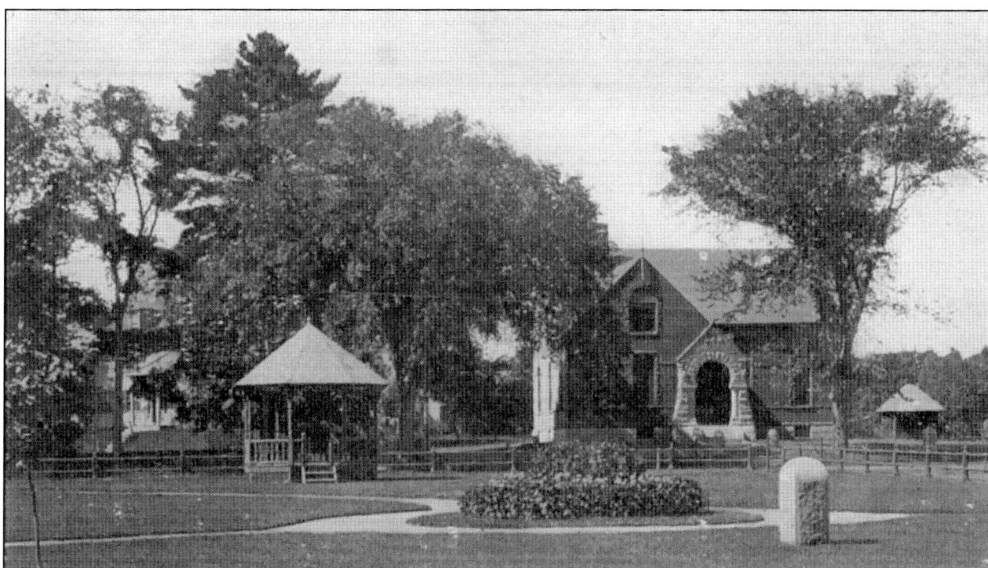

The common is the focal spot of Norton Center. Two main roads intersect nearby; several old, well-maintained houses, a church, a bank, and a library circle the common. A monument depicting the site of the first Christian church in Norton can be found on the common. The bandstand was the scene of many ceremonies and festivities through the years. The handsome brick and brownstone building facing the common was the town's public library. Designed by Stephen C. Earle and given to the town by Eliza B. Wheaton, the library was dedicated in 1888. A fine old cast-iron fence surrounds the common.

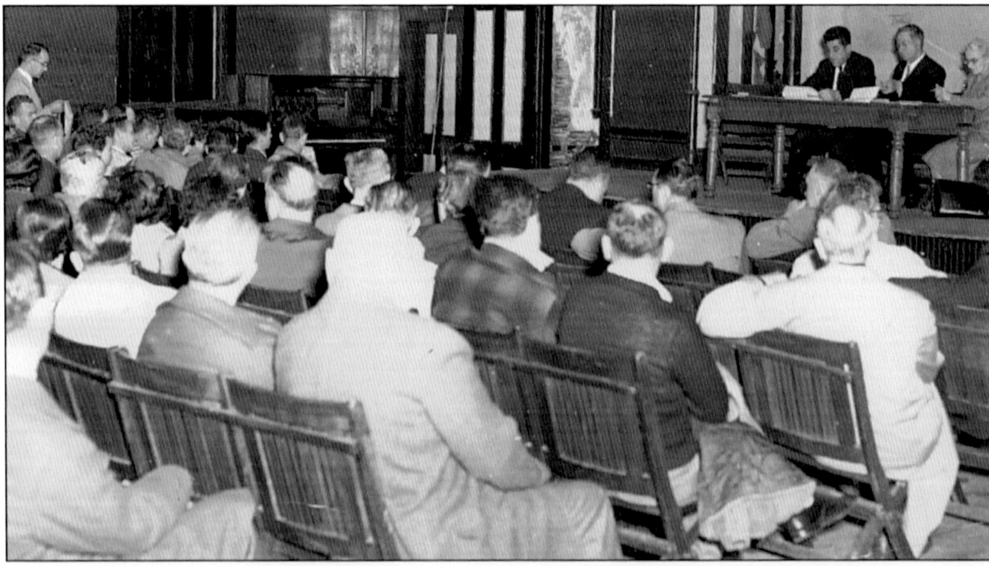

In the early years, town meetings were held at the Newcomb Town Hall on Taunton Avenue. Shown here, on April 29, 1955, is the next to last meeting to be held at that town location. On stage, from left to right, are Dr. Arthur Parker, moderator; Lester Johnson, town clerk; and Doris Durgin, Johnson's assistant. Standing at the far left is finance committee member Joe Yelle.

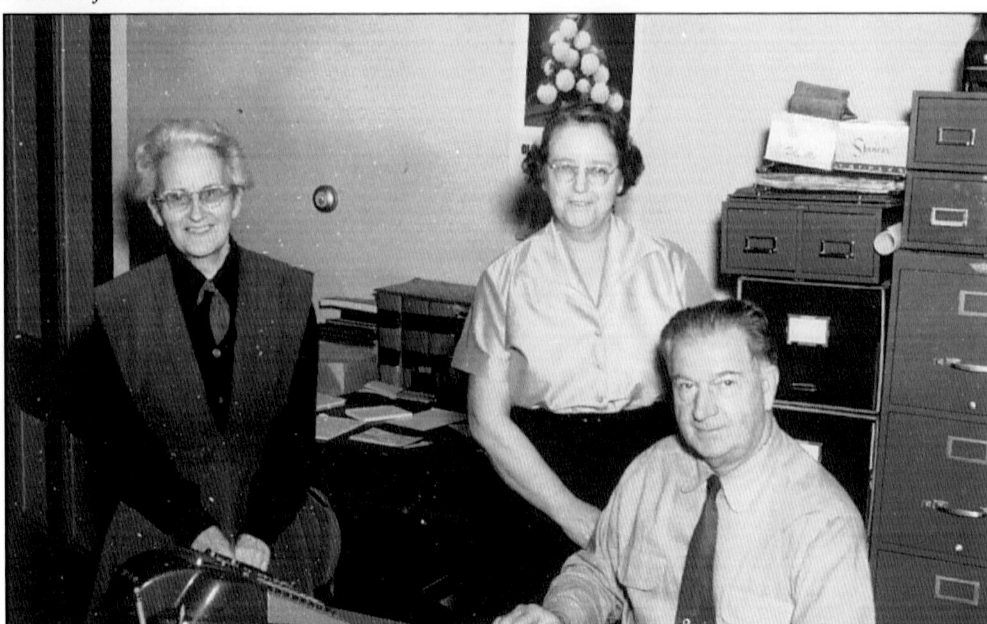

For many years these three were familiar faces in the town clerk's office. Lester Johnson served as town clerk, treasurer, and tax collector for 18 years. Doris Durgin, left, served as Johnson's assistant; she also enjoyed playing the drums and formed a small band called the Merry Maids. Annie Johnson, center, served as secretary and was also a correspondent for area newspapers for 41 years. As justice of the peace, Lester, along with his wife Annie, welcomed more than 2,000 couples to their home to be married.

In Norton during the early years, deputies and sheriffs were the law enforcement officers. Records show that as early as 1757, Benjamin Williams was deputy sheriff. In the 1800s, men were appointed as constables each year at town meeting. Frank A. Clapp served as constable from 1883 until 1944. Benjamin B. Scanlon served asconstable for 40 years. He was appointed the town's first chief of police in 1916. Scanlon retired in June 1949. He lived in the white house at Library Square, where Makepeace Hall was located.

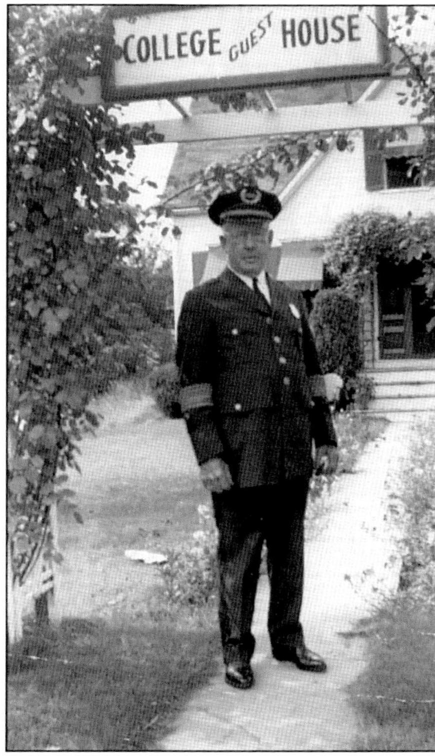

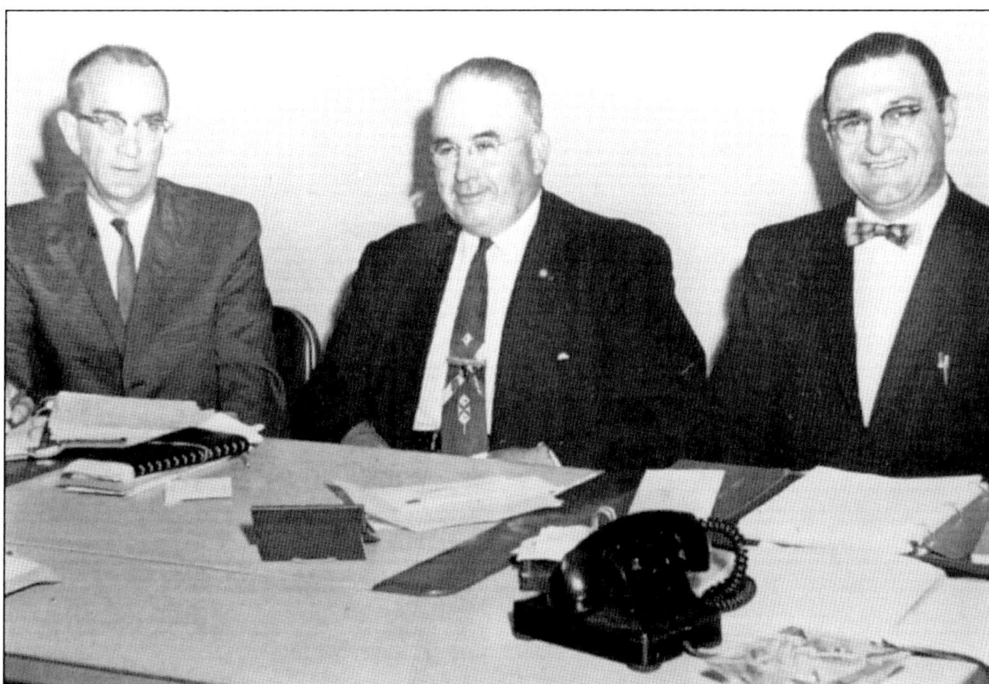

Three men who served their town for many years as selectmen were Joseph E. Yelle, John B. Scott, and Clarence P. Rich. Yelle was also postmaster of Norton. Scott was a selectman for 27 years. Rich was a selectman for 15 years.

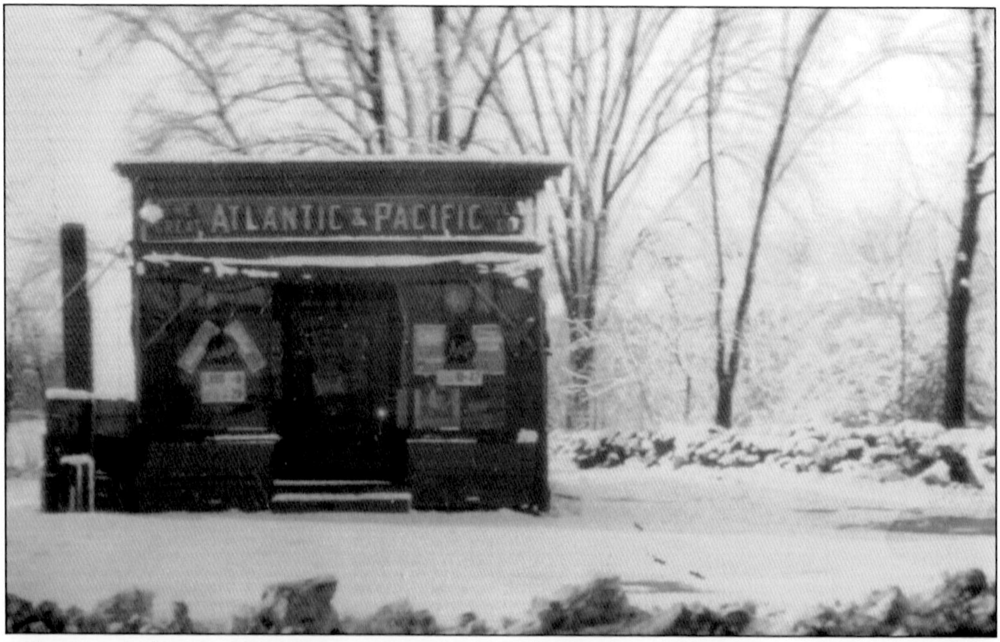

Milton and Agnes Alger began managing an A&P store on Taunton Avenue in 1922. Dr. Edgar Parks named the Wheaton College-owned house across the street "Ocean View" because it faced the Atlantic & Pacific store. When the A&P chain discontinued the business in 1939, the store became Alger's Market for several years and later was affiliated with IGA. In the 1960s, the Algers sold the market to John Fonseca, who renamed the store Fonseca's Food Center.

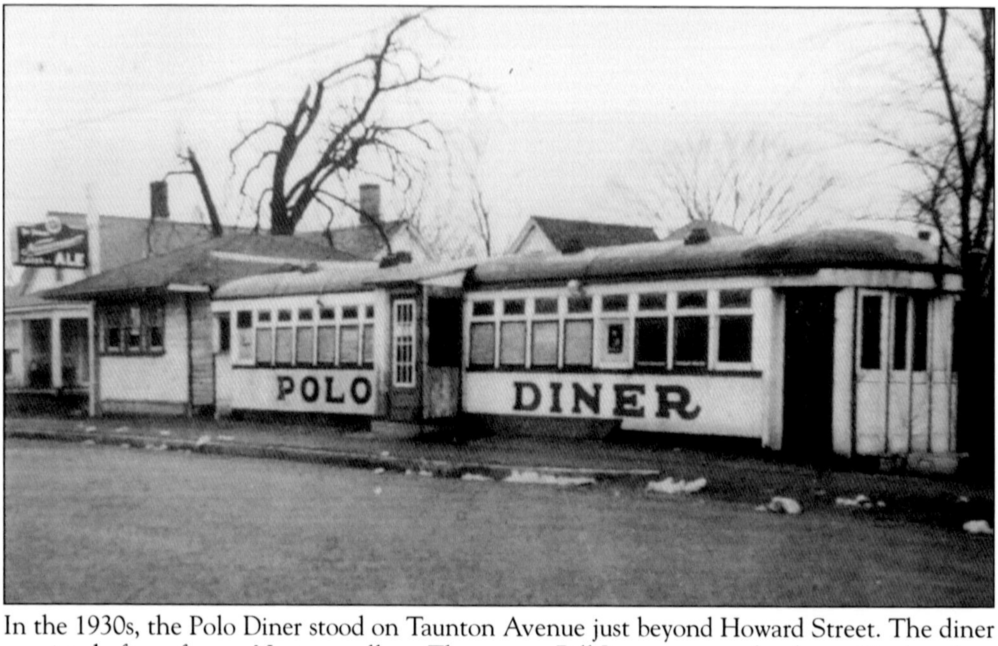

In the 1930s, the Polo Diner stood on Taunton Avenue just beyond Howard Street. The diner consisted of two former Norton trolleys. The owner, Bill Jette, was a polo player. Displayed on the walls of his diner was a collection of photographs showing him in his polo attire on the many horses that he rode during polo matches.

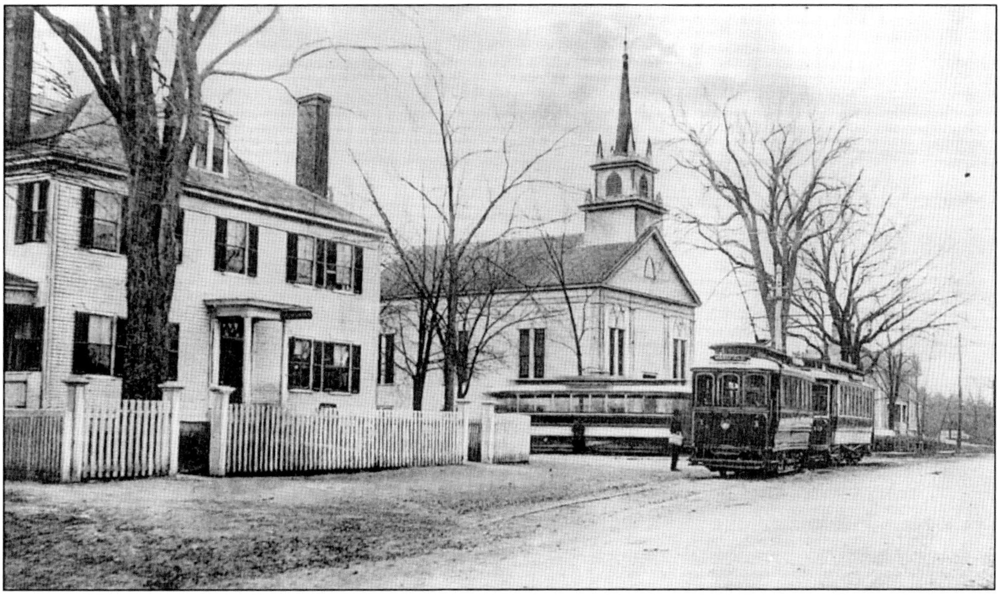

This early view of the center shows where the trolleys stopped in front of the Wheaton Inn. The former Wheaton family homestead had been a boardinghouse before it became an inn. A Paul Revere & Son bell hangs in the steeple of the First Congregational (Unitarian) Parish Church. Center School can be seen just beyond the trolleys.

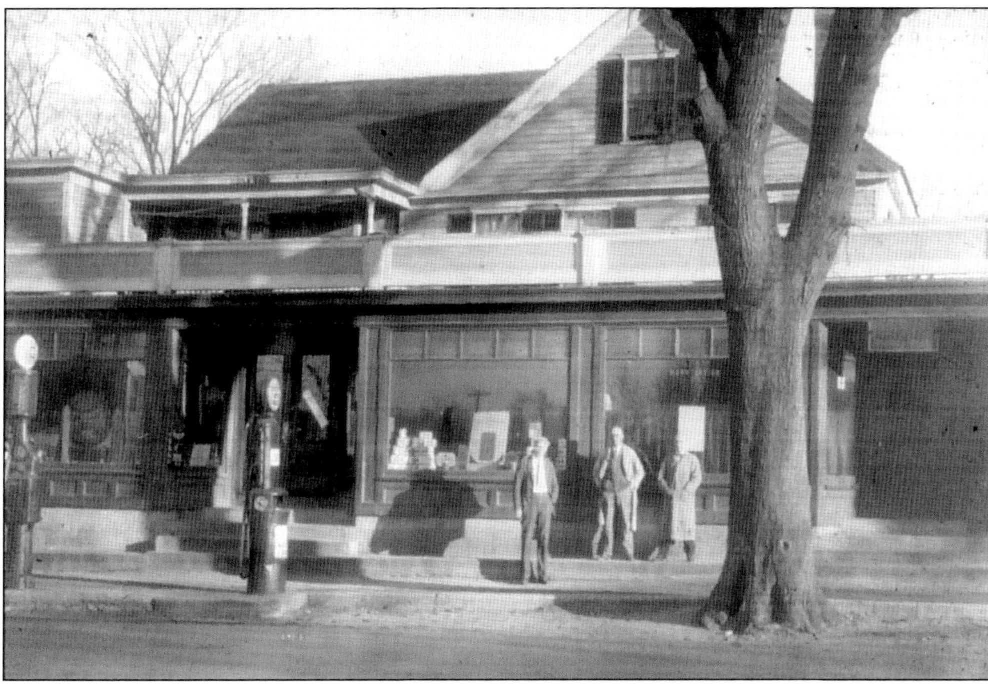

Pratt's Store was a landmark at the center until it was razed in 1963. A general country store, it had been managed under different ownership since the 1860s. For a few years, John C. Pratt, one of the last owners, was also postmaster of the Norton Post Office, which was adjacent to the store. Shown, from left to right, are Pratt; Albert Hopkins, postmaster; and G. Lester Hewitt, postal clerk. Gasoline pumps can be seen in front of the store.

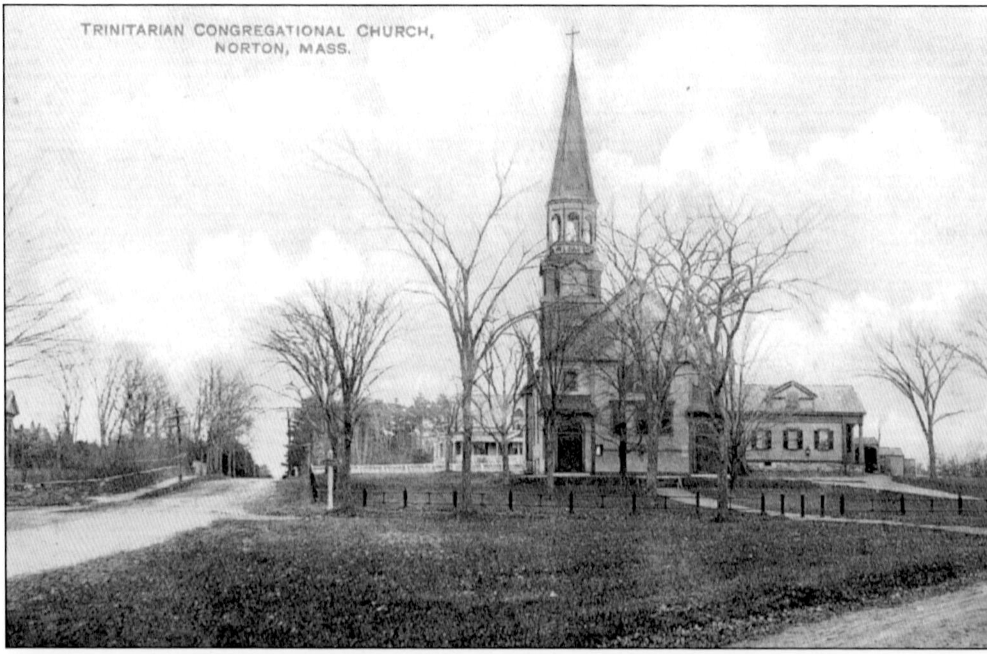

In 1832, the Trinitarian Congregational Church was organized in Norton; its first meetinghouse was built in 1834. In 1878, Eliza B. Wheaton had Wheaton College's old gymnasium moved and attached to the church's main sanctuary. In 1882, she had the entire church rebuilt at her own expense and also furnished a Howard clock for its tower. The famous architect Stephen C. Earle designed this early Colonial Revival building.

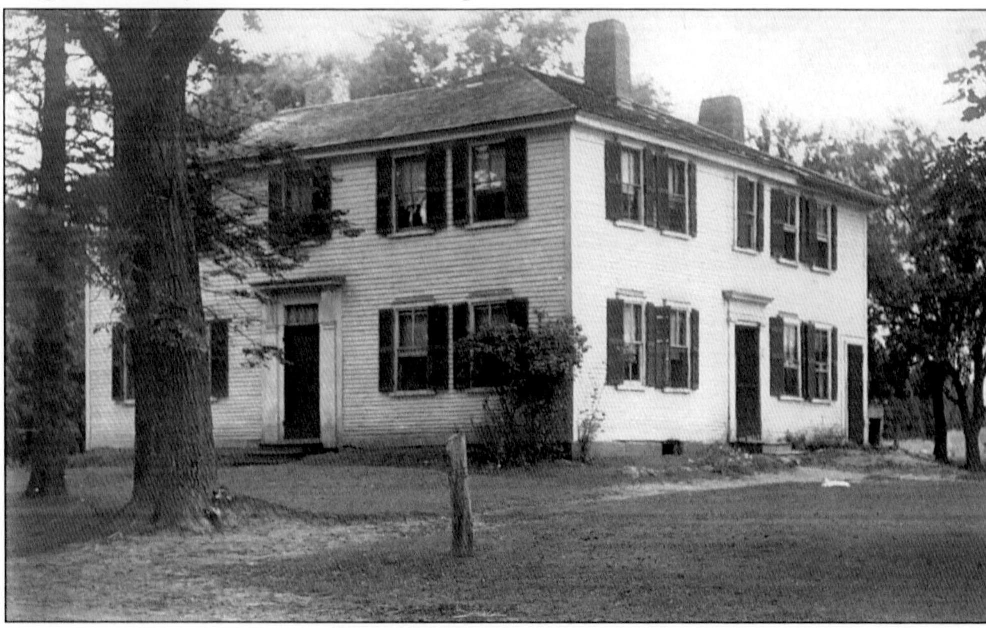

The Earl P. White House is located on Pine Street. In 1817, Norton's first post office was set up in this house with Earl White as the first postmaster. The mail was first brought to town about once a week from Taunton on horseback. Then, previous to the opening of the railroad station at East Norton, the mail was delivered by stagecoach two or three times a week.

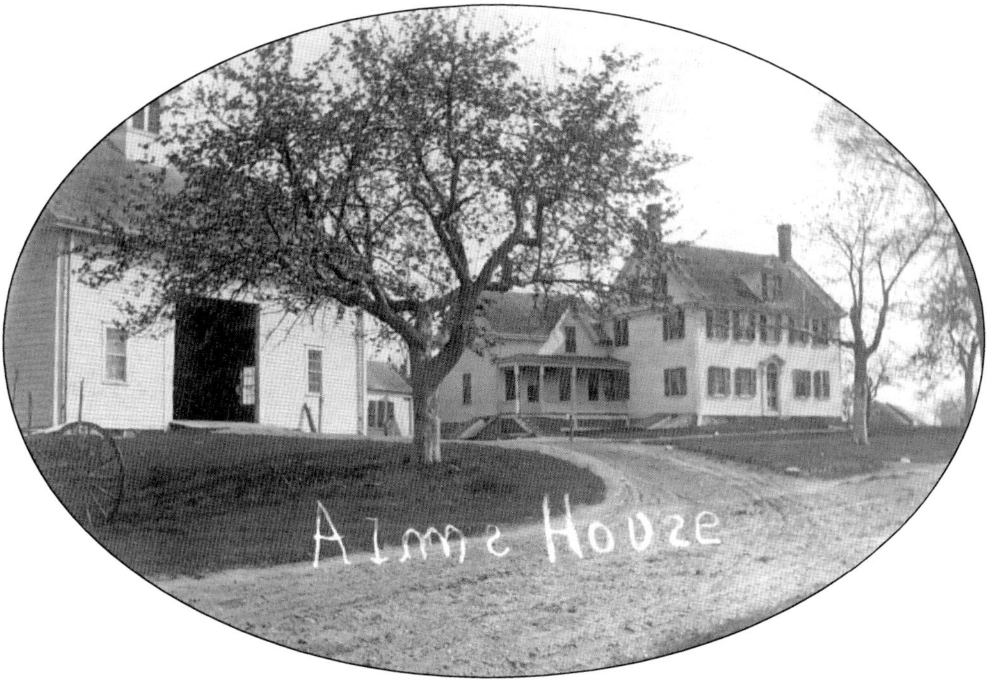

As early as 1776, there was discussion at town meetings to consider having an almshouse for the reception of the poor. It was not until 1837, however, that the town voted to purchase the John Hall Farm on Reservoir Street for that purpose. That building remained the poor farm until the town bought the Charles H. Makepeace Farm on Plain Street. This new farm, shown here, served as the almshouse from 1895 to 1910.

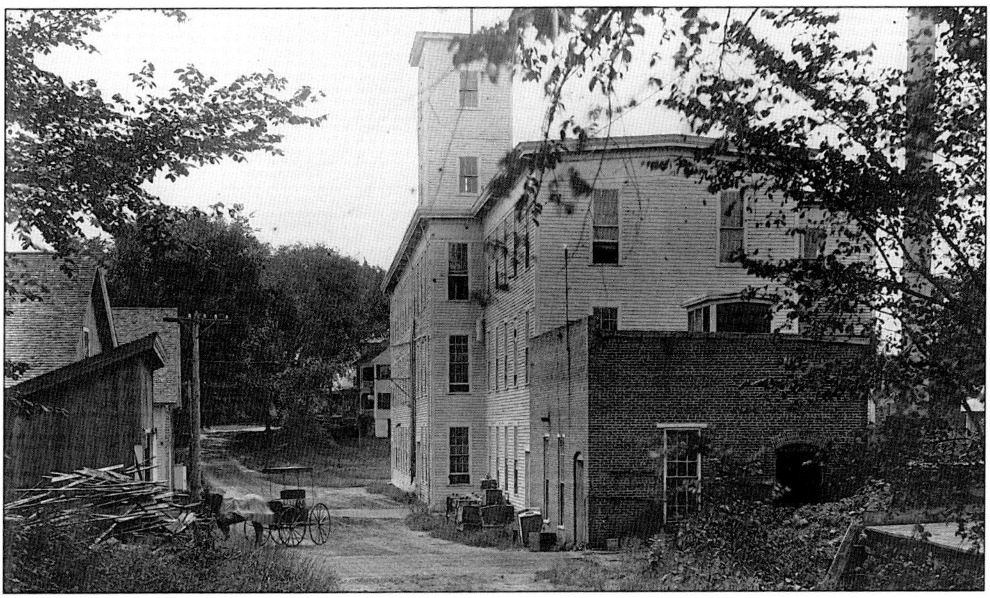

On Elm Street, a cotton factory was built by the Rumford River. The Centre Mills became a part of the Norton Mills Company. When George H. Talbot took charge of the company in 1868, he developed the Talbot Wool Combing Company. In 1958, the yarn division of Draper Brothers Company was established at this location.

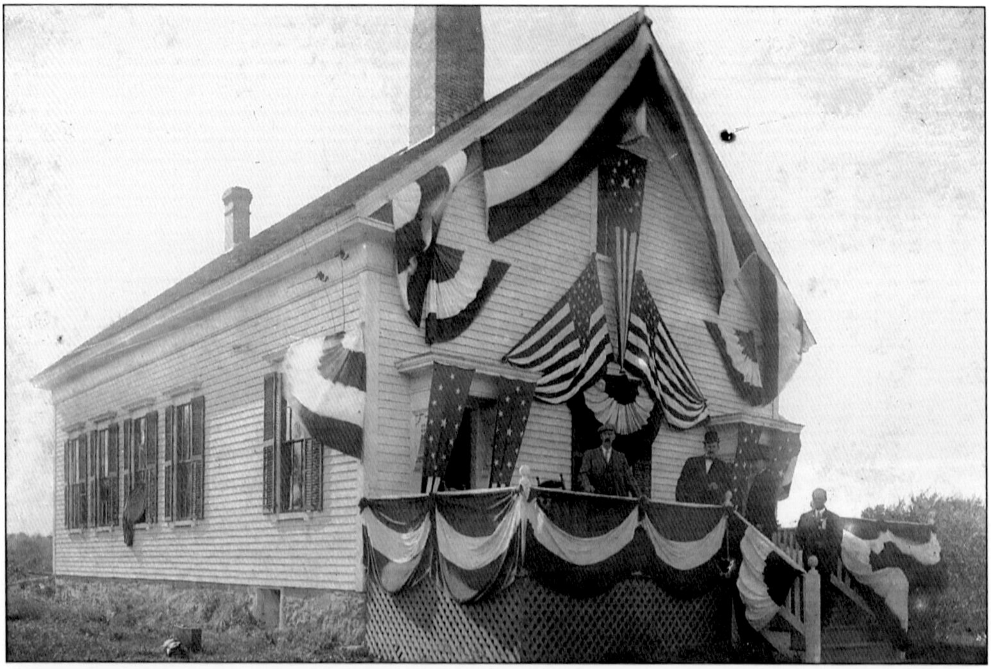

Norton had eight one-room schoolhouses, as the town was divided into eight school districts in 1781. The No. 1, Center District, Schoolhouse was located on Mansfield Avenue. The schoolhouse is shown here decorated for the town's 200th anniversary in 1911. The school closed in 1903 after the Center School was built on West Main Street, and it became the home of the Norton Grange.

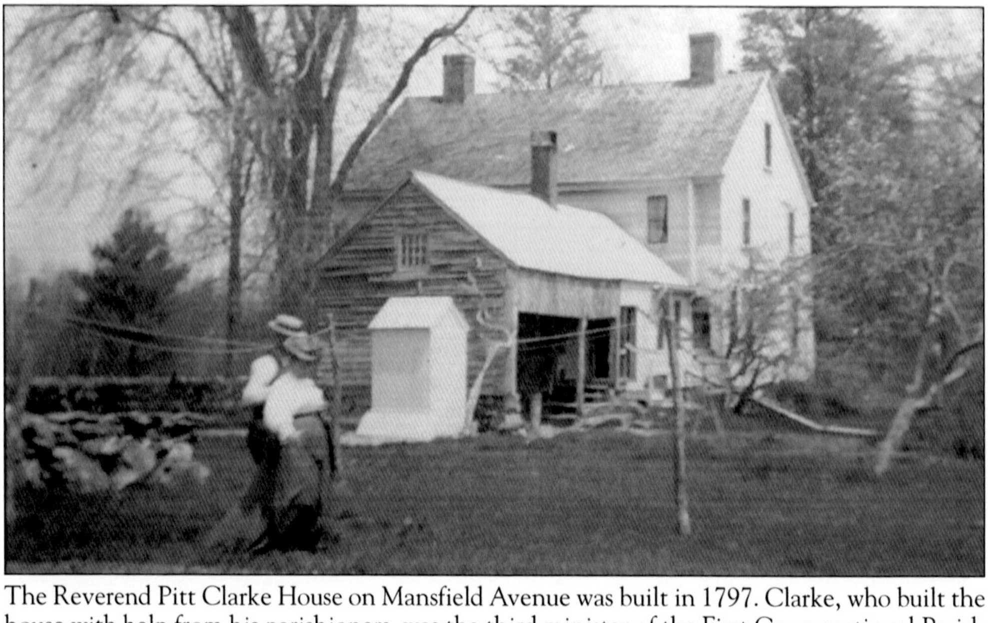

The Reverend Pitt Clarke House on Mansfield Avenue was built in 1797. Clarke, who built the house with help from his parishioners, was the third minister of the First Congregational Parish in Norton. After his death in 1835, the house passed through the hands of two families before it belonged to Nathaniel Freeman and his family for more than 90 years. The Freemans kept prize oxen on their farm.

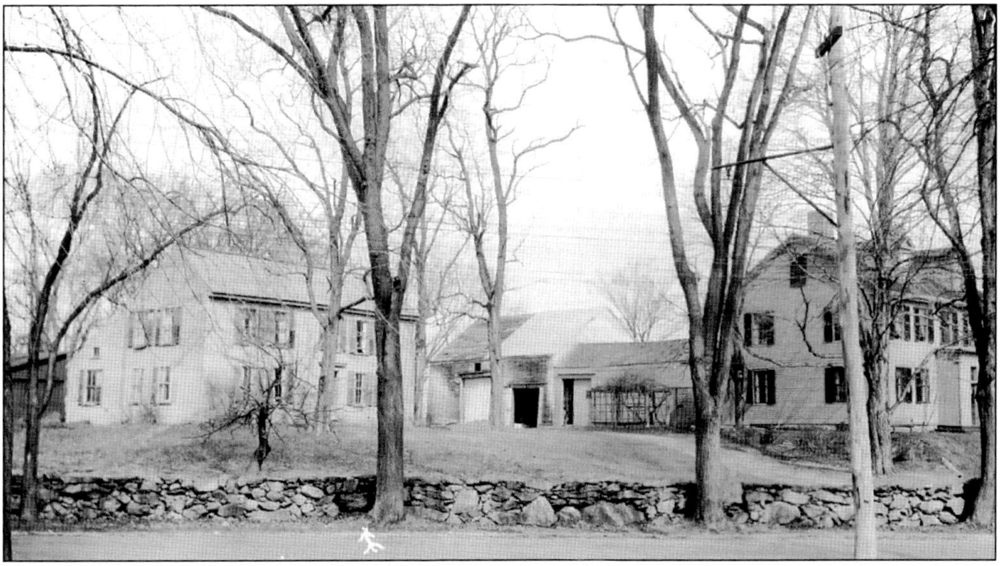

At the center can be seen the Old Parsonage, which was the home of Norton's first minister, Rev. Joseph Avery. To the right of the house is the Capt. Dauphin King House. King was a sea captain who died in 1852, during a voyage to Rio de Janeiro.

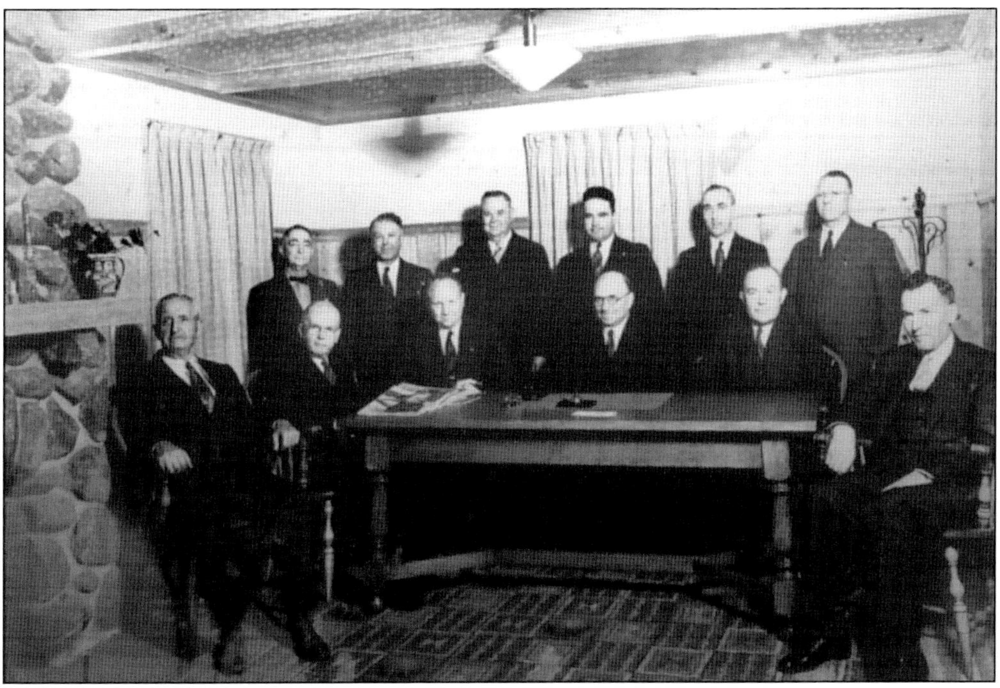

The Norton Savings and Loan Association was formed in 1890 by four leading businessmen of Norton: Austin Messinger, Andrew H. Sweet, George H. Talbot, and William A. Sturdy. The association was organized so that the people of Norton might avail themselves of the opportunity to buy and build homes. The first office was at the Wetherell store in Chartley. In 1938, the association moved to a new Cape Cod-style building next to the Unitarian church. In 1940, it celebrated its 50th anniversary with the men in this photograph on the board of directors.

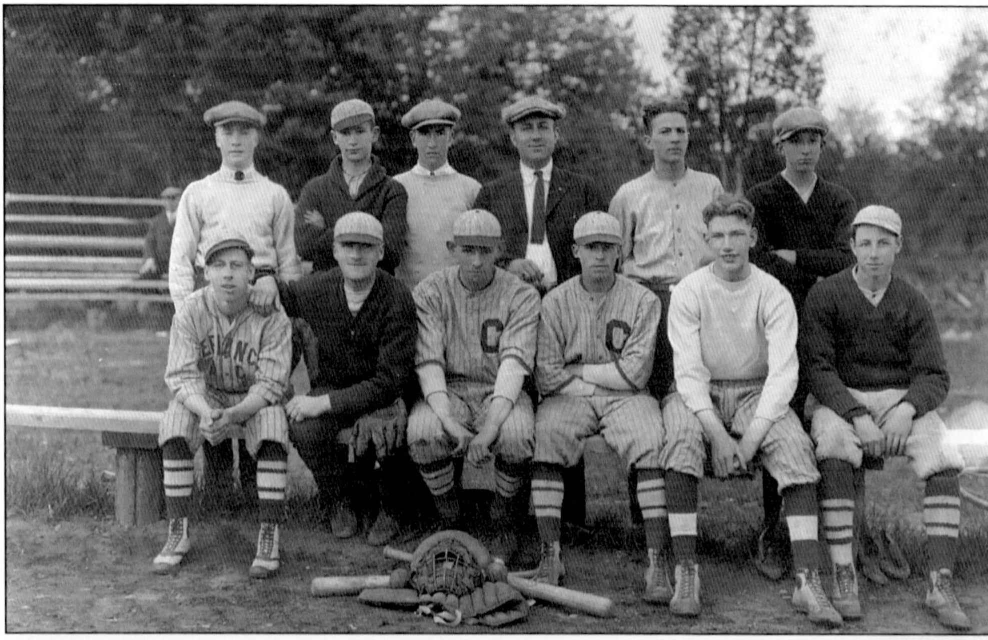

According to the late high school principal Charles Randall, the baseball team of 1924 was the best at that time ever to represent the high school. The team was 10-2 for the season. Seen here, from left to right, are as follows: (front row) William Adair, Alfred Hewins, Harold Wetherell, Lee Harper, Arthur Ross, and John Wilder; (back row) Donald Stewart, Charles Flaherty, Alex Stewart, Charles Randall, Wilfred Yelle, and Robert Young.

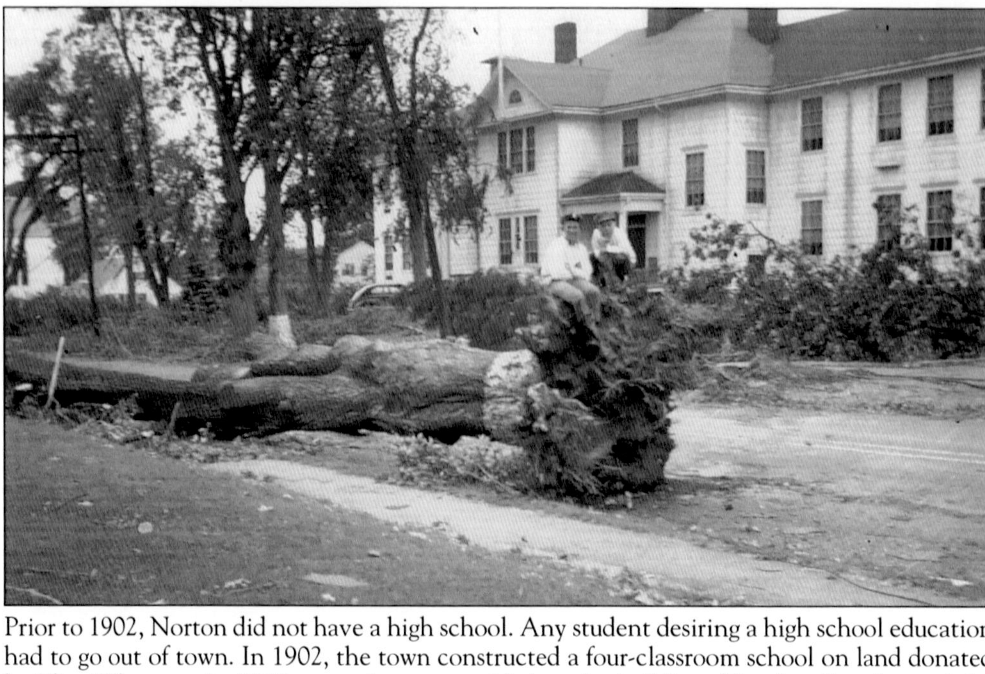

Prior to 1902, Norton did not have a high school. Any student desiring a high school education had to go out of town. In 1902, the town constructed a four-classroom school on land donated by Eliza Wheaton. In 1915, two wings were added to the building. The first floor housed the grammar school, and the second floor contained the high school. The Hurricane of 1938 destroyed many of the old trees along the main road. The building was razed in 1966.

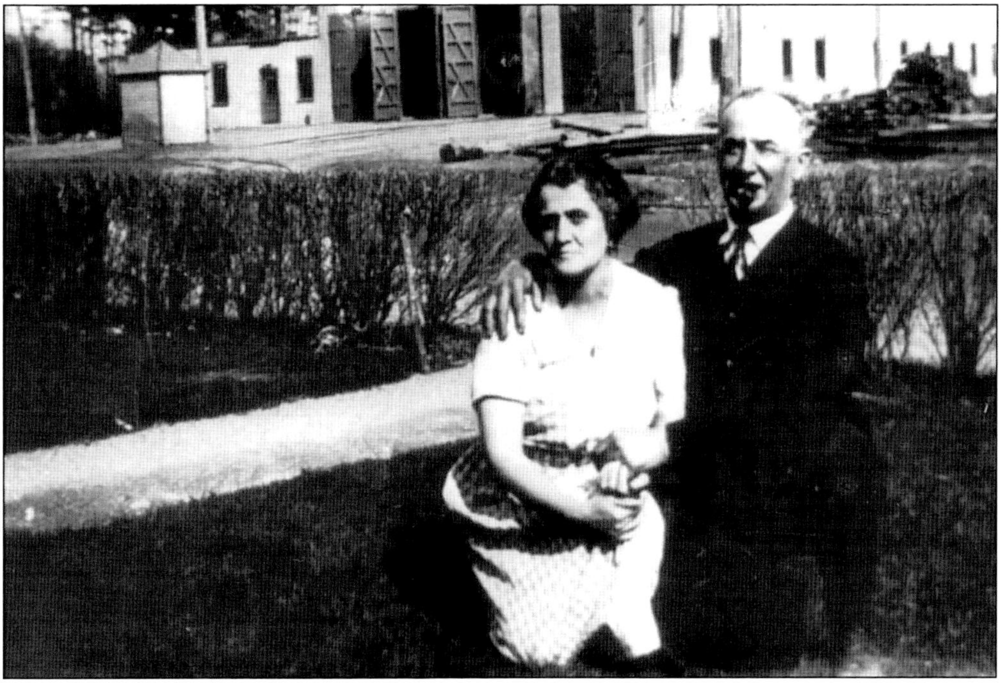

In 1898, trolley tracks were laid on the main streets to connect the four area communities of Norton, Mansfield, Attleboro, and Taunton. The car barn was situated at the center on West Main Street. The first carbarn burned down in 1914. The second barn, shown here in the background, was built afterward. Wilfred and Eveline Yelle are sitting across the street, in their front yard. Yelle was a maintenance foreman for the trolley line. The Norton, Taunton, and Attleboro Street Railway operated until July 1928.

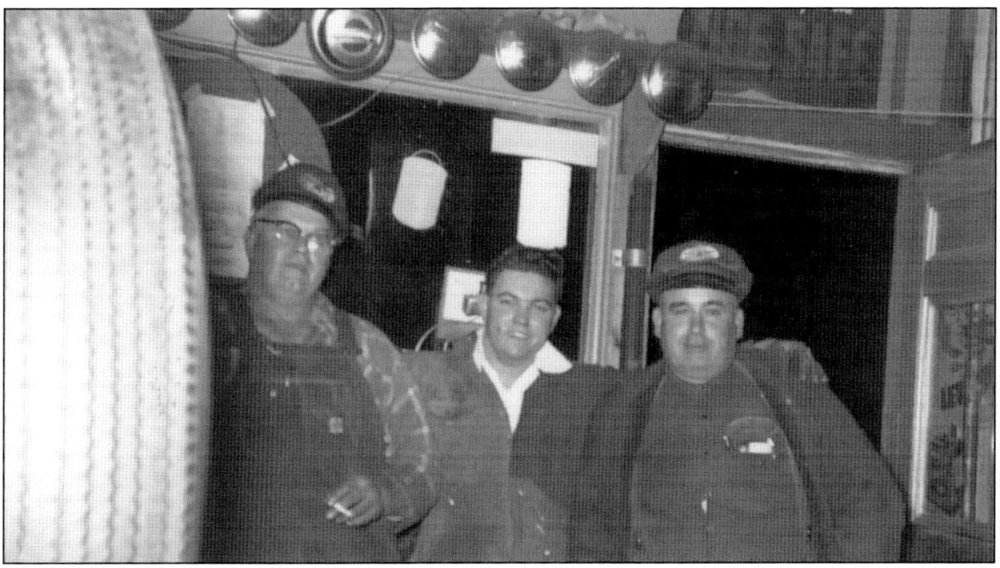

The carbarn became the Old Colony Garage. In 1938, Dave Salley sold the garage to Barney Cabisius, who named it the Norton Center Garage. John Scott, who worked for Cabisius, bought the garage in 1943. Pictured here in the garage's office, from left to right, are Scott's brother Roy Scott, Dick Liberty, and John Scott.

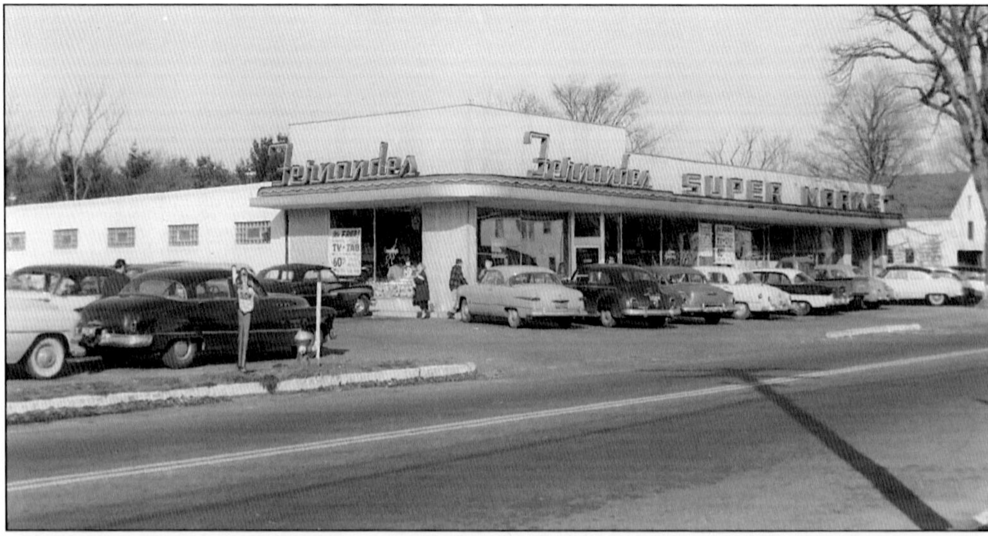

A few years after arriving in the United States from the Madeira Islands in 1924, Jose and Rosa Fernandes opened a small grocery store on the first floor of their home on West Main Street. Their store specialized in quality meats. Their children, Joe, Bea, Mary, and Vangie, participated in the expansion of the business. Eventually, the family-run business became a chain of 37 supermarkets in the state. The first supermarket was built across the street from the family's small grocery store.

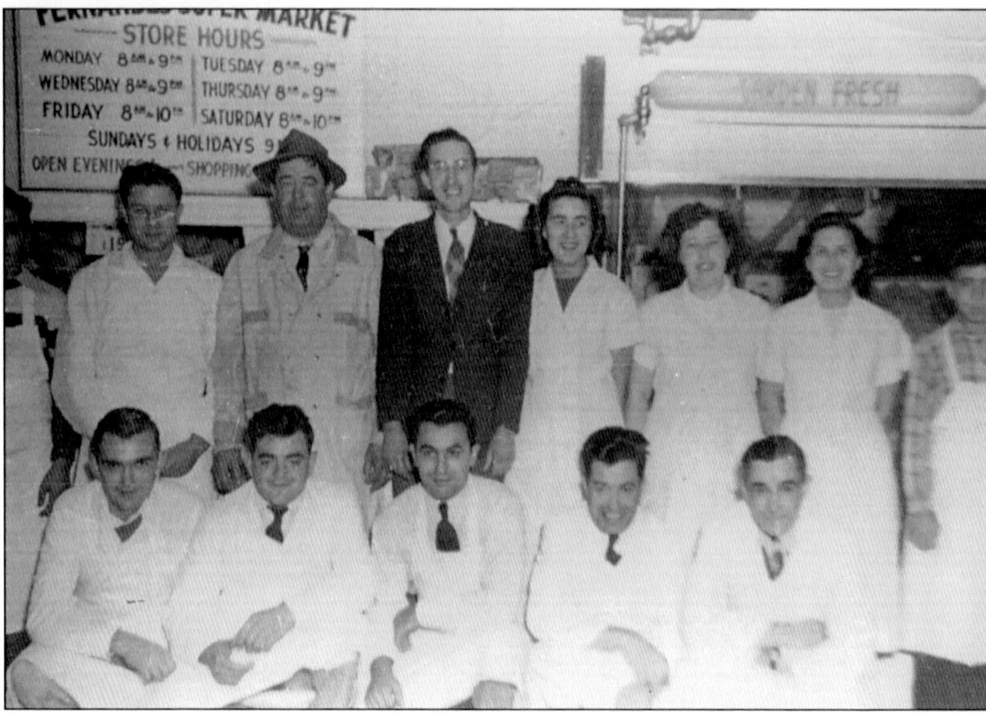

This photograph shows Jose Fernandes with his son Joseph, his daughter Vangie, and employees in the first supermarket. This store was opened in 1947. Fernandes was the president of the family business. In a quiet, dignified manner, the Fernandes family has made many contributions to the town and its citizens through the years.

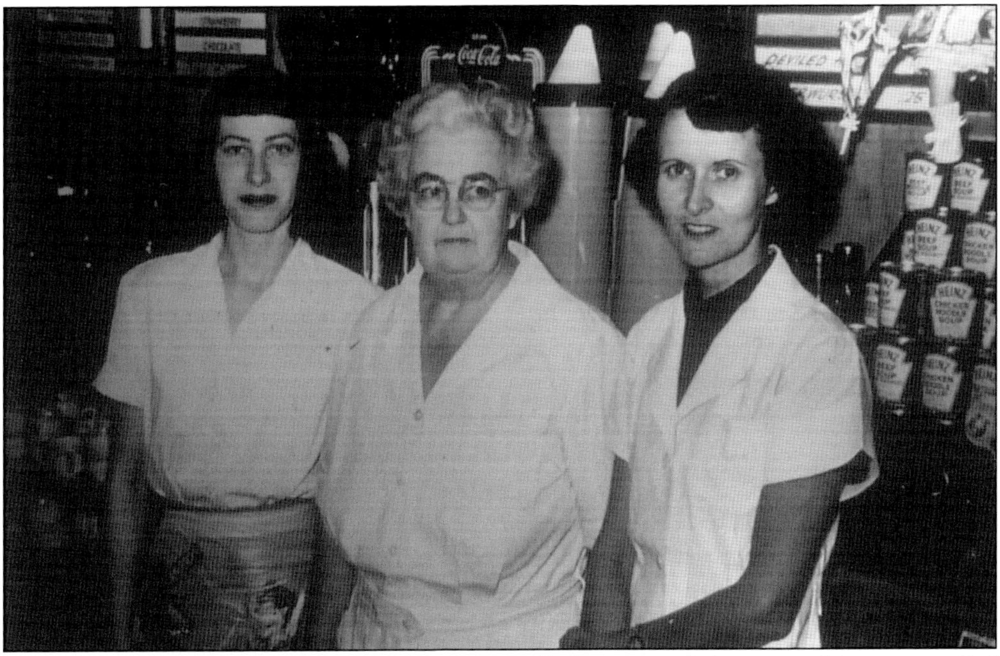

Haskins was the town's first pharmacy. Lewis S. Rubin opened the original business called Norton Perfumery in 1945. Francis "Sully" Sullivan bought the business in 1946 and operated it as a patent medicine store and soda fountain. When Malcolm Haskins, a pharmacist, bought the business in 1956, he renamed it Haskins Pharmacy. Shown here behind the soda fountain, from left to right, are Avis Brassier, Esther Spencer, and Ruth Charron.

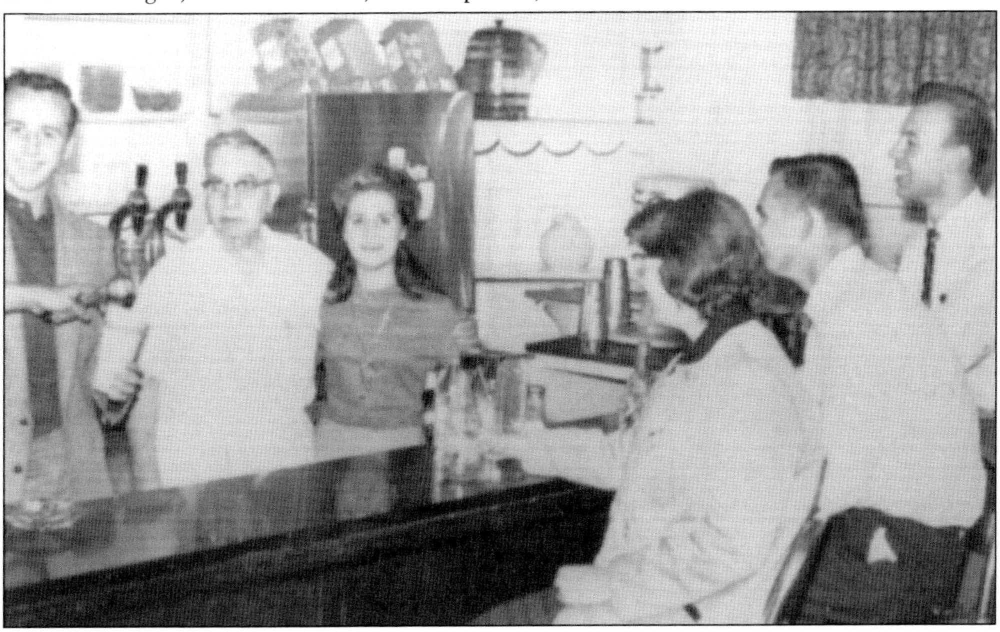

In the early 1940s, the Penesis family opened a restaurant called the Chicken Coop just beyond the Jackson House on West Main Street. The family restaurant was a popular dining spot. Patrons enjoyed Ted Penesis's fried chicken and delicious pies and rolls, and the young folk were drawn to the fountain for the newest soda creations.

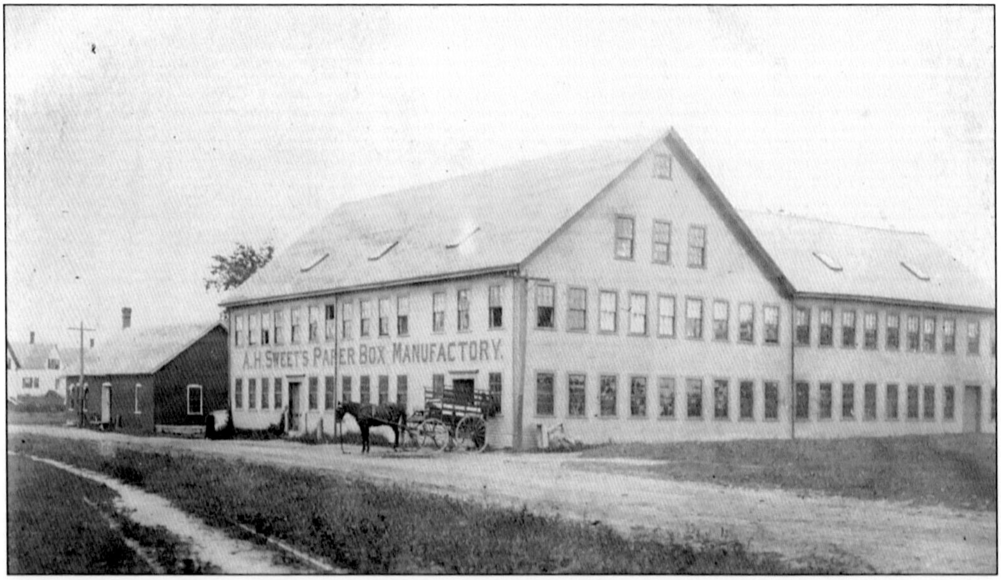

The A.H. Sweet Paper Box Company was situated on West Main Street at Box Shop Curve. This area is called Messingerville after Austin Messinger, who began making friction matches in 1858. Messinger continued in business with his son-in-law Andrew H. Sweet until 1880, when they sold out to the Diamond Match Company. Sweet then started manufacturing paper and wooden boxes in buildings on opposite sides of the street. The paper box factory burned down in 1925.

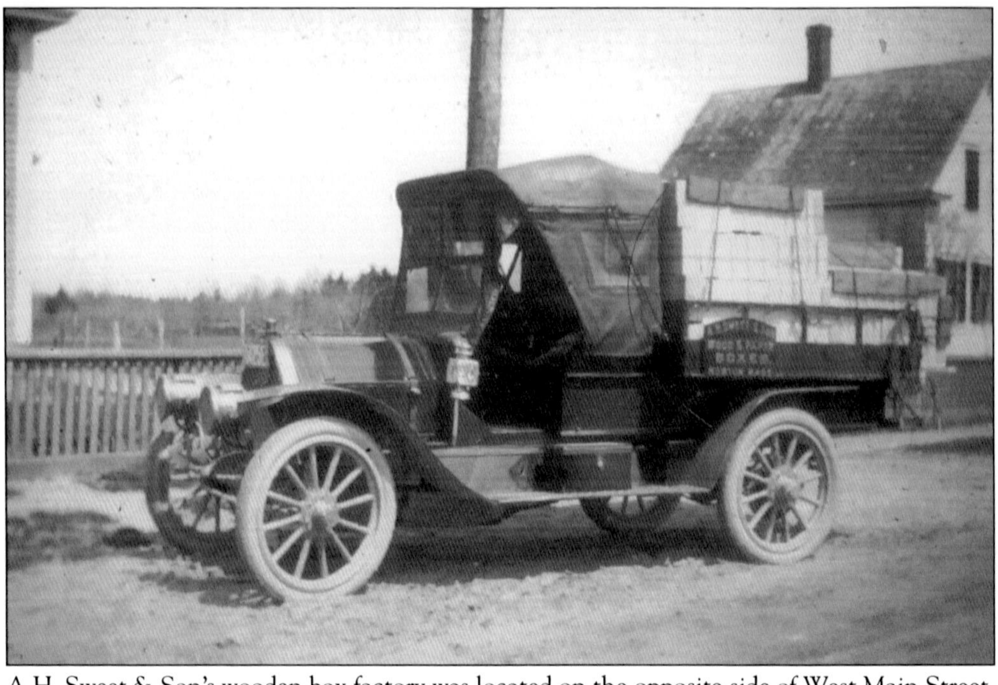

A.H. Sweet & Son's wooden box factory was located on the opposite side of West Main Street. In 1928, Sprague & Reynolds Company purchased the business. This company specialized in wooden and plywood boxes of all varieties. It closed c. 1969.

Two

BARROWSVILLE

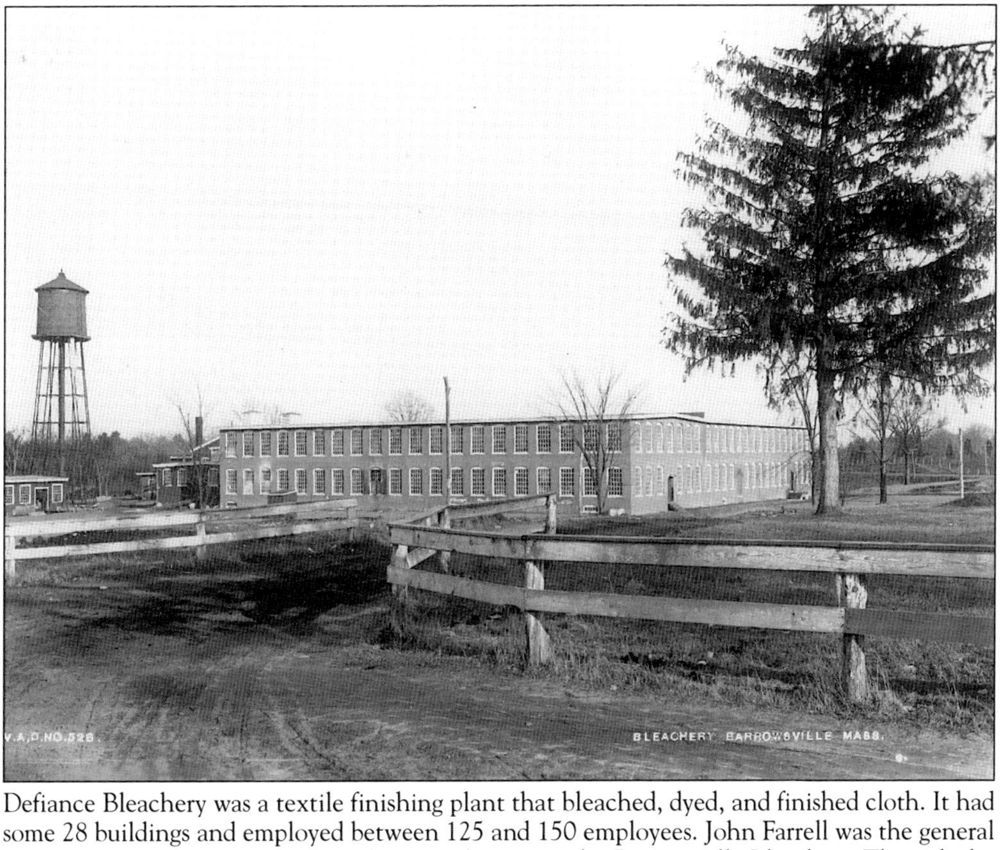

Defiance Bleachery was a textile finishing plant that bleached, dyed, and finished cloth. It had some 28 buildings and employed between 125 and 150 employees. John Farrell was the general manager for several years. Previously, it was known as the Barrowsville Bleachery. Through the years, the neighborhood prospered as more French families moved to this village to work at the bleachery. Many activities centered around the plant.

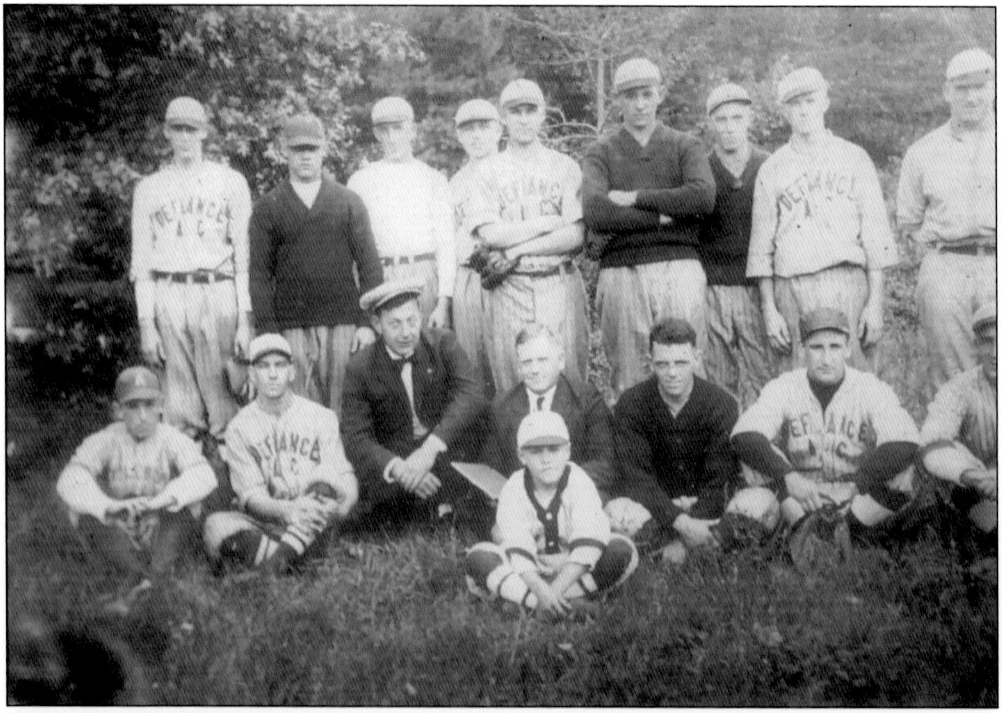

Here is the 1926 Defiance baseball team. Some of the players were George Carter, Ray Holmes, Hank Wetherell, Wally Blanchard, Lloyd Gay, Bill Flaherty, Alton Tully, and Bill Gay. Bill Taylor was manager.

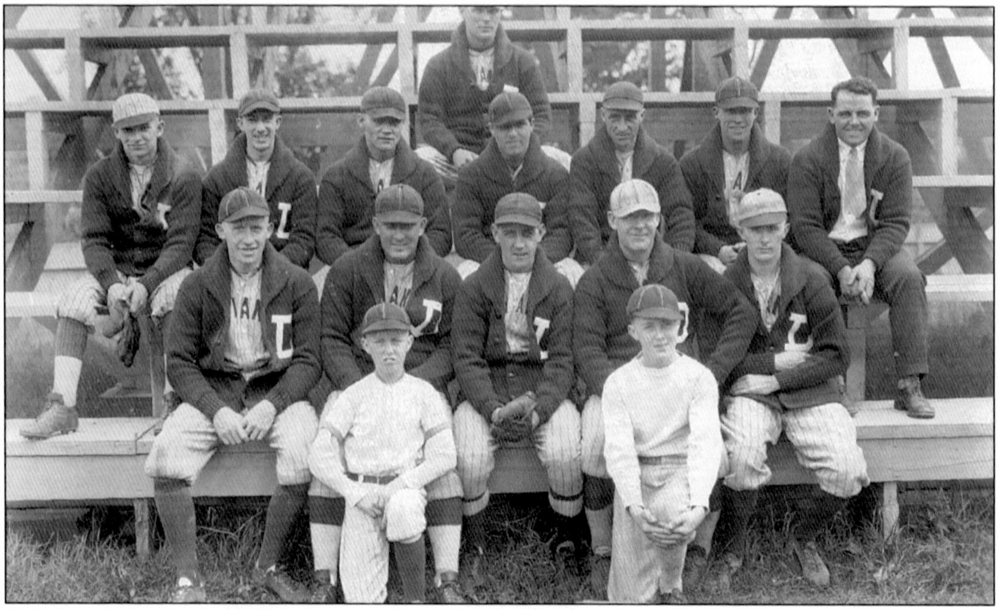

Defiance Bleachery had an outstanding baseball team. In 1927, the Defiance boys were champions of the Attleboro Manufacturers' League. The team had an exciting game that year against the Southern Bleachery champion team from South Carolina. The teams were tied until the last inning when the Southern team got the winning run.

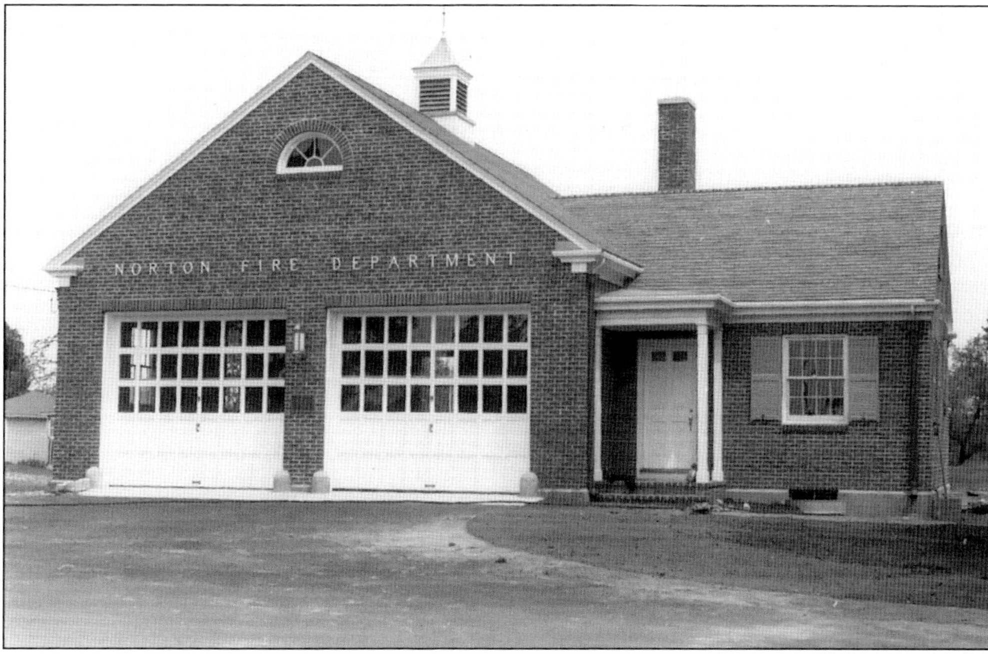

In 1953, Defiance Bleachery donated the Barrowsville Fire Station to the town. It was situated on the corner of South Worcester and Barrows Streets. The bleachery wanted to help avoid any major fires in its locale. Volunteer firemen manned Station 5; some of them worked at the bleachery.

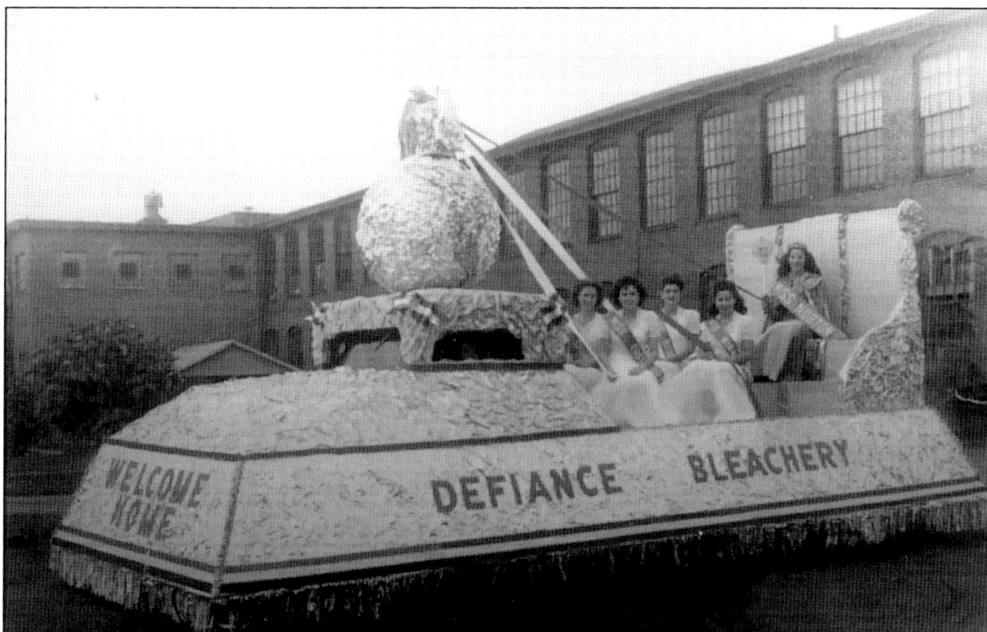

Defiance Bleachery participated in the Welcome Home Parade of October 1946 for the returning veterans of World War II. Ida Bliss was Miss Norton, Hazel Gomes was Miss Winnecunnet, Emma Sears was Miss Barrowsville, Gertrude McGovern was Miss East Norton, and Lillian Flanagan was Miss Chartley.

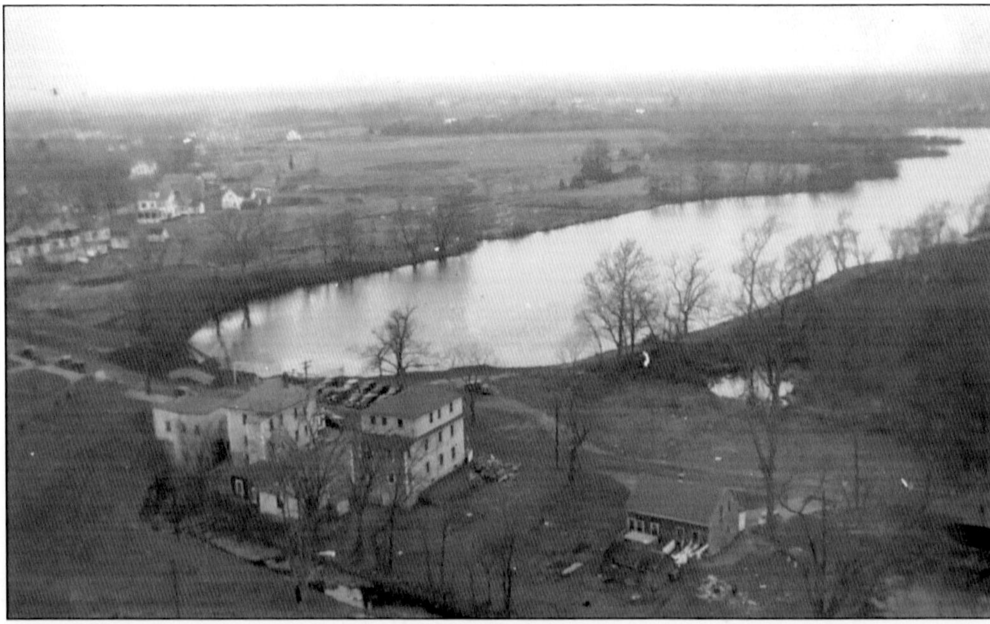

This 1940s view shows the neighborhood along Barrows Street and Barrowsville Pond. The picture was taken looking toward South Worcester Street.

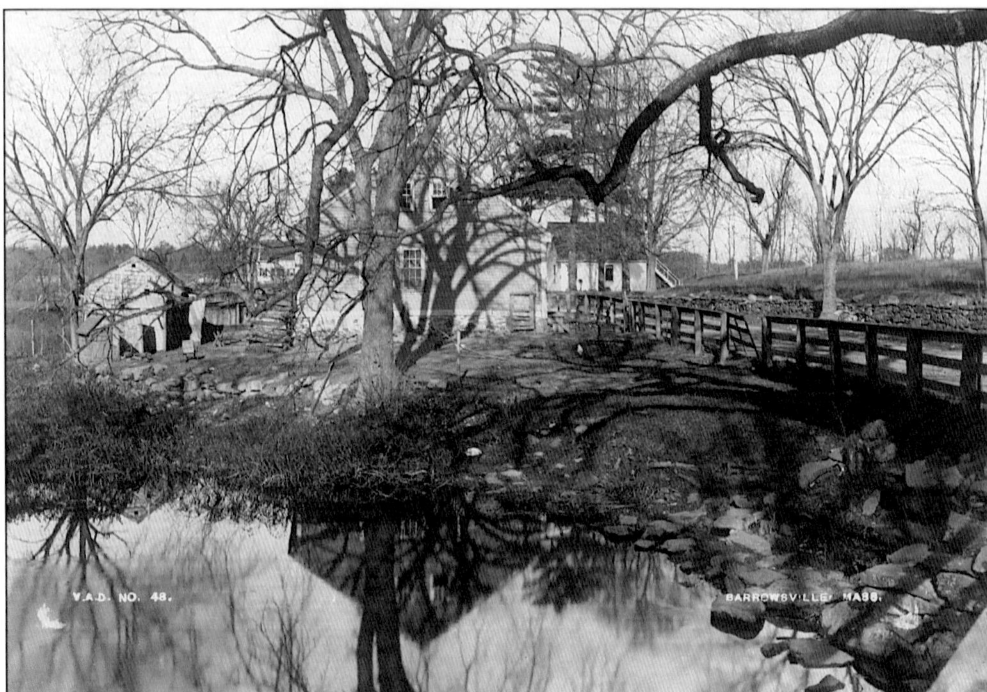

This early view of the Barrows Street bridge was taken looking east. The wooden bridge was laid on stone piers.

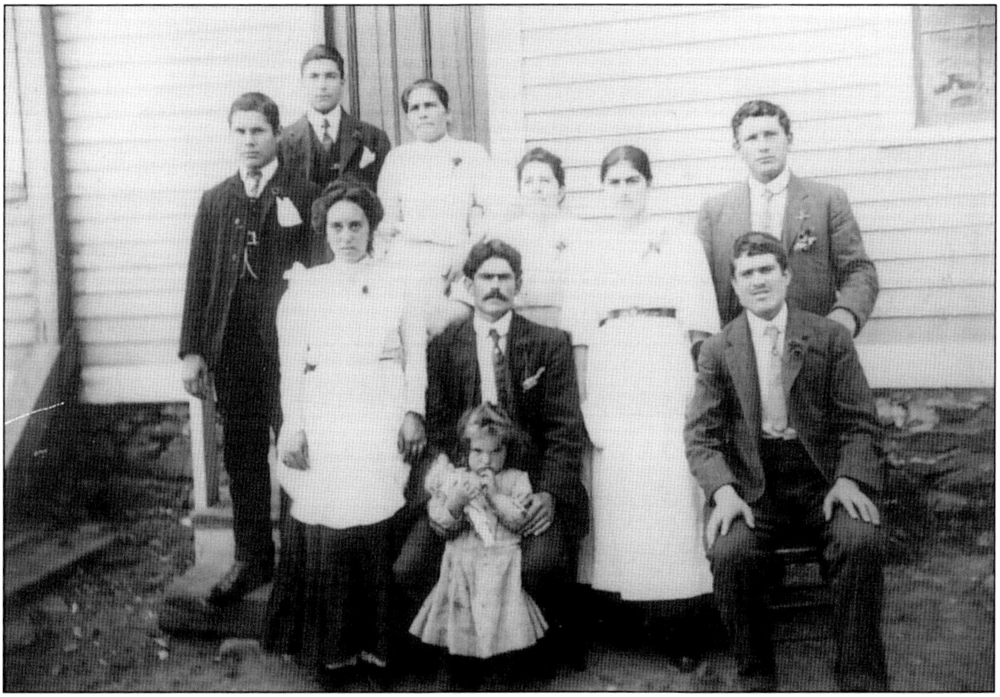

Oscar's Lunchroom was a very popular eating place, enjoyed by the neighbors. Workers employed at Defiance Bleachery, which was located behind the house, often dropped in during their lunch hour. This family is posing in their Sunday clothes on the front steps of their mill house near the lunchroom.

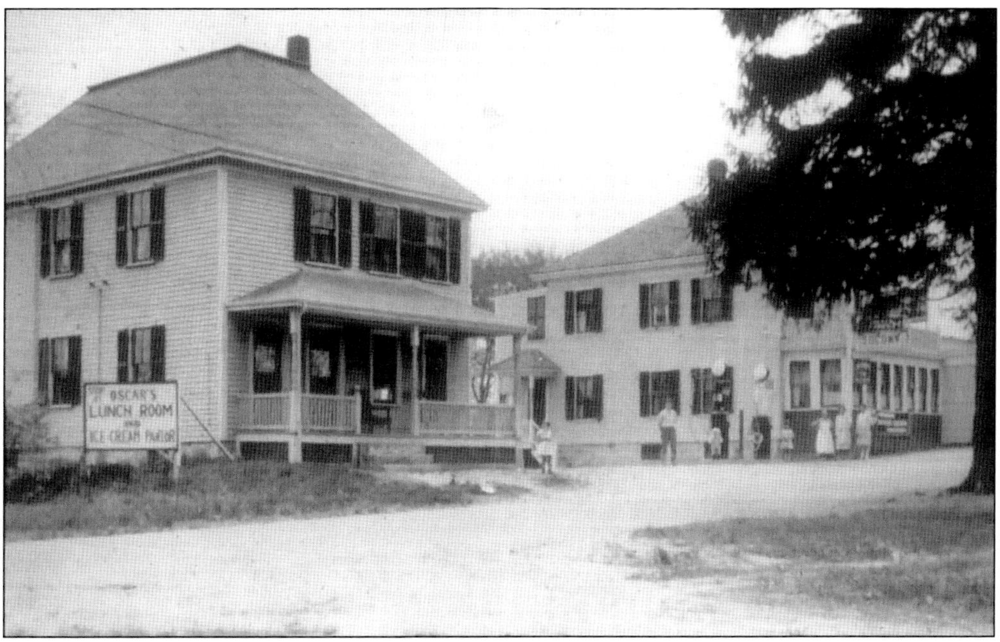

From the 1930s to the 1950s, Oscar and Blanche Bellevance ran a lunchroom in the small front addition to their home on Barrows Street. They served light lunches, sandwiches, and ice cream accompanied by music from their jukebox.

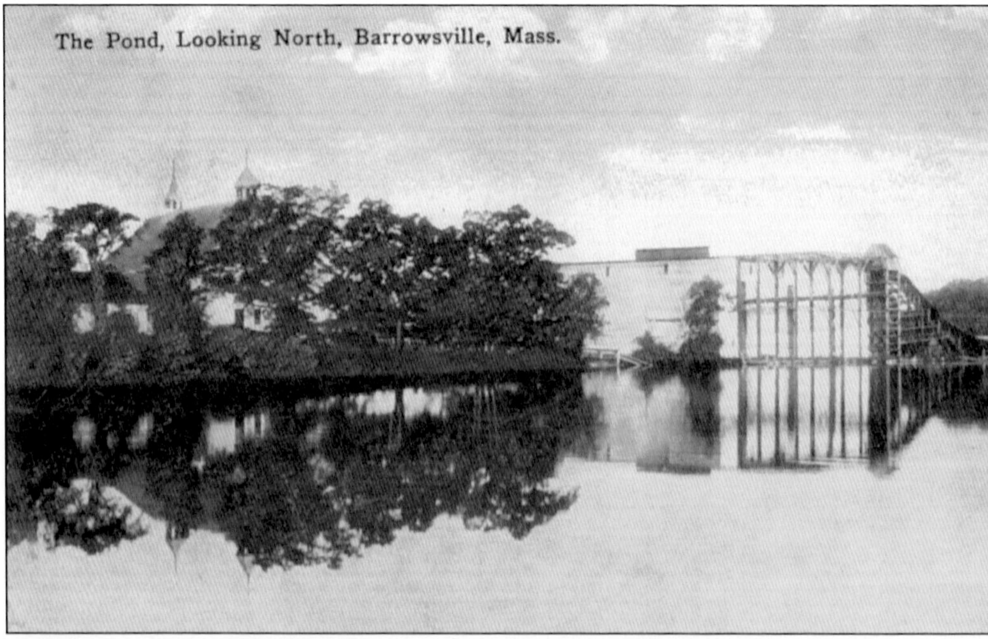

In the early 1900s, a large ice-harvesting operation was situated on Barrowsville Pond. It was owned by the Providence Ice Company. A spur track from the railroad main line ran to the icehouses, where freight cars were loaded with blocks of ice for shipment. The ice-harvesting industry disappeared with the development of electric refrigeration.

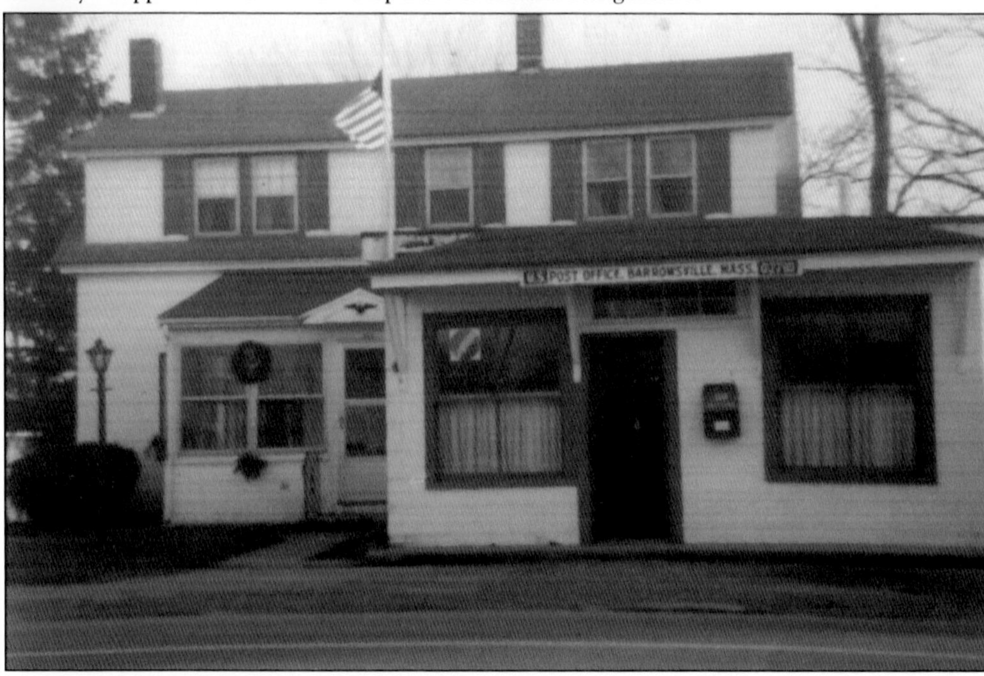

This image shows the Barrowsville Post Office. From 1915 to 1920, Frank and Mary McGinn operated the post office and had a general store at this location. In 1920, Joseph P. Bartley was appointed postmaster and served until 1953. His wife, Margaret Bartley, was his assistant. After his death, daughter Anna Shea served as postmaster for 27 years.

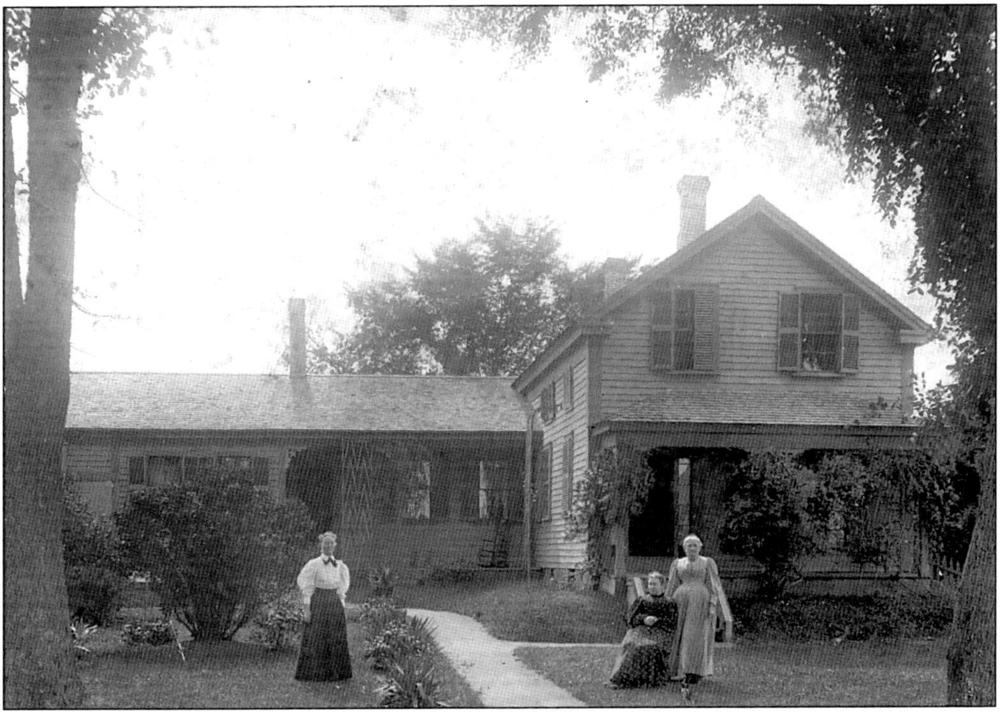

Henry and Martha Freeman lived in this family homestead on South Worcester Street. He was the postmaster and had the post office in his home. Florence Freeman was his assistant.

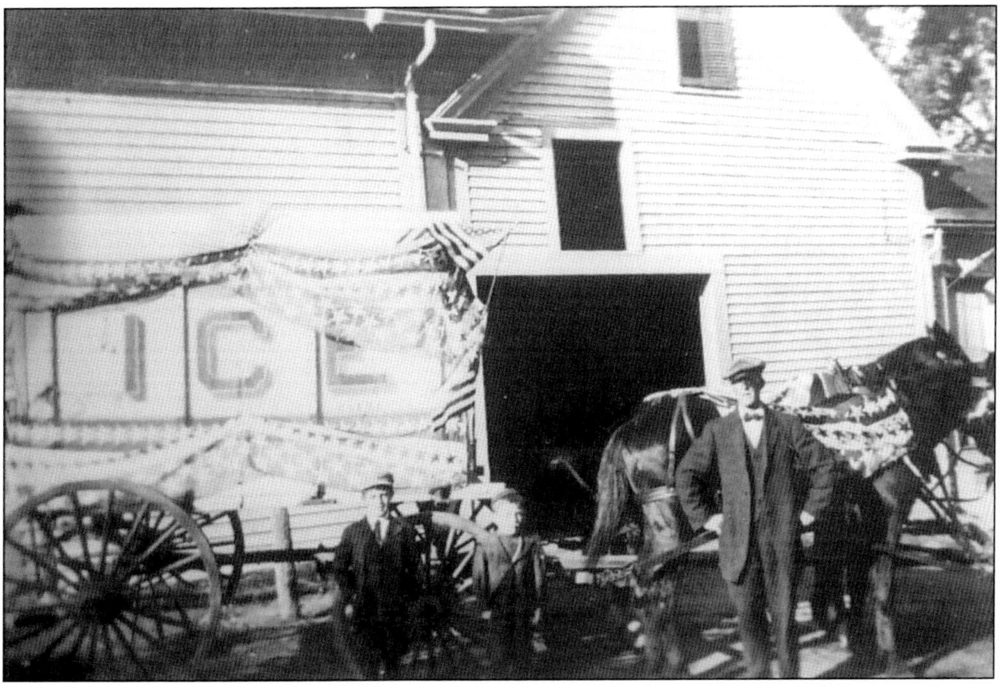

The Norton Bicentennial Parade of 1911 passed along South Worcester and Barrows Streets to Taunton Avenue. This decorated ice wagon, seen in front of the Freeman House, was in the parade.

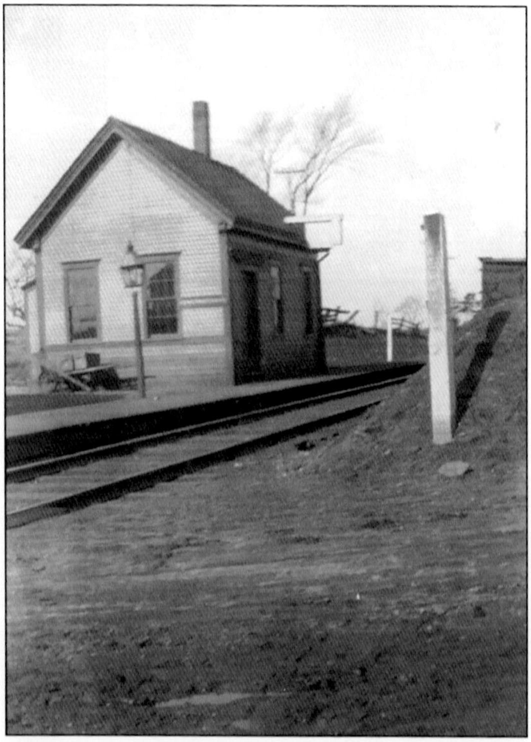

The Barrowsville Railroad Station was situated on South Worcester Street near Barrows Street. In 1900, the station agent was Savillion Bates. The first post office in Barrowsville was located in the old depot; the postmaster was S.H. Bates. Notice the kerosene lamppost by the track. After the station closed, the building became a private residence.

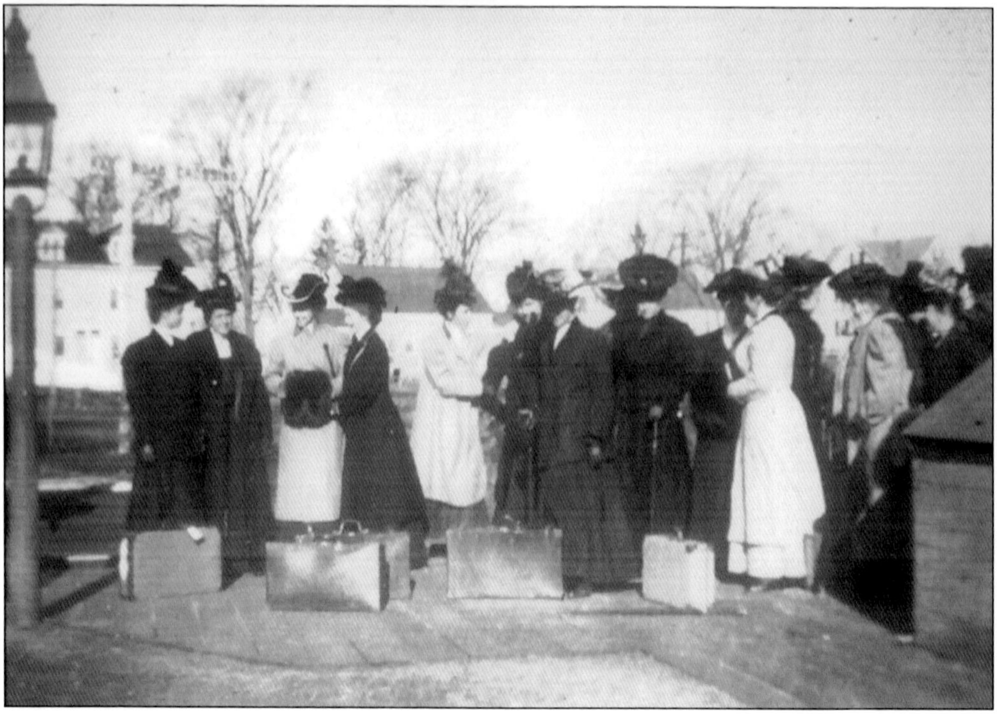

This is a 1906 scene of some Wheaton Seminary students waiting for the train at the Barrowsville Railroad Station. They were traveling to Attleboro or Providence for the Christmas holiday.

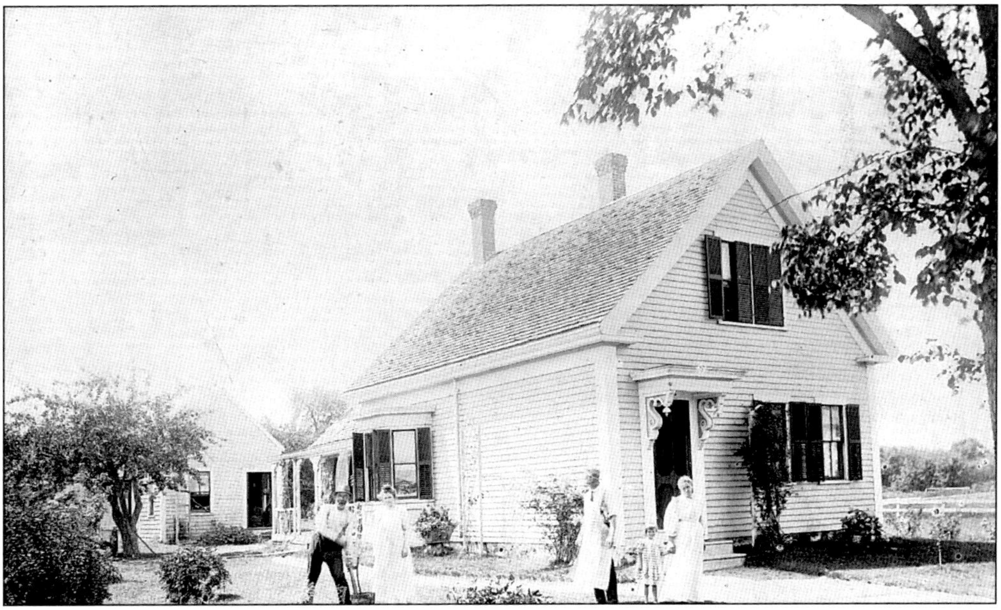

Abbie and William Allen Lane lived in this farmhouse on South Worcester Street. Lane was the brother of Abbie and Ella Lane who lived at Goose Brook Farm. He was a farmer who was quite active, serving on several town committees. He was also past master of the Norton Grange.

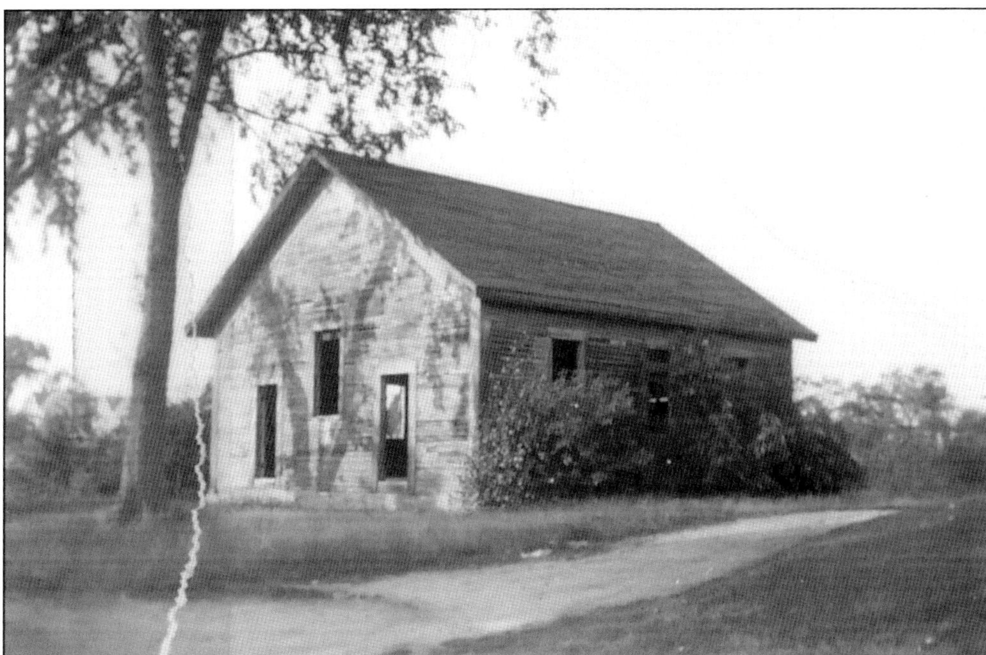

In 1850, some members of the Rehoboth Reformed Methodist Church organized the Wesleyan Methodist Church in Barrowsville. For some 15 or more years, the church held services in this meetinghouse located on South Worcester Street. Rev. Solomon P. Snow and the ten members of the church dedicated this meetinghouse on May 8, 1854. The building no longer stands.

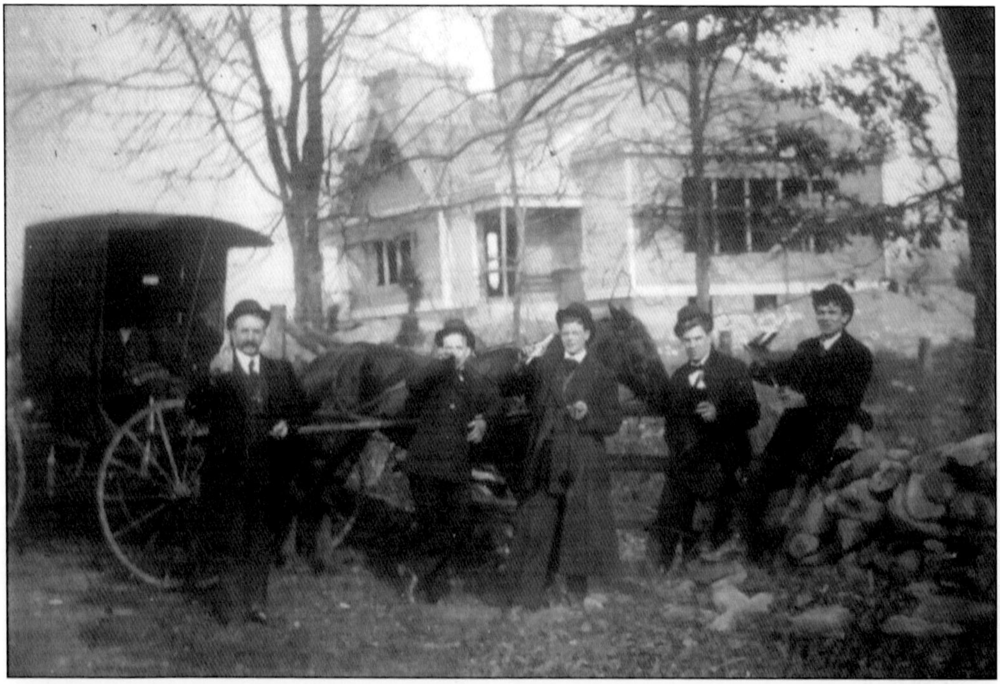

In 1906, the Barrowsville School was built to replace the No. 4 School. It had a center hall and a recitation room in the rear, with two schoolrooms on each side. Martha Crane was the principal, Ethel Ratcliffe was the grammar school teacher, and Katherine Butler taught the primary grades.

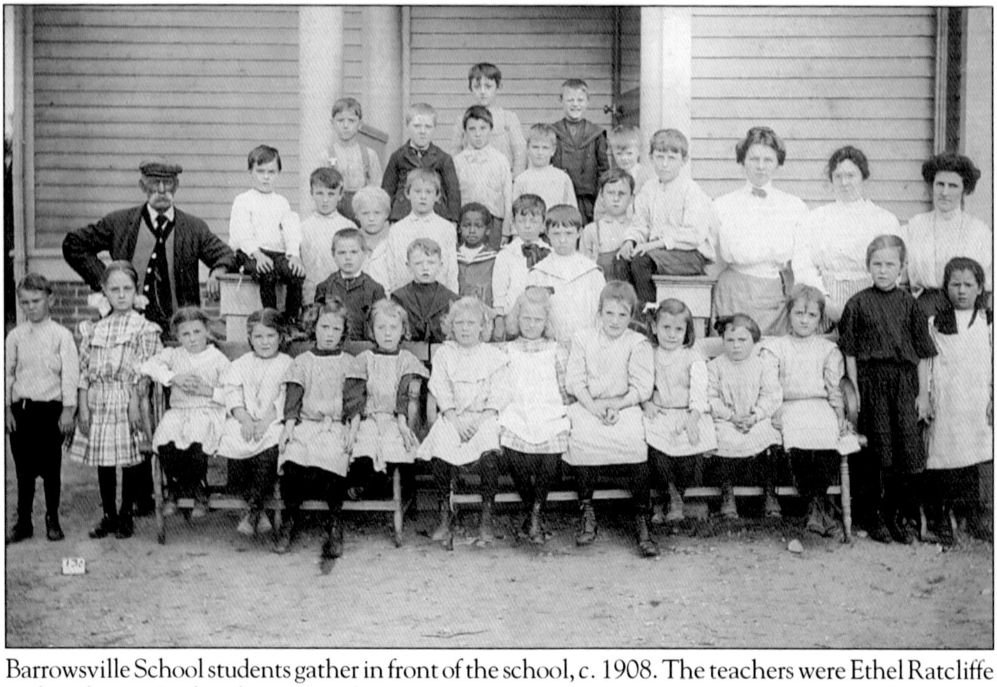

Barrowsville School students gather in front of the school, c. 1908. The teachers were Ethel Ratcliffe and Katherine Butler, the principal was Martha Crane, and the janitor was John Adair.

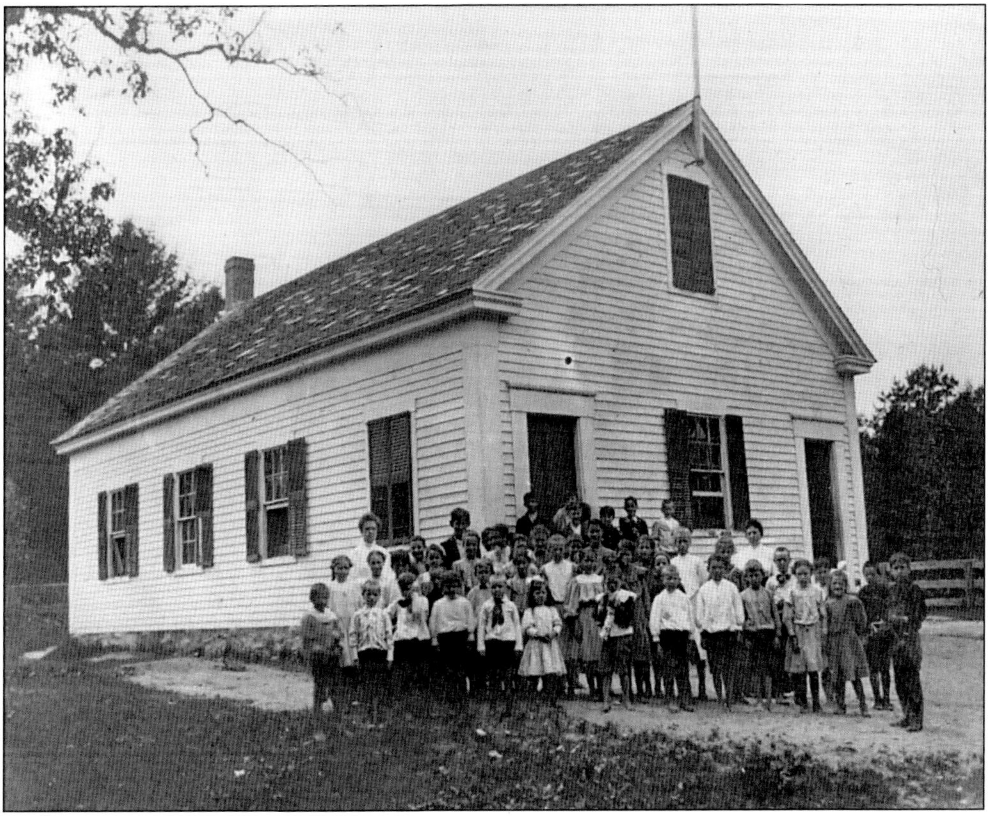

District No. 4 Schoolhouse was located on Dean Street. With more families moving into the village, the one-room school with eight grades and two teachers became increasingly overcrowded. It closed *c.* 1906, and the building became a private residence.

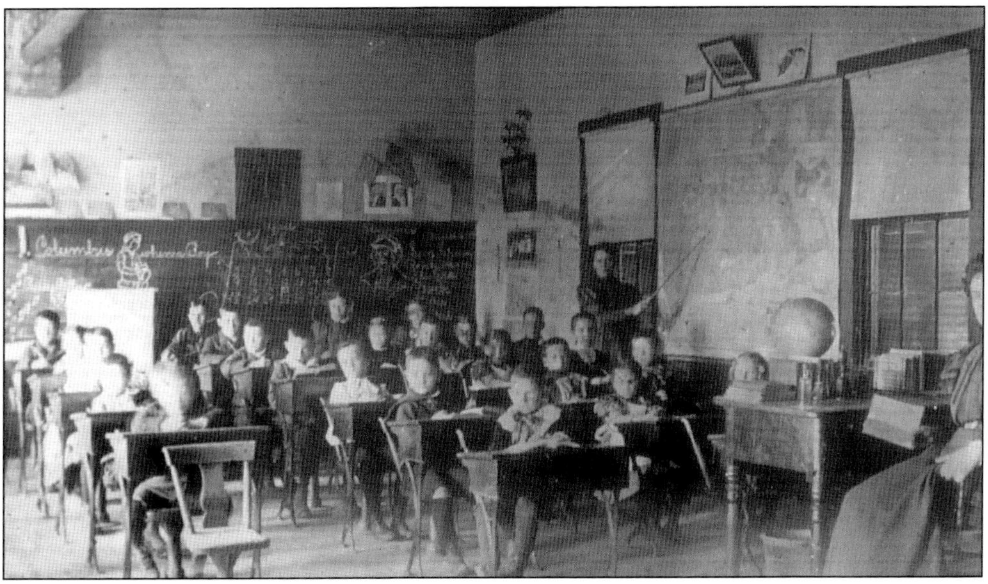

This is the interior of District No. 4 School, *c.* 1899. Minnie Folsom, just visible on the right, taught 41 students during the three terms.

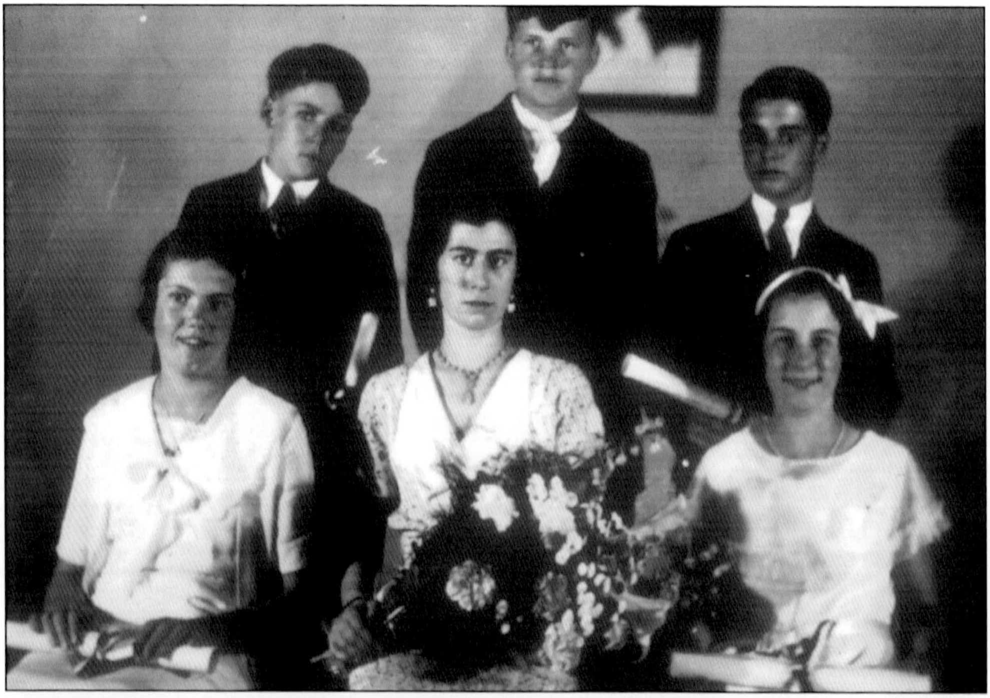

In 1932, there were five eighth-grade graduates from the Barrowsville School. The boys were Roland Bellevance, John Sears, and Armand Brown. The two girls were Doris Bellevance and Catherine Garrity. Florence Hickey, center, was their principal and teacher.

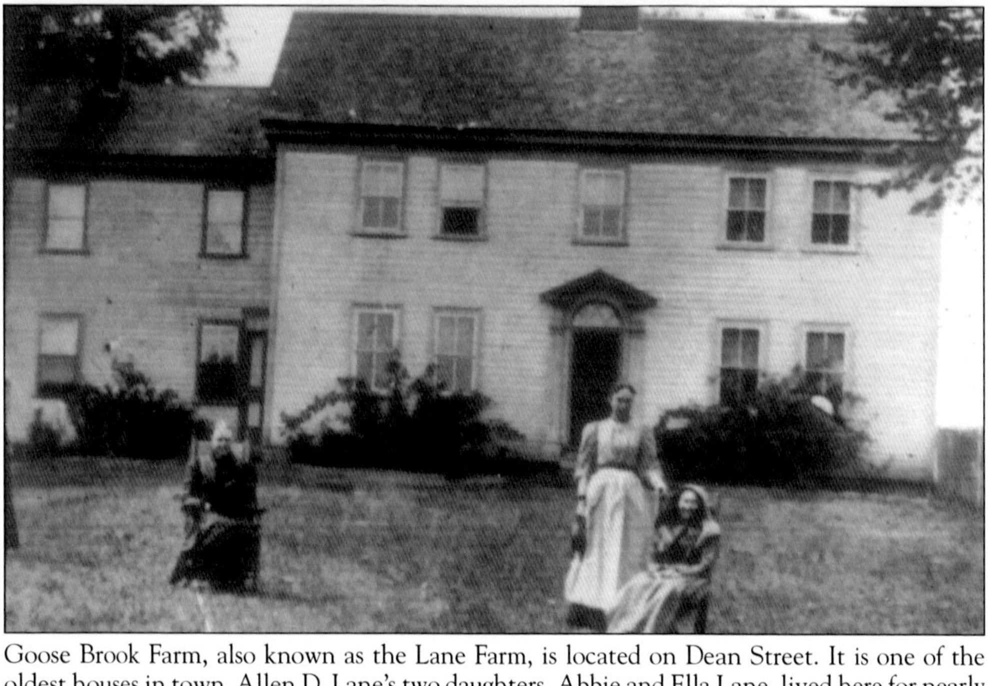

Goose Brook Farm, also known as the Lane Farm, is located on Dean Street. It is one of the oldest houses in town. Allen D. Lane's two daughters, Abbie and Ella Lane, lived here for nearly 90 years. Through the years, great care has been taken by the different owners to preserve this early New England farmhouse.

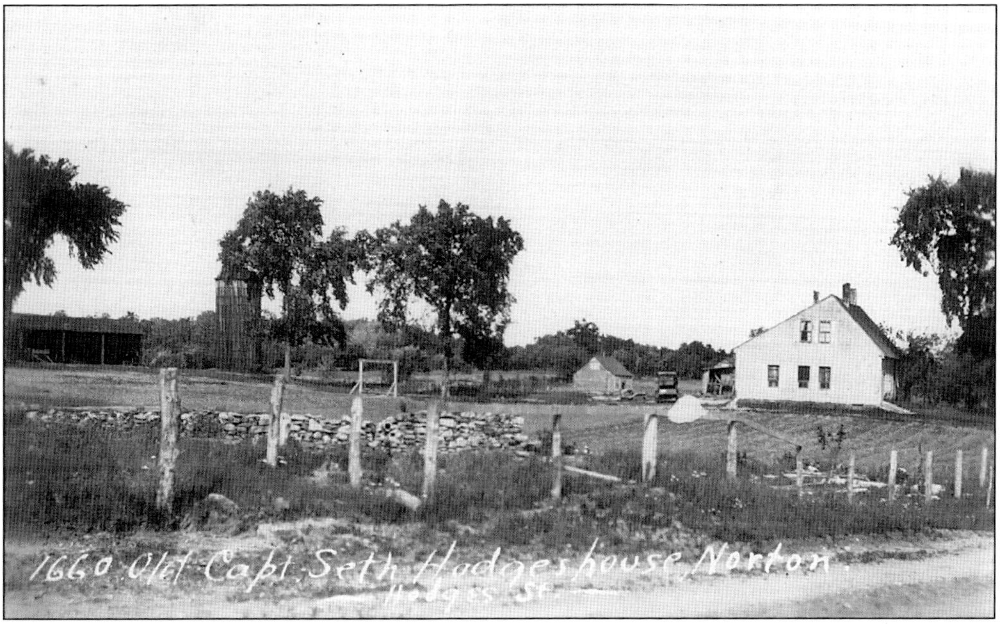

In Barrowsville, there is a street 2.6 miles long that runs from the Taunton line to the Attleboro line. In the early years, the Hodges families owned the majority of the houses on the road. This road was appropriately named Hodges Street.

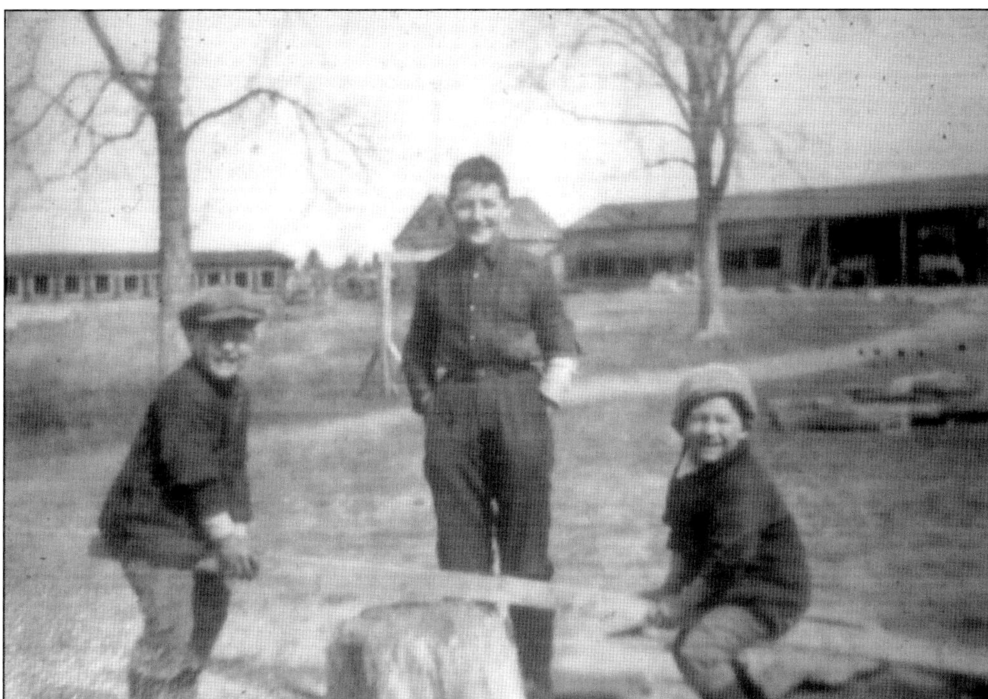

For many years, the Rubin Family operated the Rubin Egg Farm on East Hodges Street. The three Rubin brothers, Ralph, Arthur, and Lewis, were ingenious boys who made their own seesaw out of a board and tree stump.

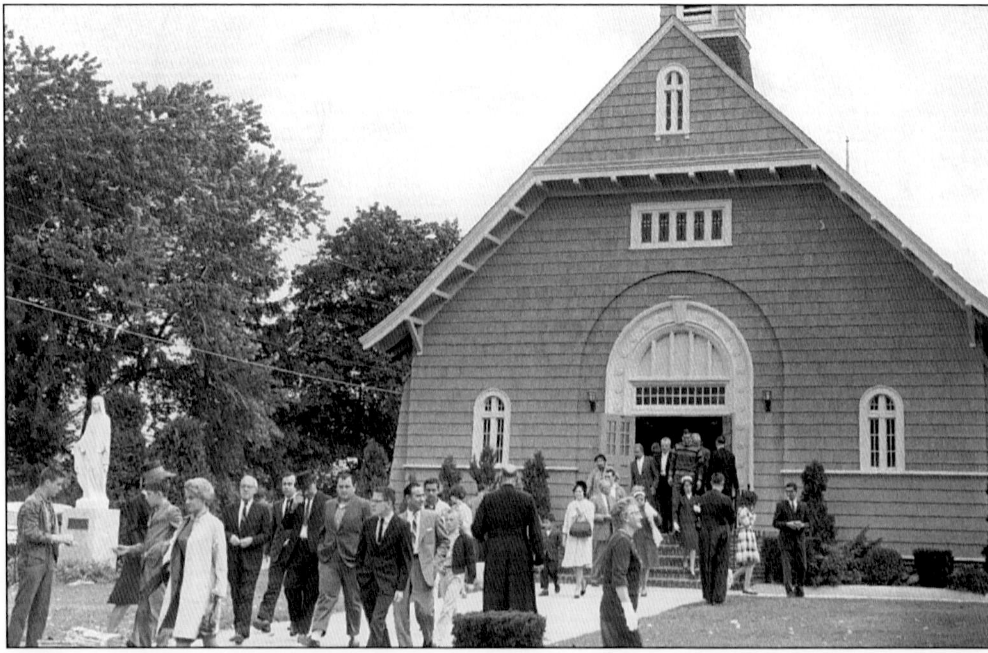

In February 1925, the first services were held in the new St. Mary's Catholic Church on South Worcester Street. A farmhouse across the street was converted into a rectory. Rev. John McNamara was appointed the first pastor. In this picture, Fr. Thomas Daley is greeting the parishioners as they leave the church.

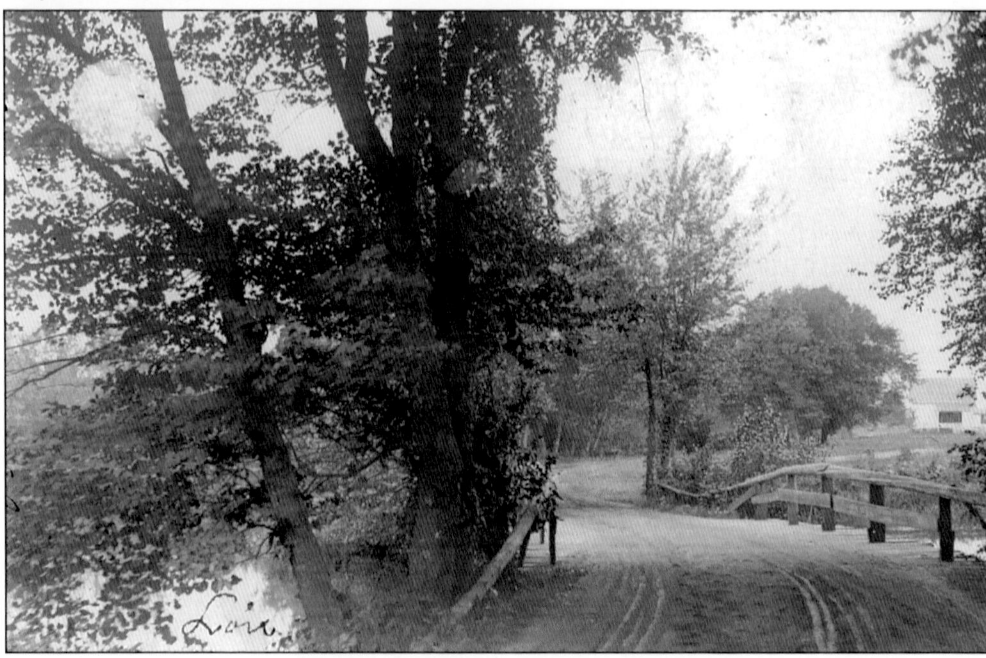

Over the years, the bridge on Power Street has been called the Ann Cobb Bridge or the Witches' Bridge. There are stories that witches lived in town during the early years. These witches, such as Ann Cobb, dealt in the black art and caused trouble for anyone who displeased them. Sometimes they made cattle disappear or made wheels fall off wagons.

Three

CHARTLEY

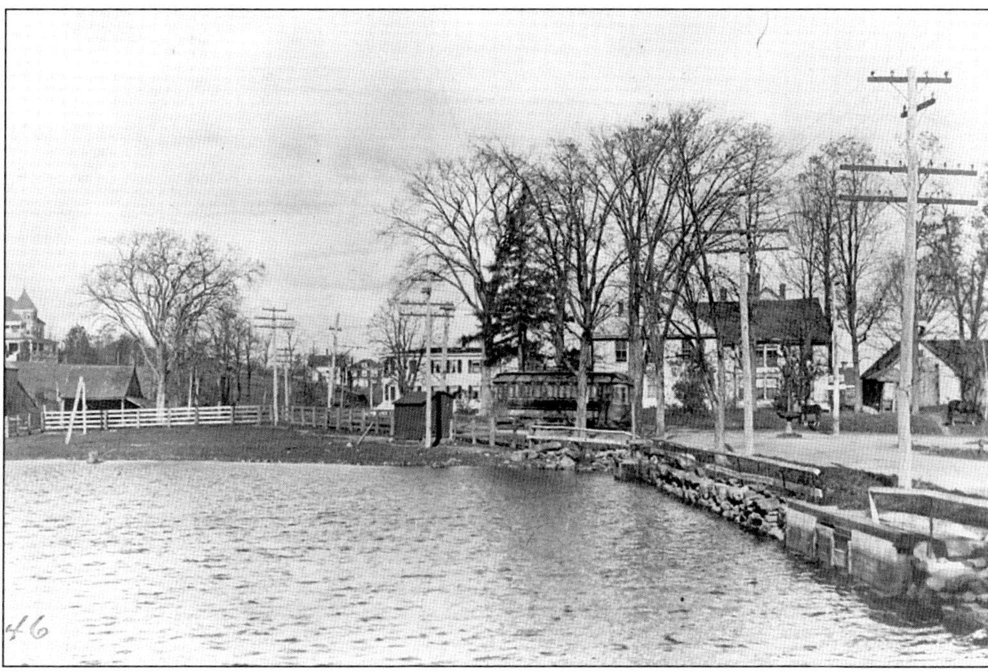

Here is a view of Chartley Corner, taken from Bottomley's grocery store window, *c.* 1910. Note the trolley heading up North Worcester Street. Frank Barney's house can be seen on the hill at the left. At the right is Judge Leonard's mansion. Chartley Corner was a crossroad of activity. People came by trolley and train to work in the jewelry shops and laundry. The pond was a gathering spot for swimming, fishing, boating, and skating.

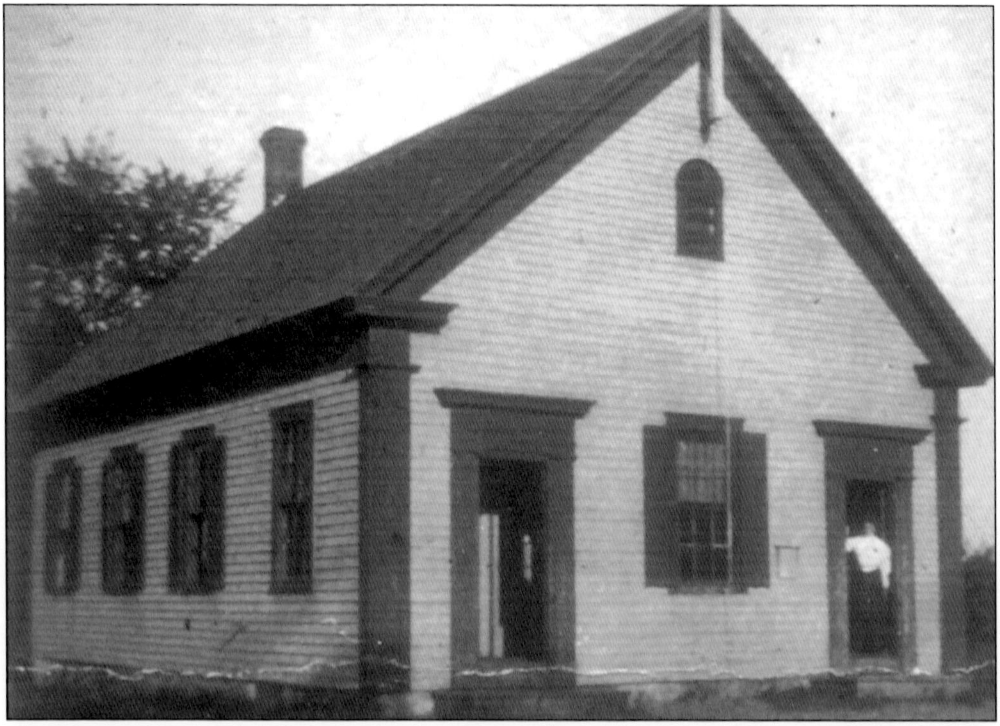

The District No. 2 Schoolhouse was situated at Valentine's Corner. Alice Sturdy became the teacher in 1892 and taught here for a few years before transferring to the No. 1 Schoolhouse. The enrollment averaged about 27 students. The school was closed in 1902 when it became overcrowded.

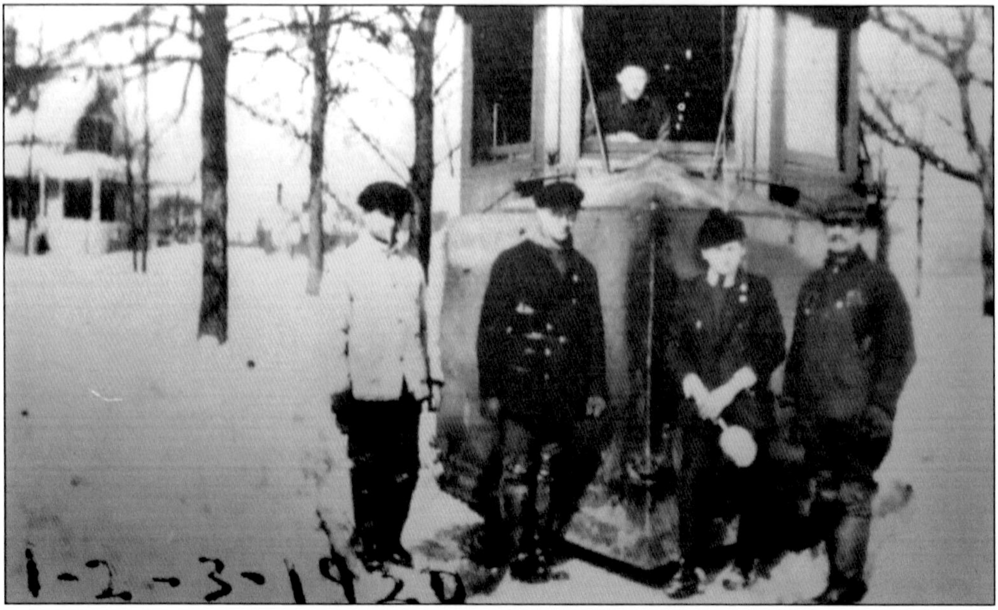

This trolley snowplow is on North Worcester Street. During the winter, the snowplow would clear the tracks. The motorman was Carl Bottomley. Standing here, from right to left, are Wilfred Yelle, Archie Leonard, Benedict Yelle, and an unidentified man.

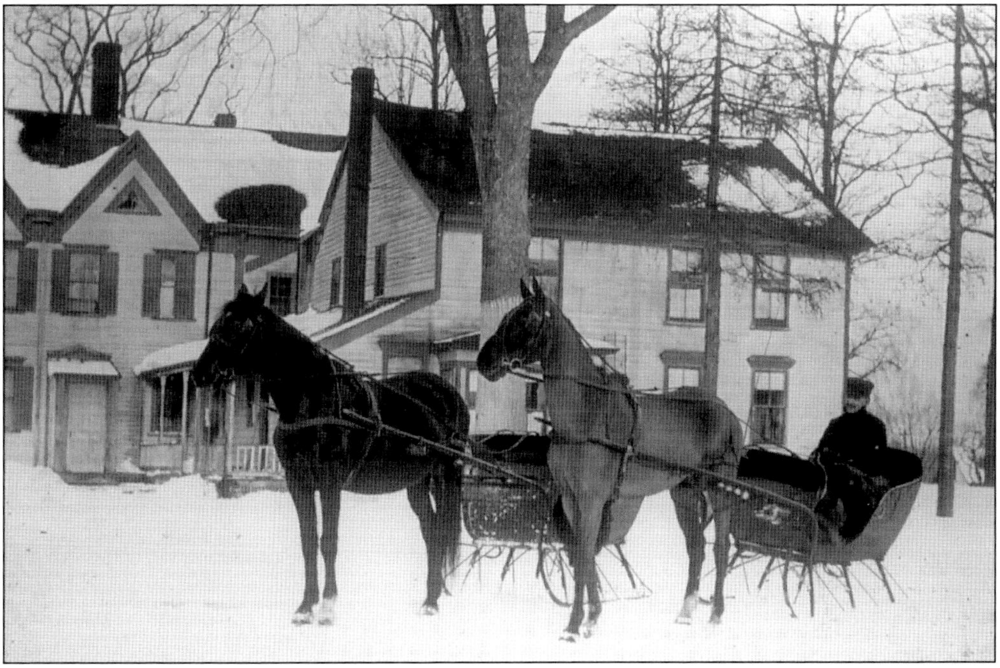

Here, James B. Wetherell stops in front of the Leonard Mansion during a sleigh ride. The mansion was burned down by the fire department in the early 1960s.

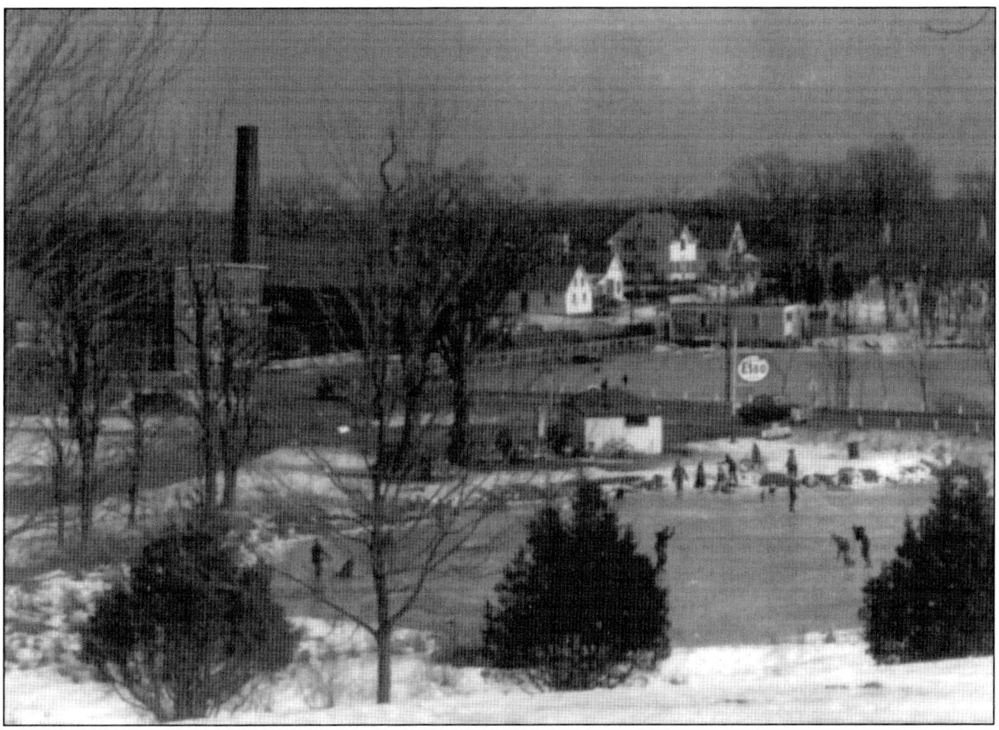

This view of Chartley Pond taken from Barney's Hill shows skaters enjoying a day of fun. Local youngsters played hockey and had bonfires on the ice to keep warm. When Old Colony Road was constructed, it divided the pond into two bodies of water.

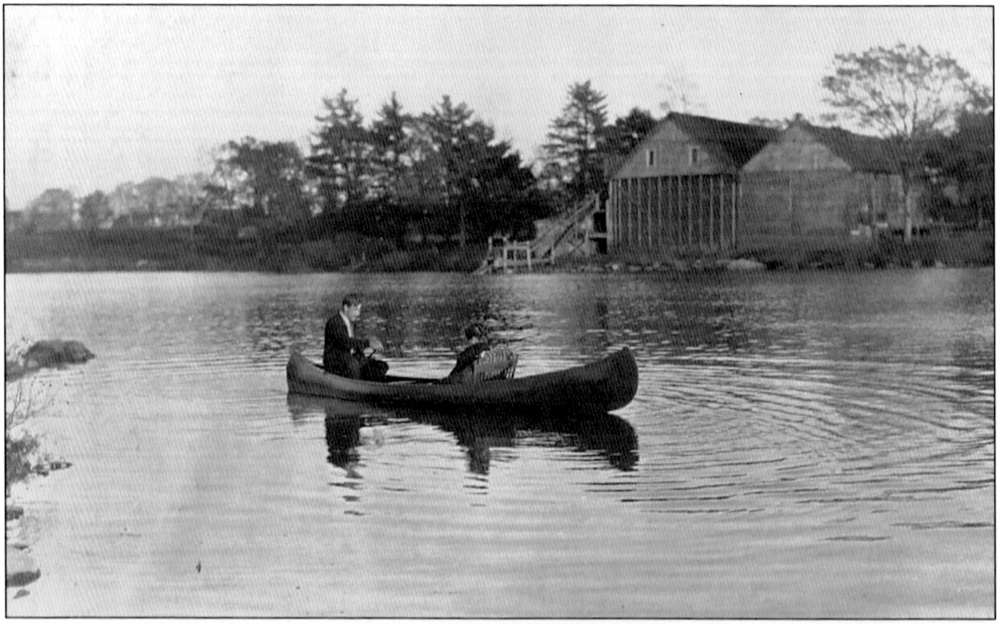

In summer, Chartley Pond's tranquil waters were ideal for canoeing, boating, and fishing. In the background are the icehouses originally owned by Oliver Lane. During the winter, large crews cut blocks of ice from the pond and loaded them into the icehouses.

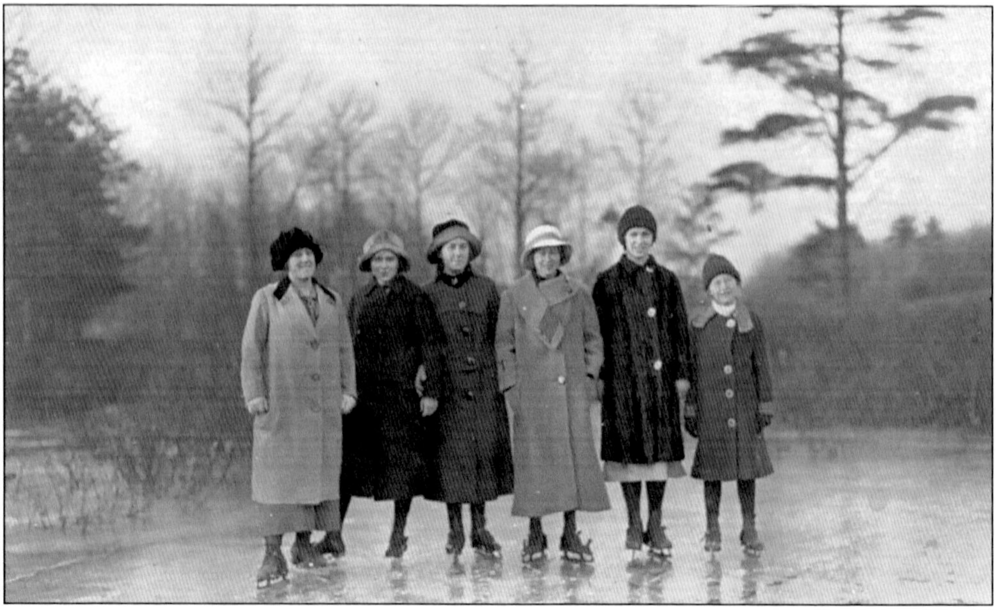

These six young ladies, Ruth Barney, Fanny Lane, Marion Bottomley, Doris Mondor, Zaidie Burgess, and Gladys Willet, enjoyed skating on Chartley Pond.

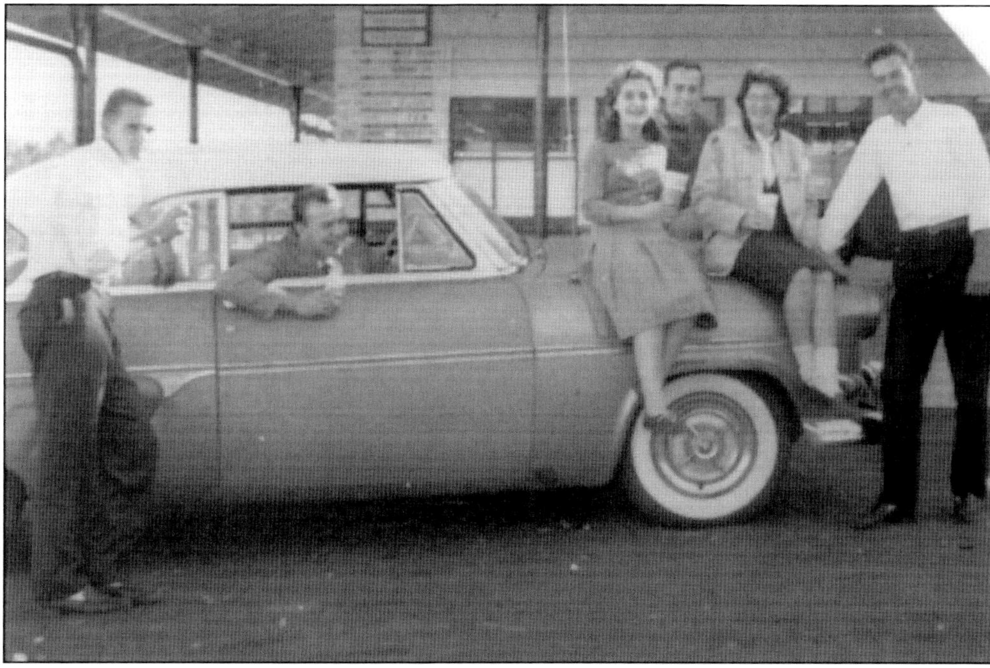

On the hill overlooking Chartley Pond, Everett Leonard ran an ice-cream stand. It was a popular spot for teenagers to gather after school. Leonard began the business in the early 1930s.

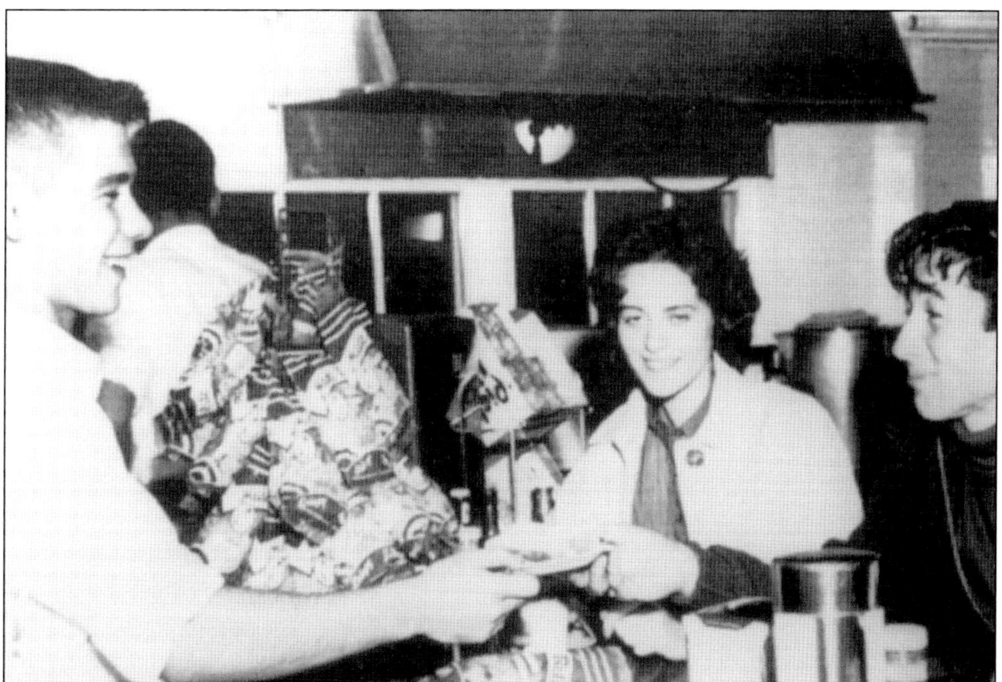

Inside Everett Leonard's ice-cream stand was a small counter and a few booths. People came here to enjoy good food and conversation.

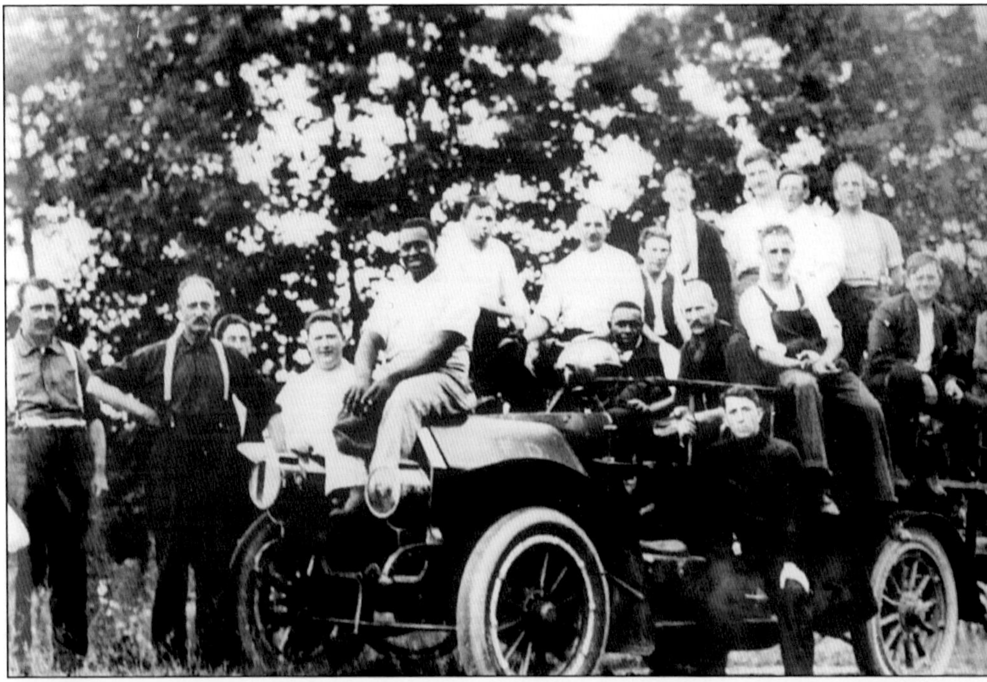

In 1898, the Norton Volunteer Fire Department was organized. This Knox truck was purchased *c.* 1916 and equipped as a fire truck. Frank Smith, sitting behind the wheel, was the second fire chief.

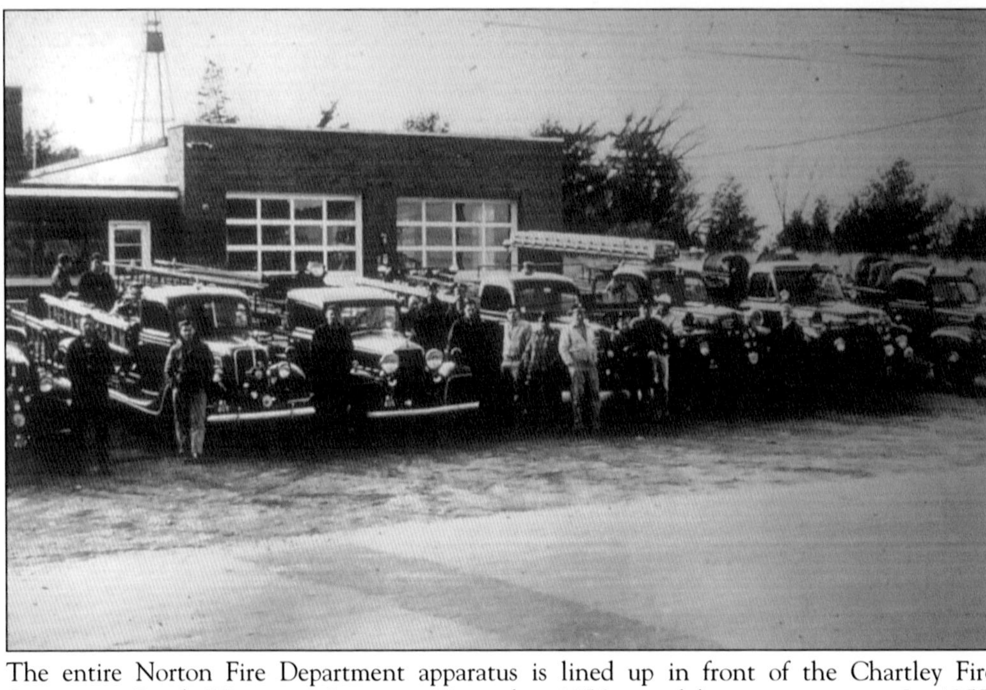

The entire Norton Fire Department apparatus is lined up in front of the Chartley Fire Station on South Worcester Street in November 1956 to celebrate its opening. In 1955, Chief Harold Wetherell donated the land for the new station. William F. Fales constructed the building in 1956 at the cost of $28,000.

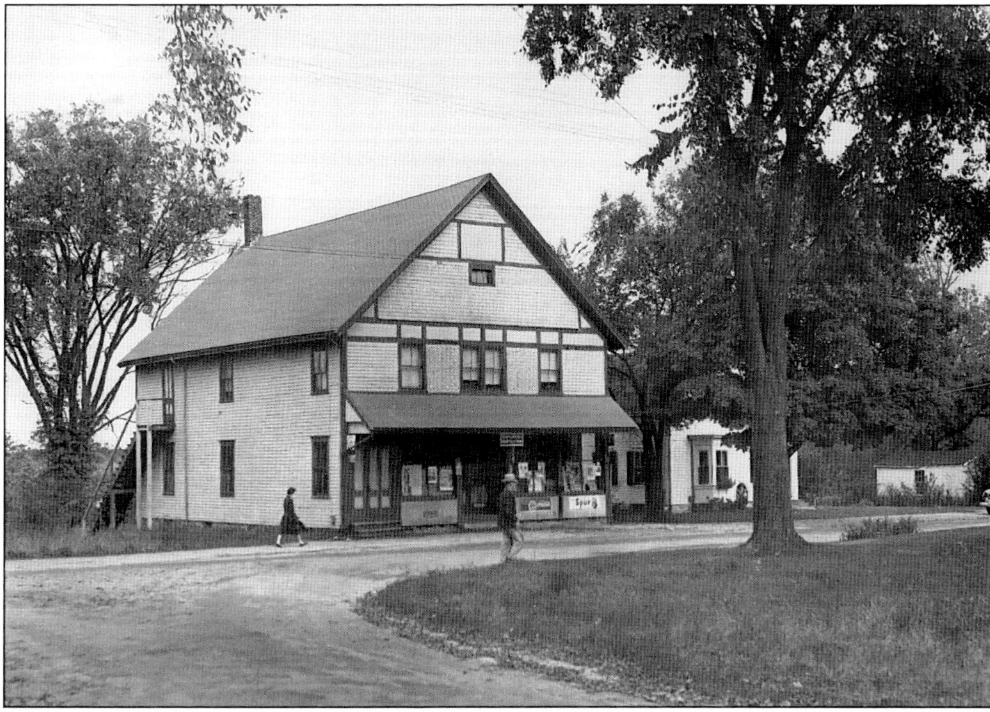

The Chartley Post Office was located in the Wetherell Store on South Worcester Street. For many years, men in the Wetherell Family were the postmasters. The Wetherells also operated the general variety store. Many functions were held in the hall upstairs. The ladies of the Methodist church presented their plays there.

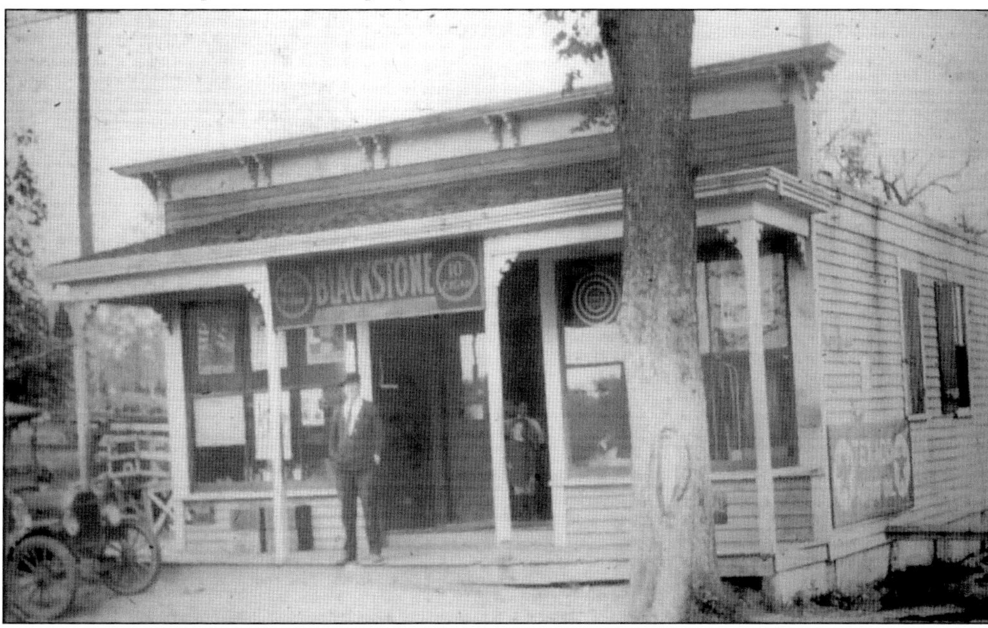

Edward "Doc" Roberts stands on the porch of his store by Chartley Pond on South Worcester Street. Joseph Bottomley built this store c. 1904, ran it until 1917, and then sold it to Roberts. Later, the building became known as the Sportsman Cafe.

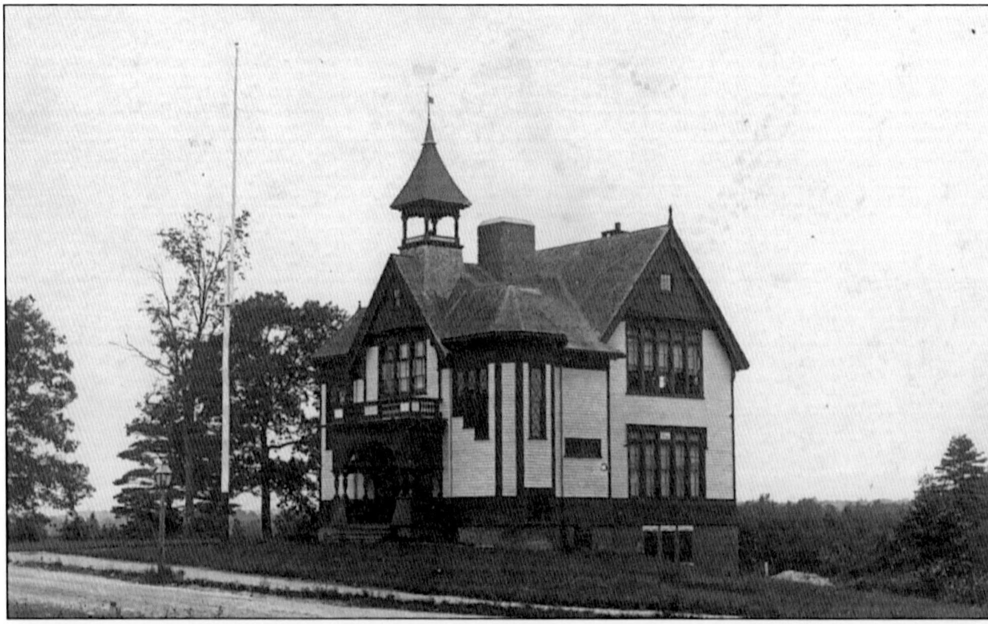

In 1890, the town accepted this school building and all its furnishings as a gift from William A. Sturdy. Known as the Sturdy School, it was a graded primary and grammar school. When Sarah Sturdy retired in 1937 after 20 years as principal of the school, Henri Yelle succeeded her and held the top post until he entered the service in 1941.

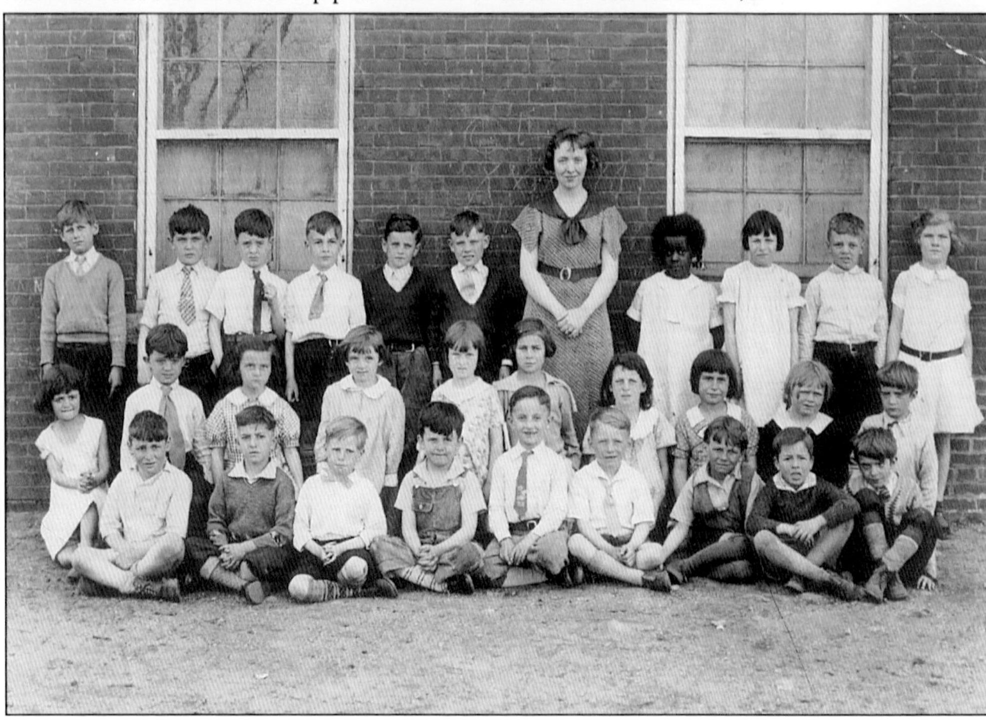

This picture was taken in 1933 of the first and second grades of the Sturdy School. Among the students are Carl Bottomley, Howard Pike, Homer Roy, Mary Devlan, Allen Richmond, Irene Facey, and Robert Jackson. Evelyn Chassee was their teacher.

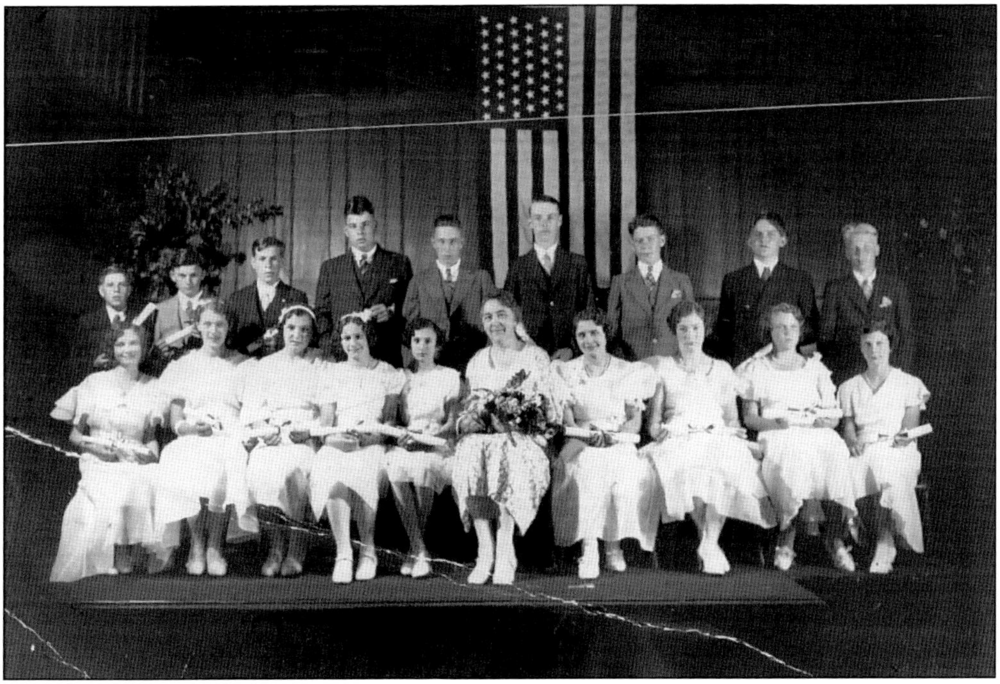

The graduation class of the Chartley Grammar School poses in 1933. Sarah Sturdy was the principal. The three Norton grammar schools held combined graduation exercises at the Trinitarian Congregational Church. School Supt. Lawrence G. Nourse presented the diplomas.

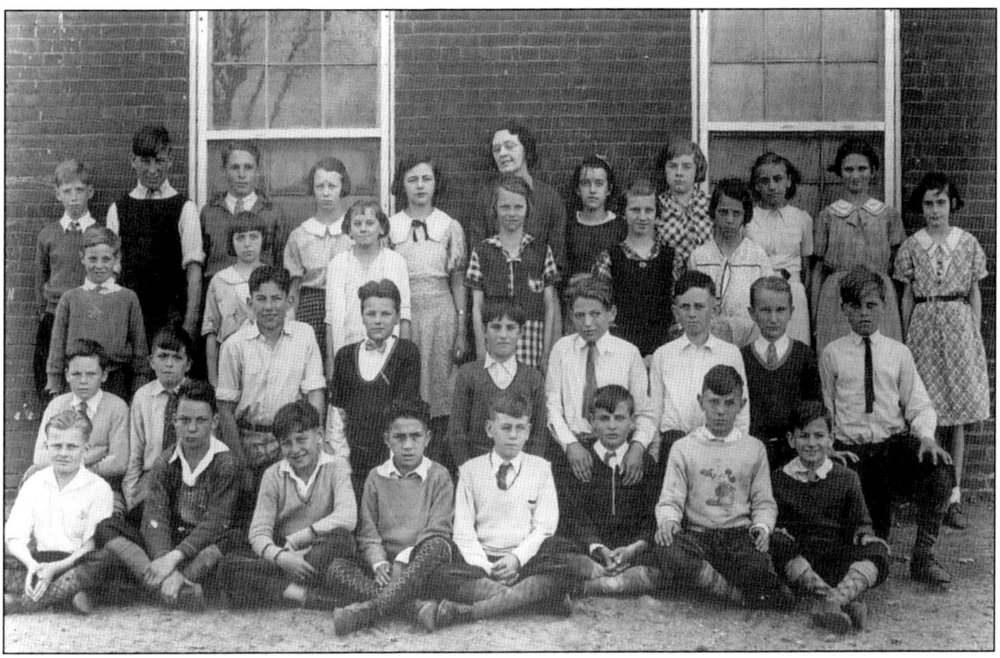

This photograph was taken at the rear of the Sturdy School in the fall of 1934. The pupils are fifth- and sixth-graders. Their teacher, Mildred Witherell, is standing in the center of the back row.

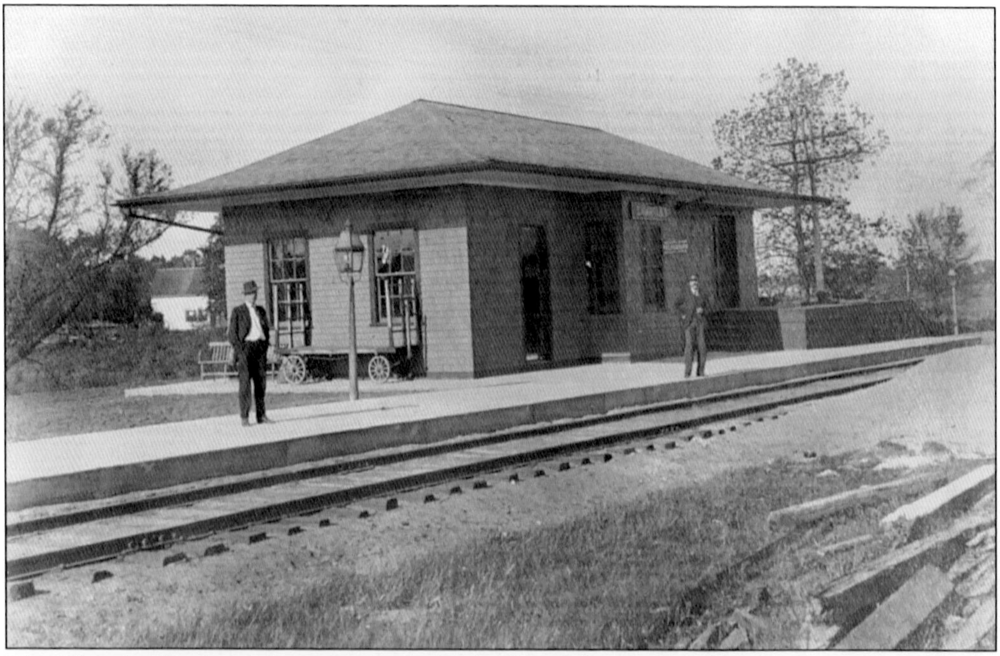

The Chartley Railroad Station was located on Maple Street. There was a time when as many as 20 passenger trains operated between Taunton and Providence to accommodate employees of the jewelry factories in the Chartley area. Express and passenger services were discontinued *c.* 1931.

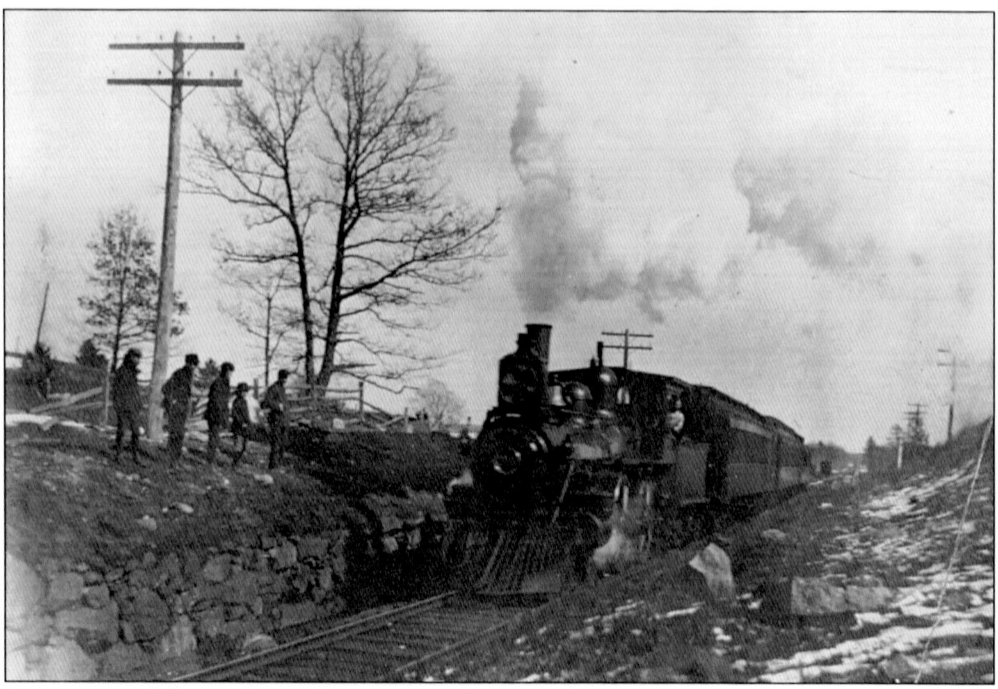

Some young folk watch a passenger train leaving Chartley Station, heading for Attleboro. Train connections with Boston via Attleboro were excellent. The 6:15 evening train made connections with the Fall River Line boats to New York.

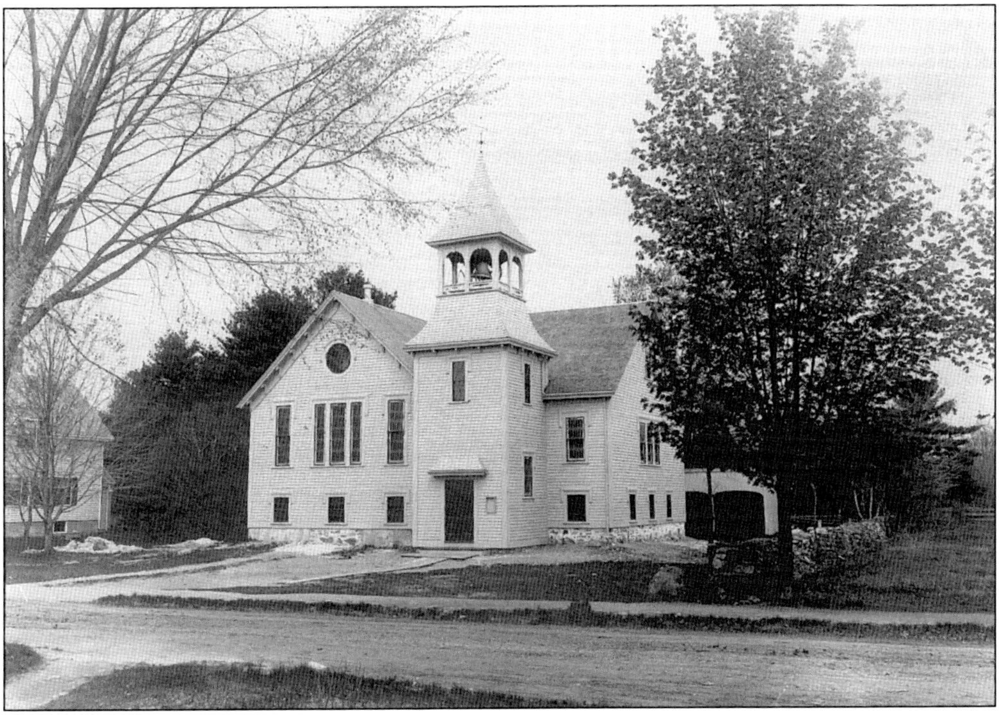

The Chartley Methodist Episcopal Society was organized in 1875. For years, members met in private homes in the neighborhood. The chapel was raised *c.* 1900, a wing was added, and the bell tower was built. Notice the buggy stall sheds in the rear. The church is now known as the Chartley Methodist Church.

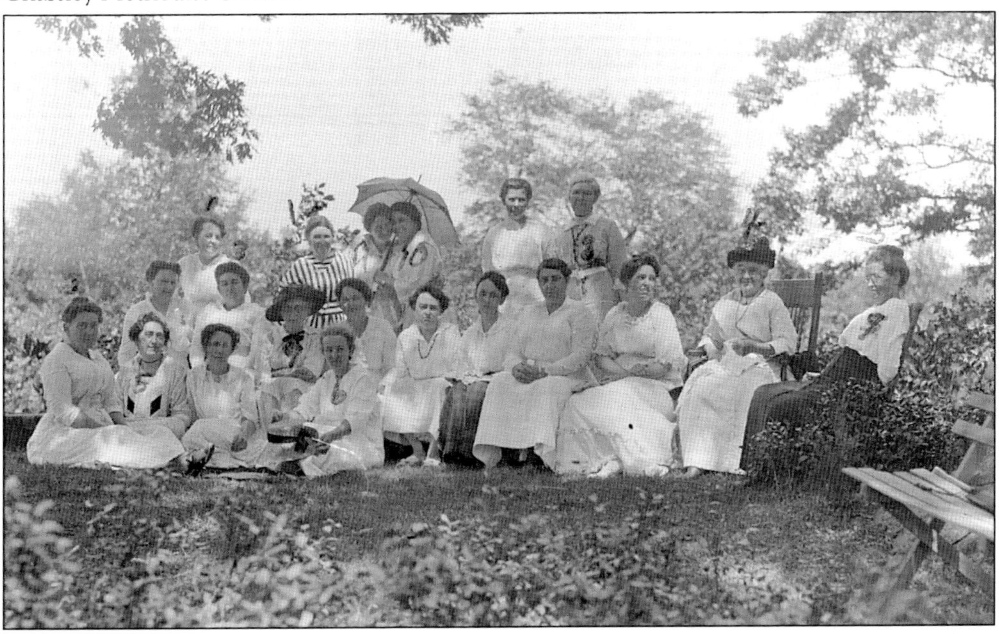

Women of the Ladies' Aide Society of the Chartley Methodist Church contributed much to supporting the church. They earned money by having sales, fairs, suppers, and by presenting plays. Their May breakfasts and strawberry festivals were most popular.

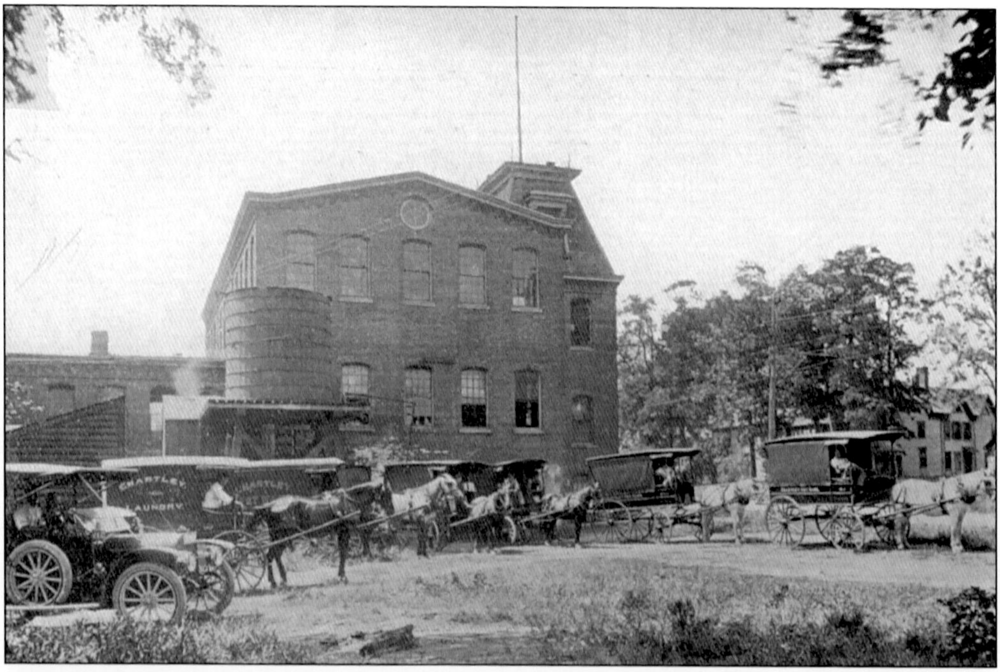

Homer L. Lane and his brother Howard owned the Chartley Wet Wash at Chartley Corner. Their extensive fleet of wagons transported laundry to businesses, hotels, inns, and residences throughout the local towns. Later, the laundry moved into a new building, which the brothers had built across from T.J. Holmes.

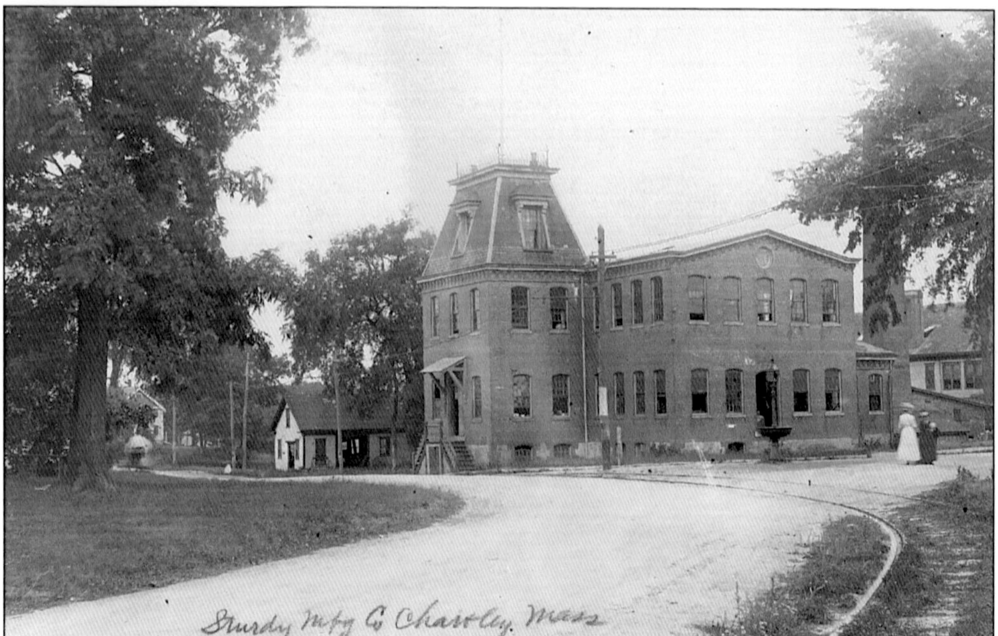

W.A. Sturdy & Co. operated a jewelry business in this building at Chartley Corner. The company manufactured jewelry, such as cuff and collar buttons. To the left of the building, Bill Dunn's blacksmith shop can be seen.

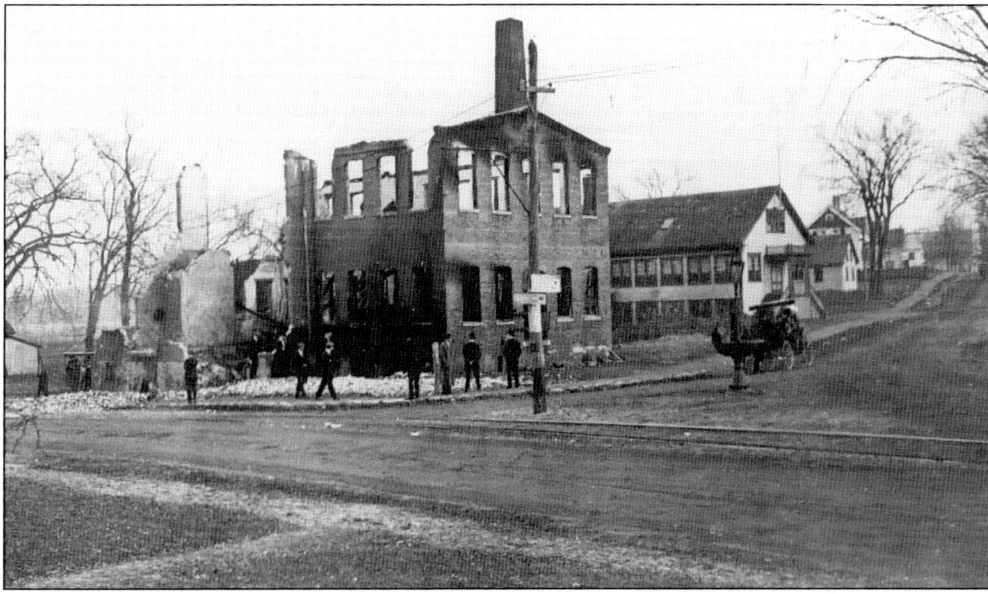

On December 7, 1911, this brick building was destroyed by fire. Notice the horse trough to the right of the building.

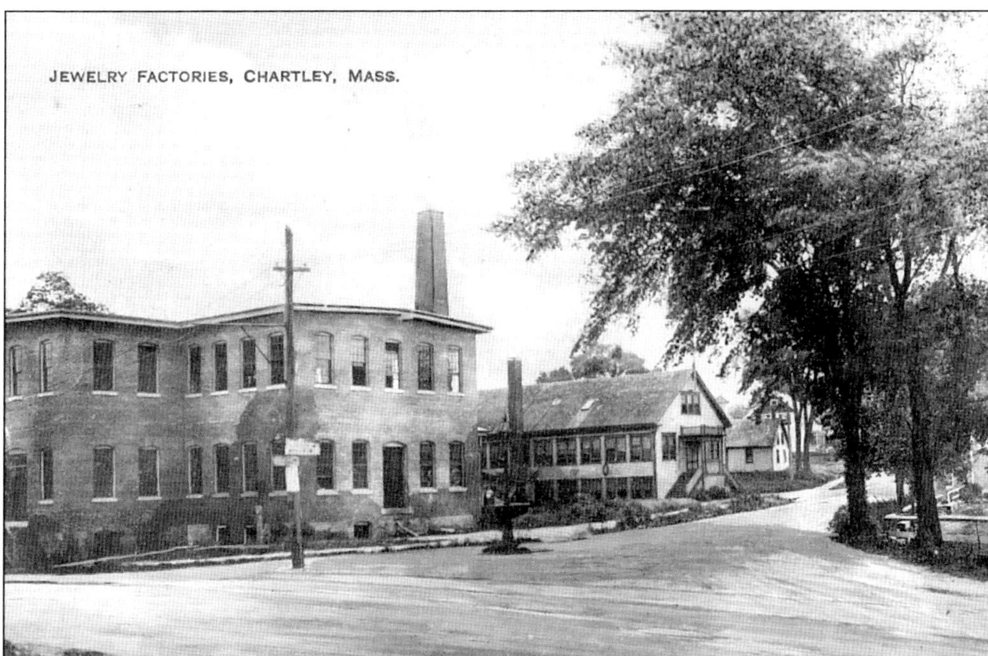

In 1913, W.A. Sturdy merged with Sturdy Brothers and the company became known as Sturdy Brothers Manufacturing Company. The company moved into a shop on South Worcester Street. By 1925, the Sweet Paper Box Company was located in the Sturdy Building.

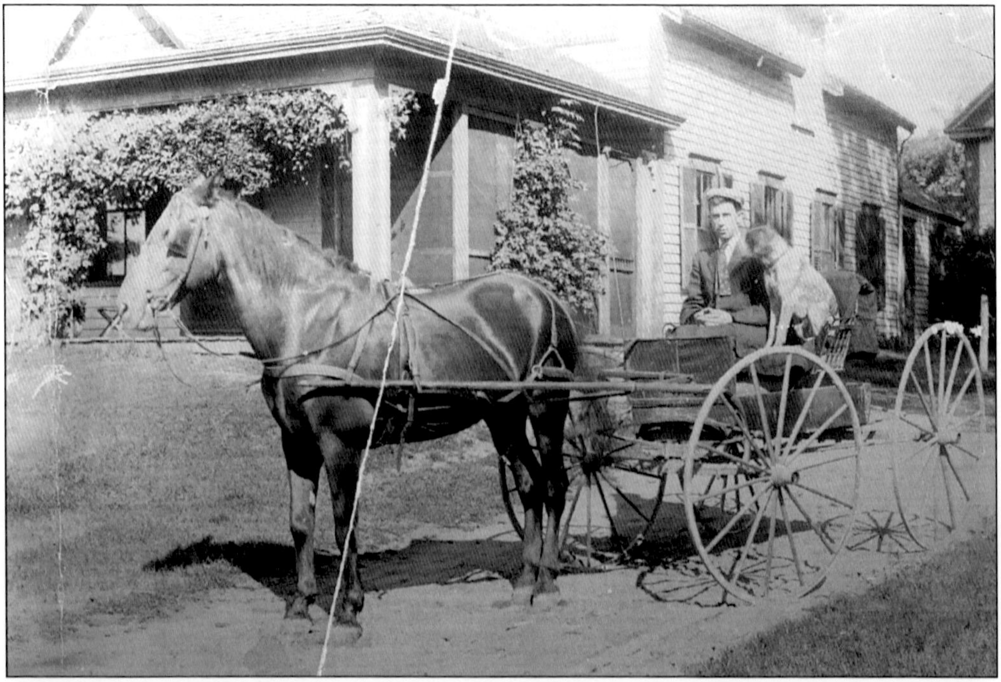

Donald Ulmer and his dog are in front of his father's house on West Main Street by Oak Street. Ulmer farmed 30 acres of his family's land to produce vegetables, which he sold at his roadside stand.

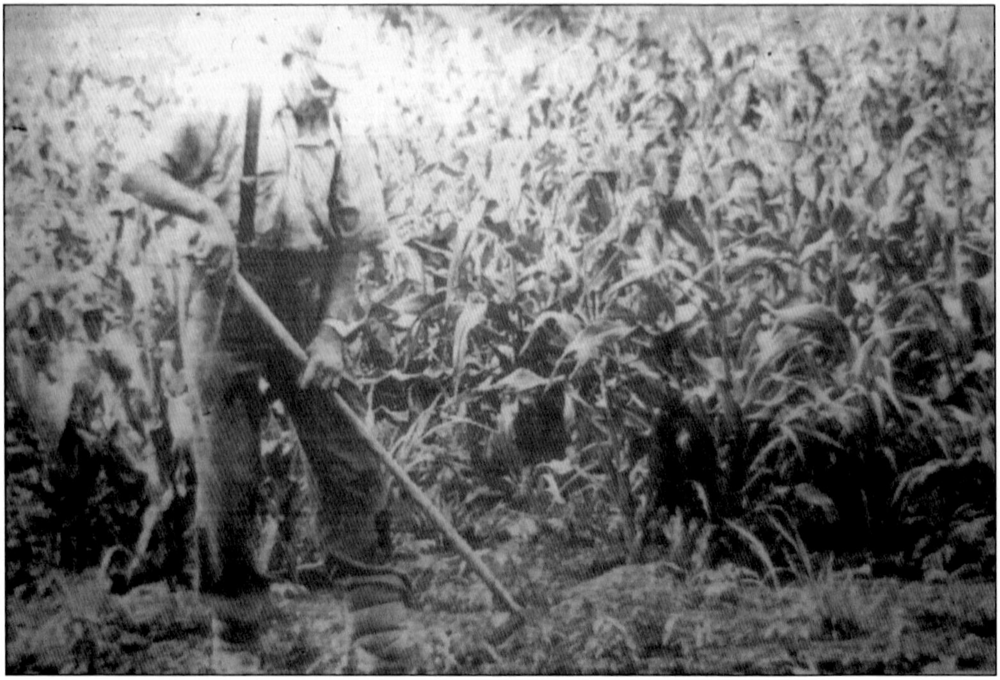

Donald Ulmer spent most of the daylight hours working in his fields. Many local youngsters earned pocket money picking strawberries in Ulmer's fields and across the street at the Sousa Farm.

Four
EAST NORTON

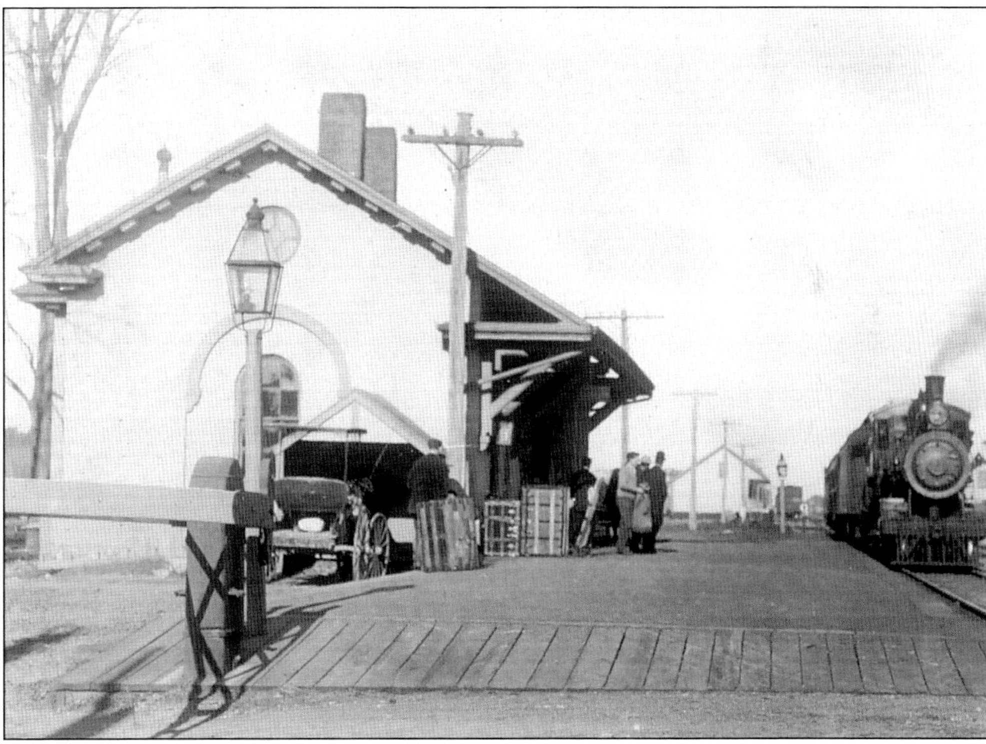

This photograph depicts the Norton Railroad Station as it appeared in the early 1900s. It was one of the few railroad stations designed by Richard Upjohn, one of America's first great Gothic architects. The station had two waiting rooms separated by the ticket office. The Taunton branch of the New Haven Railroad went by this station. As many as 14 passenger trains daily came through Norton. The number of daily trains gradually declined until passenger service stopped completely in 1938.

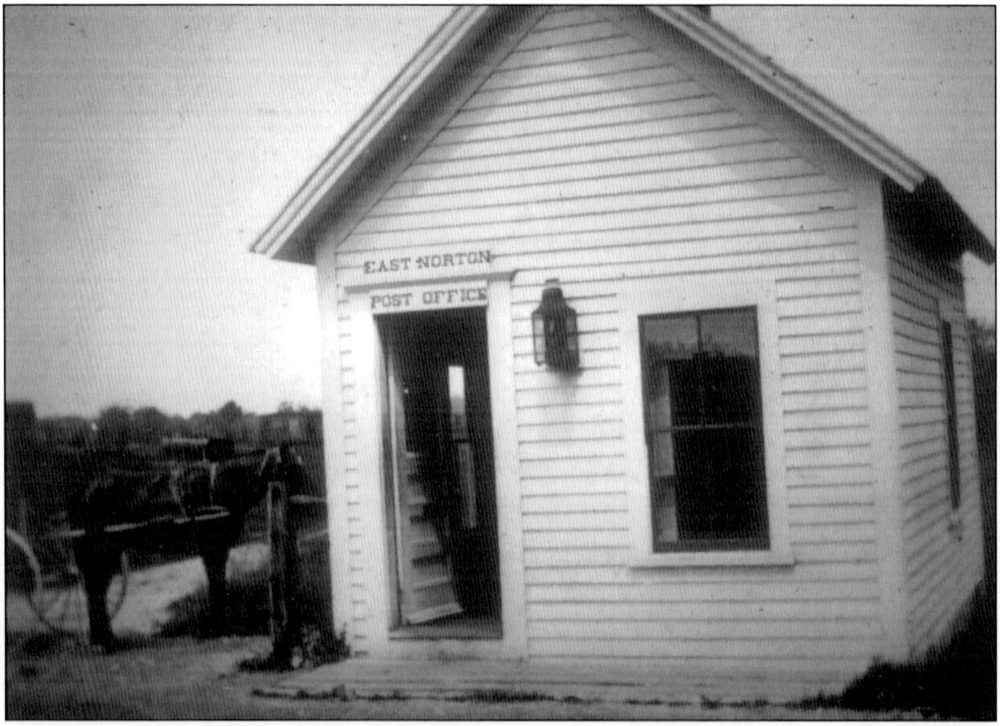

In the early days, the East Norton Post Office was located in a small building to the east side of the railroad tracks. When Charles Bruce became postmaster in 1926, the office was moved into one of the waiting rooms of the station. He remained the postmaster until the post office was closed in 1943.

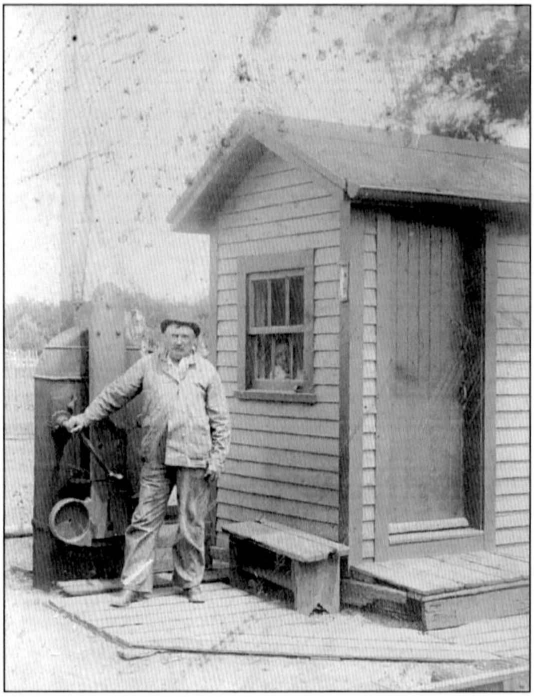

Before they were electrified, railroad crossings were guarded by flagmen. The flagmen had small buildings next to the tracks where they stayed while on duty. Usually, there were three shifts so that the crossings were covered 24 hours a day.

Husband and wife Alton and Drusilla Ring Foster are shown in their costumes for the town's 250th anniversary. Both were founding members of the Norton Historical Society and were instrumental in the restoration of District No. 3 Schoolhouse, which became a museum for the society. She was the longest-serving district health nurse for the town and was also the school nurse. He was the son of Howard and Jessie Hunt Foster, who lived in the Hunt family farmhouse on South Washington Street.

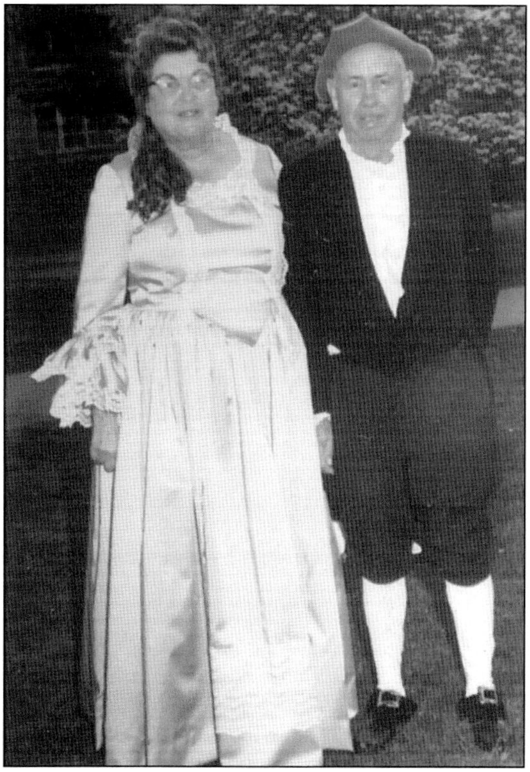

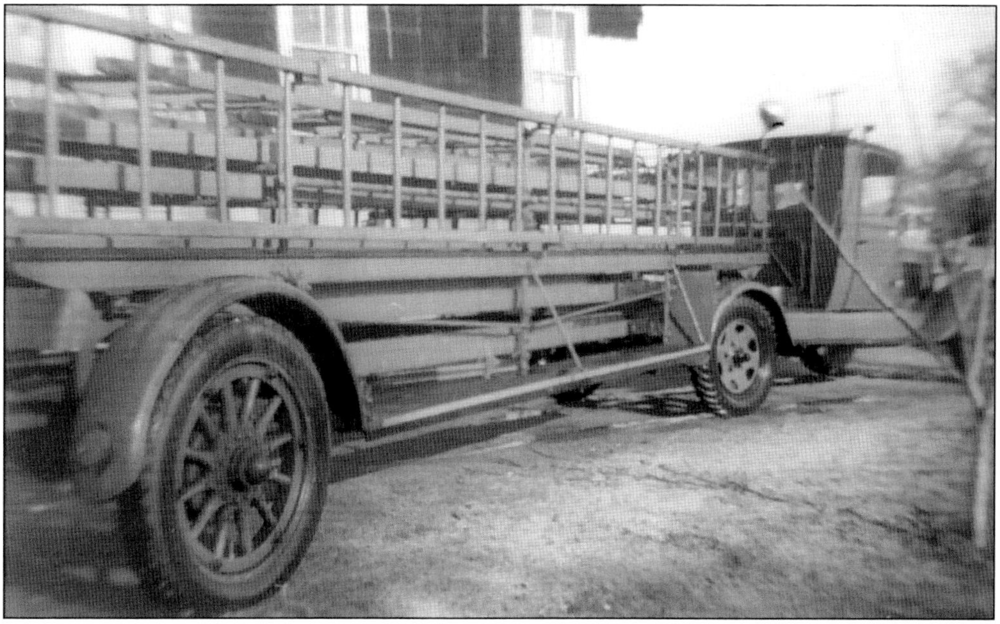

Howard Foster served as fire engineer for the town. He was ingenious in repairing and improving fire trucks and apparatus. In 1935, Foster, Stephen Benaski, and Harold Wetherell, built this ladder truck out of an older horse-drawn ladder truck, another truck, and a cab. They transferred the ladders to the truck chassis, attached the cab, and came up with a serviceable truck.

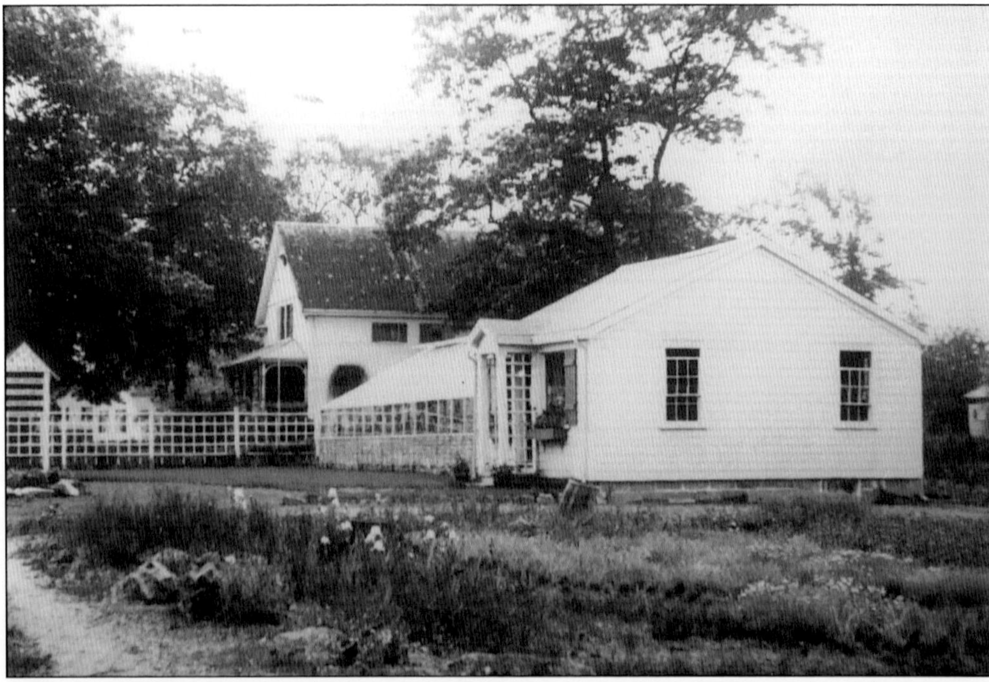

Charles and Ethel Bruce resided in this house on East Main Street. Bruce, his father, and his brother constructed the house in 1907. Bruce was an outstanding, well-respected, lifelong resident of the town. As a hobby, he established a florist business in 1933. He raised plants and flowers in his greenhouse, specializing in geraniums. He closed his business in 1964.

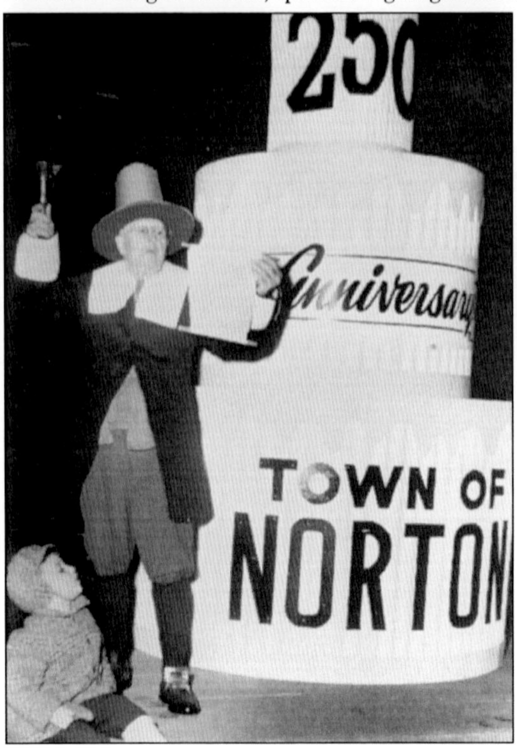

In 1961, when the town celebrated its 250th anniversary, Charles Bruce was appointed town crier for the event. A selectman for eight years, Bruce became assistant station agent of the Norton depot in 1903. In 1908, he was made agent and served for over 45 years in that position. Bruce was an active, longtime member of the Norton Grange No. 218 and was grange master in 1927 and 1928.

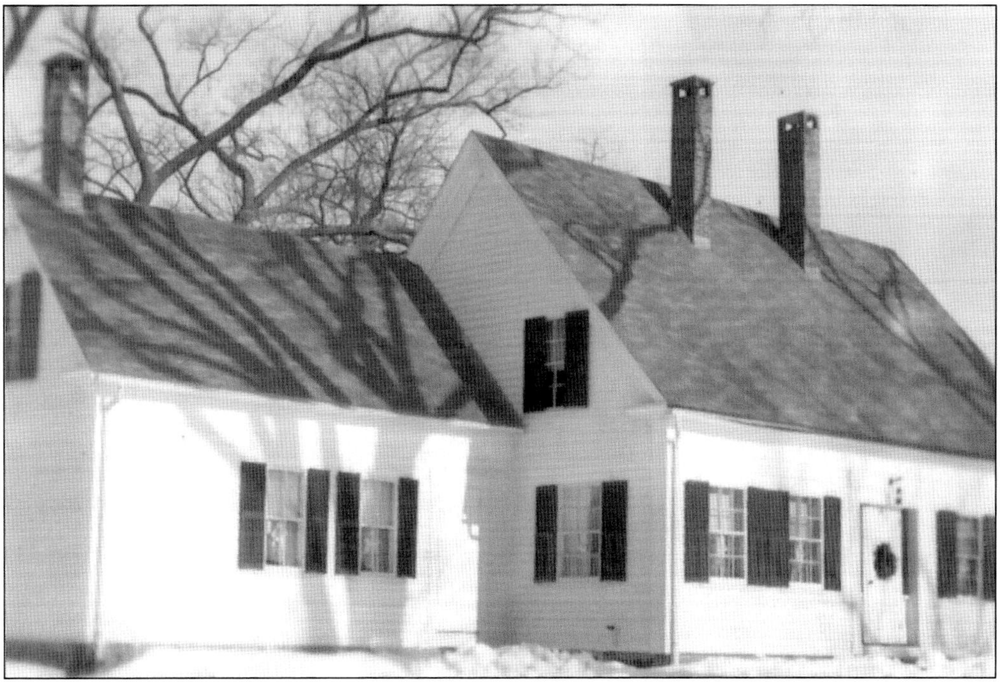

George Perry lived in this house at the entrance of North Washington Street. Perry served his town in many capacities. He was the first postmaster in East Norton and station agent at the train depot for 11 years. He served as selectman for 10 years, moderator for 15 years, and auditor for 10 years. He was marshal at the graduation exercises of Wheaton Seminary for 20 years.

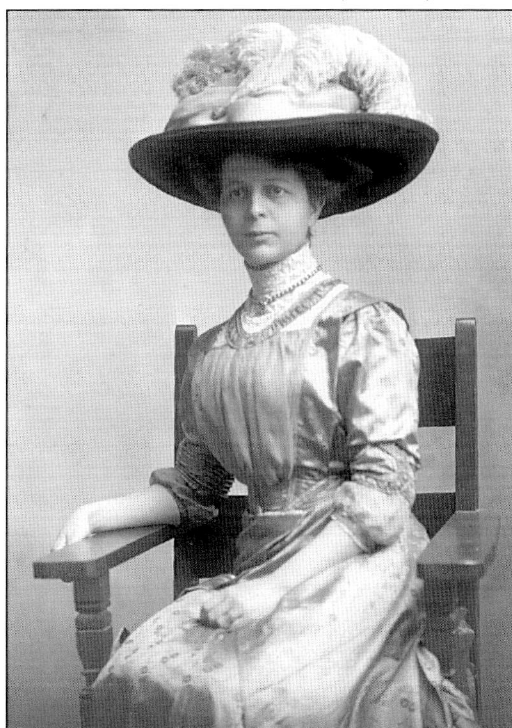

Mabel H. Perry, the daughter of George Perry, was a teacher and principal in Taunton. For many years she was a member and secretary of the Norton School Committee, and for 12 years she was president of the Norton Public Library. She was known around town for the stylish hats that she always wore in public.

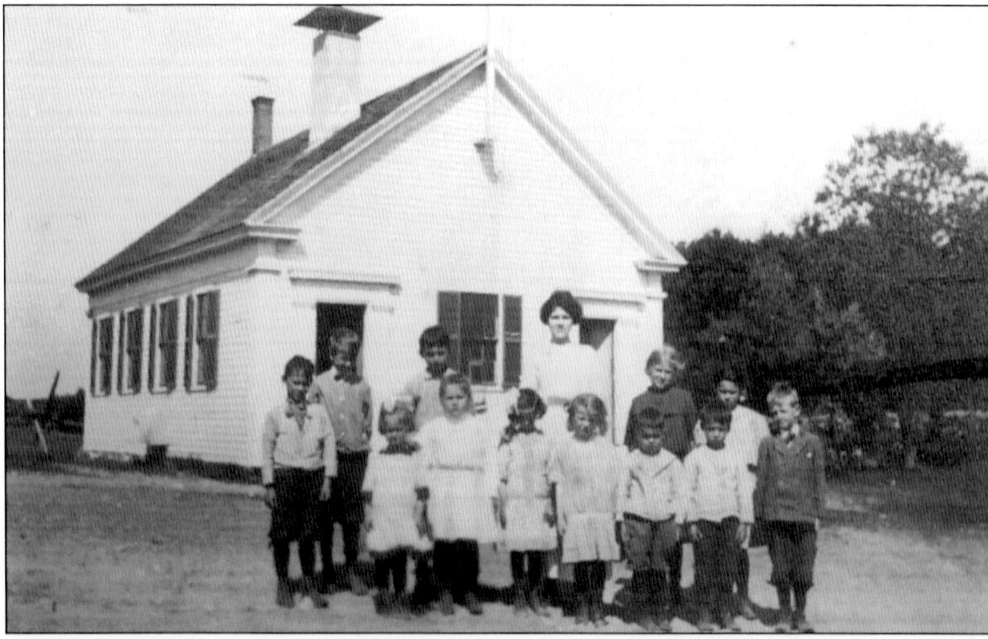

District School No. 5 was located on the corner of Newcomb and North Washington Streets. This photograph, taken in 1913, shows Miss Burke standing in front of the school with her class. The children are members of the Beebe, White, Scott, Foster, and Sweet families. The school closed in 1916. The building was moved to its present site on West Main Street in 1925. Before it became the Senior Citizens Center, it was used as a fire station.

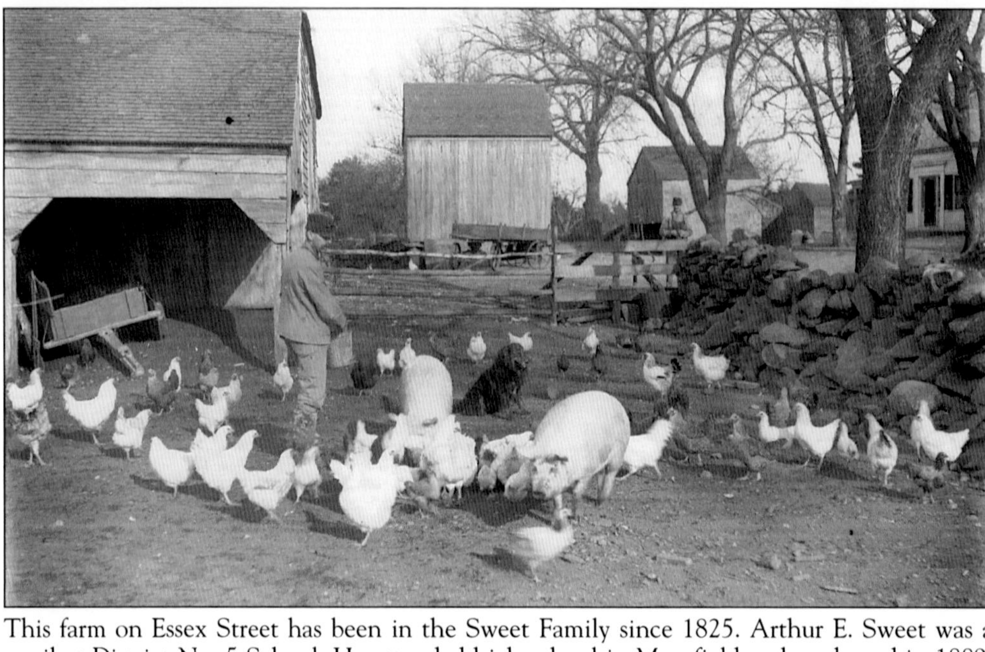

This farm on Essex Street has been in the Sweet Family since 1825. Arthur E. Sweet was a pupil at District No. 5 School. He attended high school in Mansfield and graduated in 1889. He traveled daily by foot or horseback. He was an active member of the Trinitarian Church, serving for many years as treasurer and deacon. He also was a member of the Norton Grange for more than 50 years.

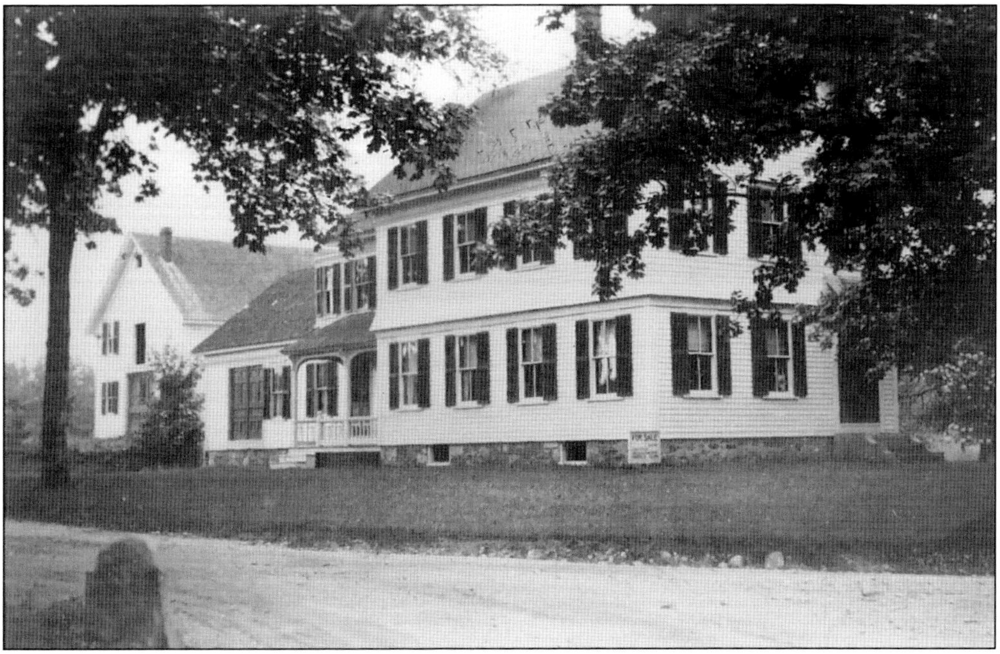

At the corner of North Washington and Cobb Streets is the Foster Homestead. Alexander Foster had a machine shop in the attached buildings, which he erected. Generations of the Foster men have been mechanical geniuses. Son Walter Foster and grandson Frank worked in this shop using many of the ancestral tools. They not only repaired machinery and restored wooden furniture but also added a long list of inventions to the Foster name.

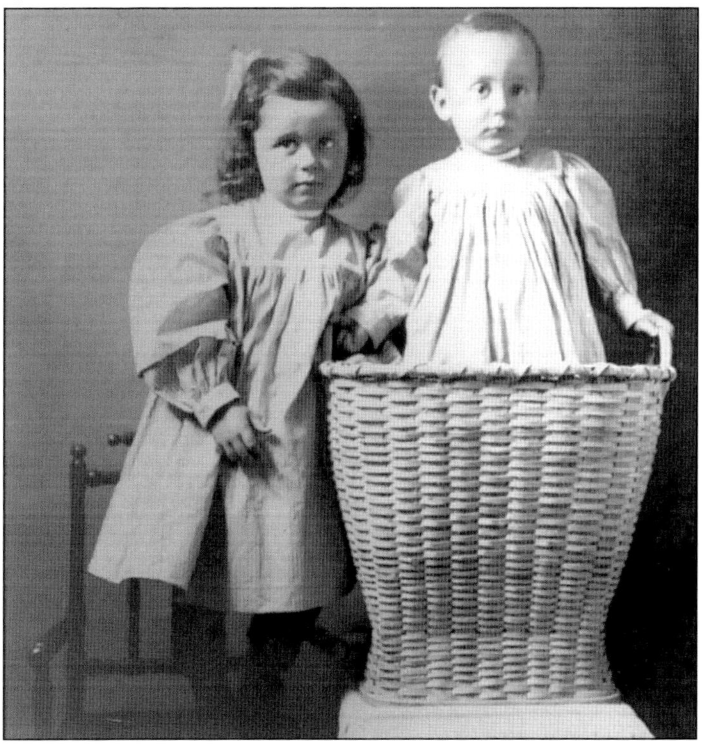

Ida and Clinton Foster were the children of Walter and Kate Foster. They lived in the Foster Homestead, which was close by Bruce's basket shop. Clinton is standing in a Bruce basket. Walter Foster had three wives and 11 children.

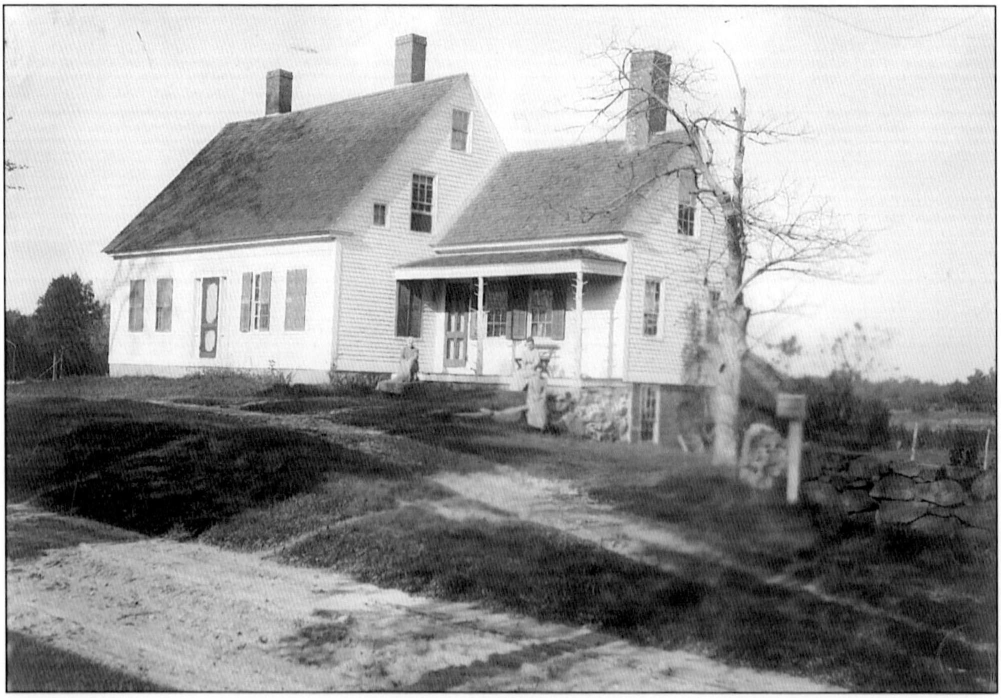

Daniel Parker, an early doctor in Norton, built this house on North Washington Street. He acquired about 60 acres of land on both sides of the road to add to his farm. When George Bruce bought the farm in the 1870s, he began a basket-making business.

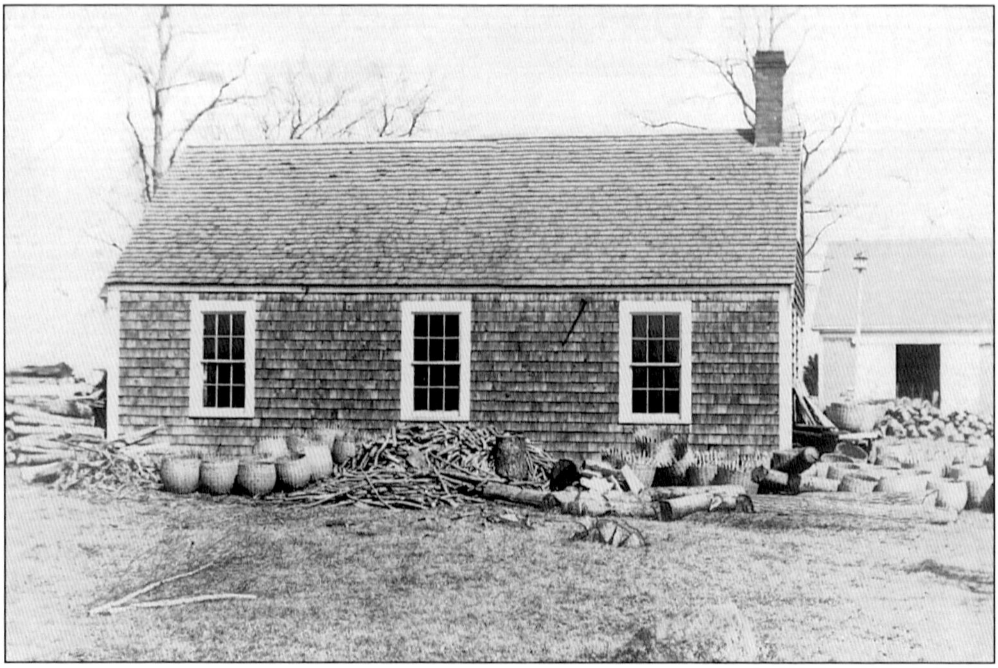

The basket shop was across the street from the Bruce Farm. The Bruce family made baskets of all shapes and sizes, using strips of oak, ash, or walnut from trees in the local woods. The logs were kept in water until they could be used.

George "Strawberry" Bruce was not only a basket maker but also a farmer. He was known for the delicious strawberries that he grew. Bruce is pictured weaving pliable strips of wood into a basket. To start the basket-making process, Bruce split logs into small sections called bolts. The bolts were then run through a splitting machine to make the long strips. The strips were made pliable by steaming them over a boiler.

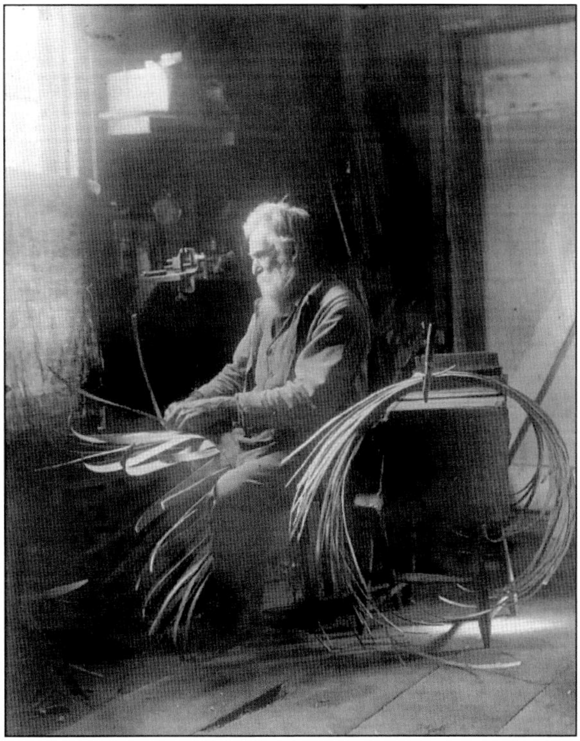

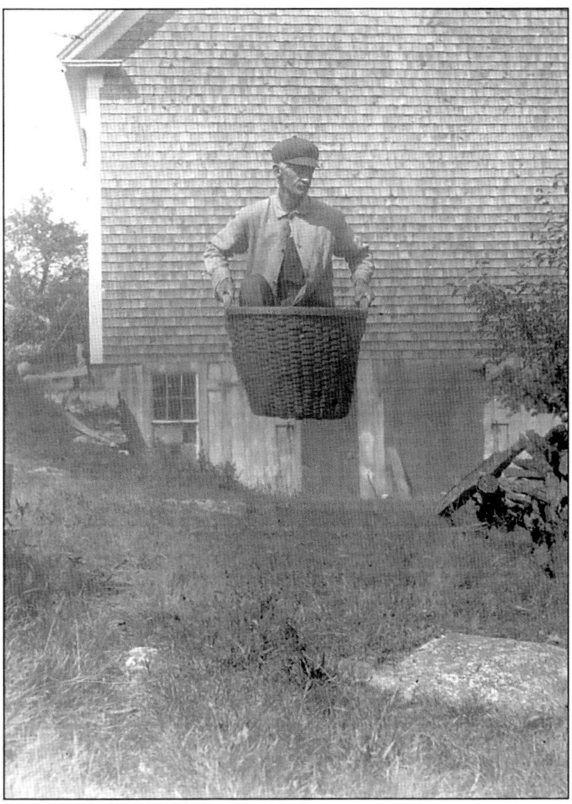

Basket making seems to run in families. George Bruce's son Elmer Bruce was also a basket maker. His hobby was photography, and he enjoyed posing in many of his trick photographs. Here, he appears to be floating across the yard in a large laundry basket. The forms on which some of the baskets were built were called drums. Basket makers produced these drums from white pines.

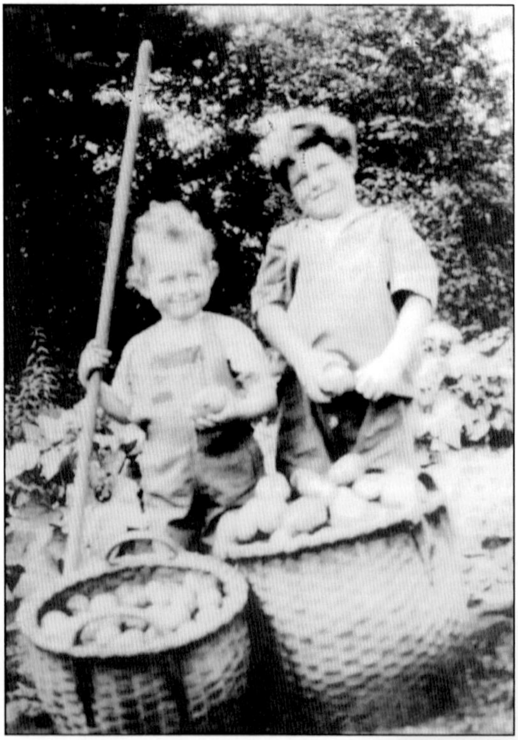

The Bruce baskets could be found in many Norton households. Sometimes, a new bride would receive a Bruce basket as a wedding gift. These baskets were very sturdy for many different uses. Here, Charlotte Goff and her cousin Pearl Billows have dug a couple of basketfuls of potatoes from the family garden.

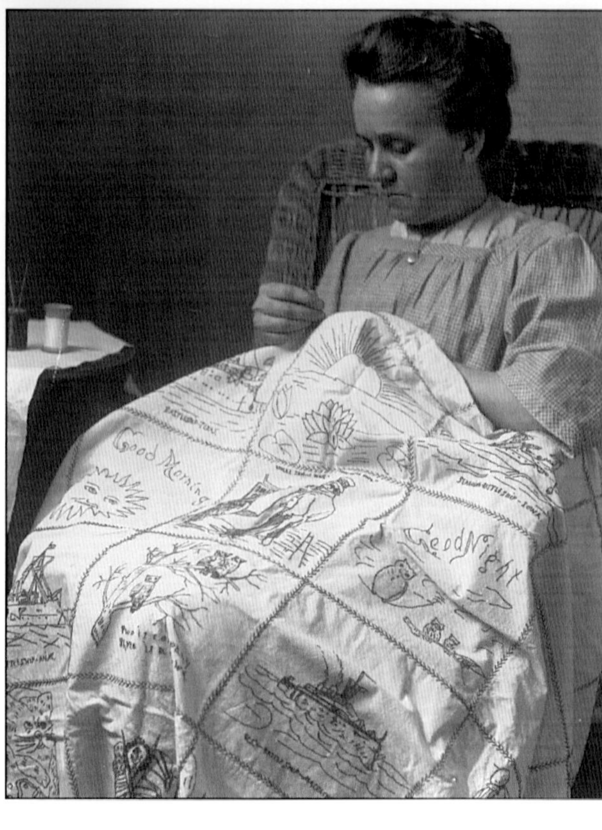

Minnie Bruce was the daughter of George Bruce. Like many women of her times, she was adept at handiwork. She spent her evenings embroidering a pictorial bedspread that depicted events of interest to her. This glass-negative image was taken by her brother Elmer Bruce.

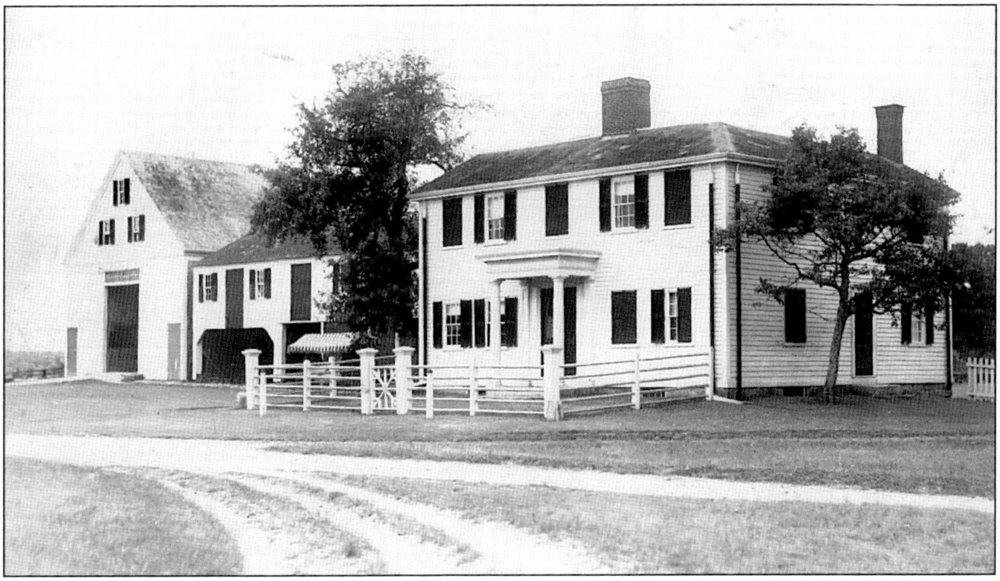

Harriot A. Newcomb lived in this stately home at the corner of Newland and Newcomb Streets. The daughter of Nathaniel Newcomb, she bequeathed her house and a sum of money to establish a nonprofit home for aged women of the town. In 1923, the Newcomb Home for Old Ladies opened. In later years, the home accepted men and couples. In 1966, the Newcomb Home merged with the Daggett-Crandall Home of Attleboro to form the Daggett-Crandall Newcomb Home. The old homestead no longer stands.

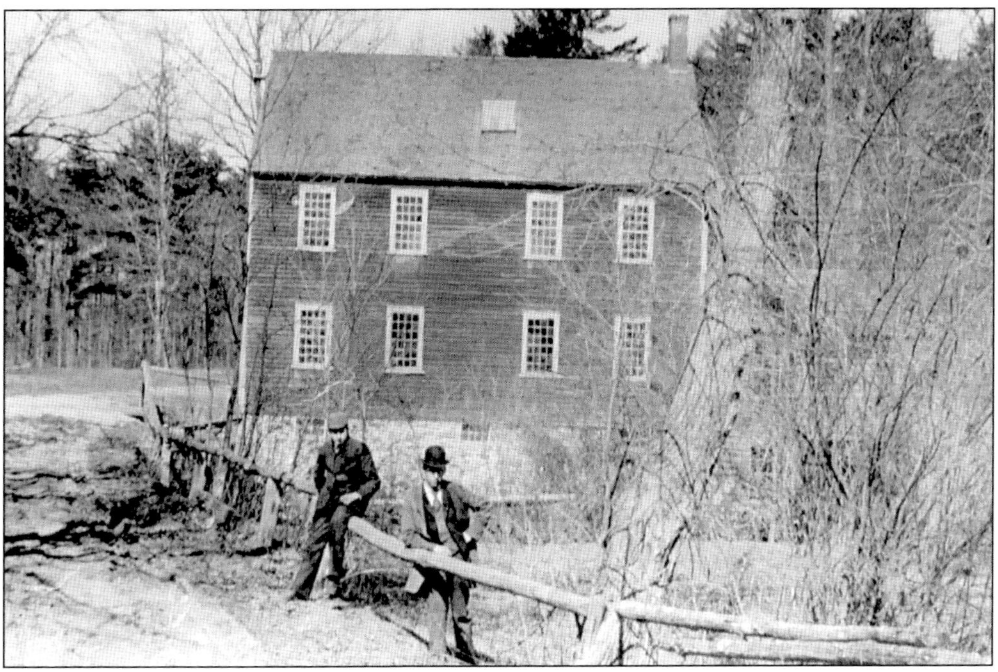

Nathaniel Newcomb owned a cotton mill on Red Mill Road by the Canoe River. Although the building is gone, the stone foundation can be seen beside the bridge. The Land Preservation Society of Norton owns and maintains several acres along both sides of this dirt road. The town designated Red Mill Road as a scenic road in 1978.

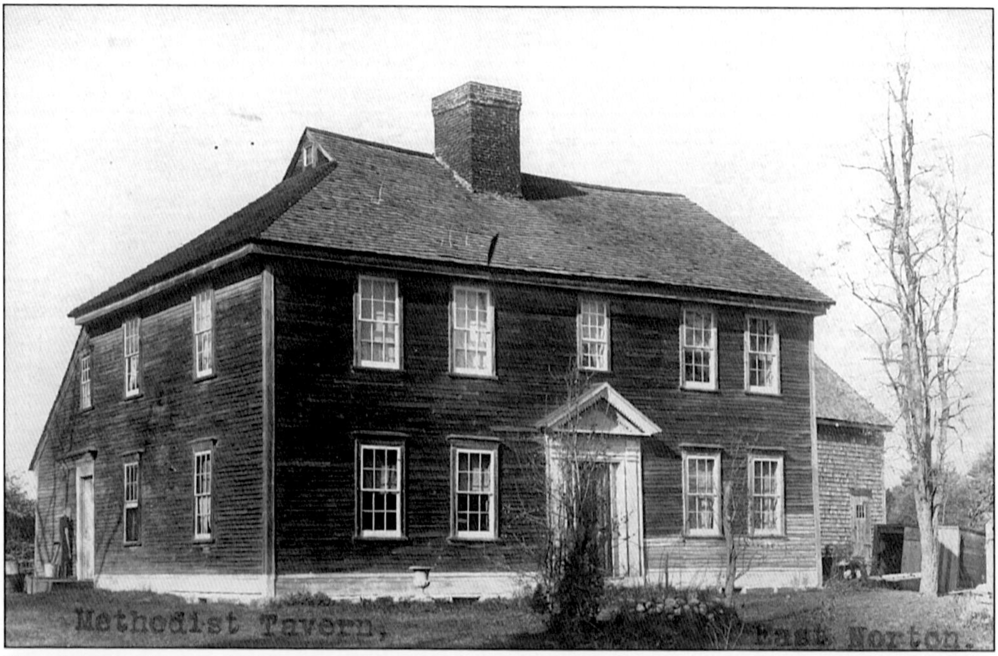

The Joseph Newcomb Homestead can be seen on Burt Street. This home remained in the Newcomb family until the 1950s, when it was sold after the last descendant passed away. During the early years, this home served as a schoolhouse, a tavern, and a stagecoach stop for the Boston-to-Taunton run. It was also the earliest Methodist meetinghouse in the area.

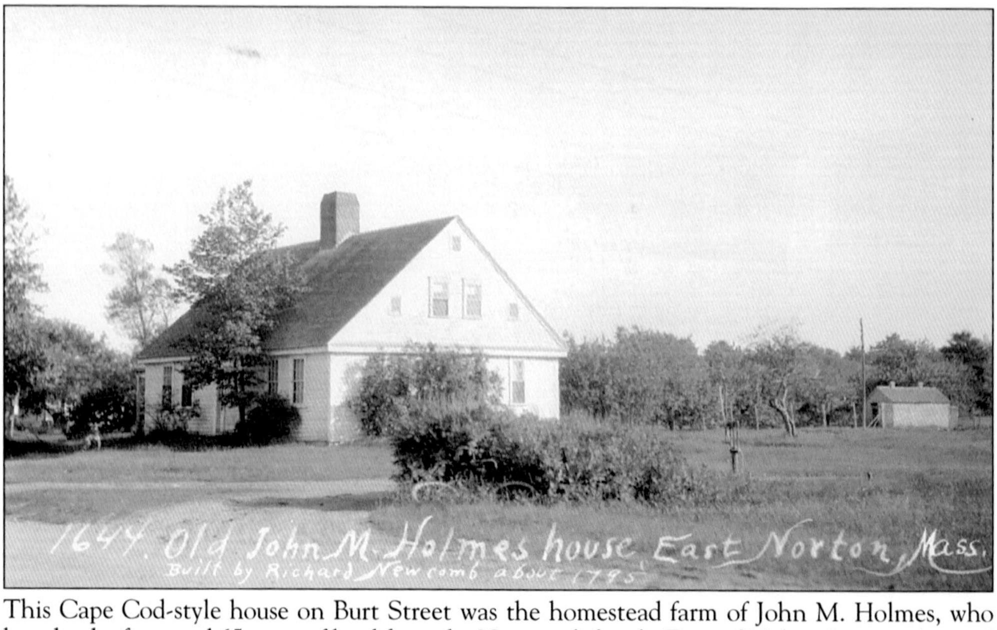

This Cape Cod-style house on Burt Street was the homestead farm of John M. Holmes, who bought the farm and 65 acres of land from the Newcomb family. Four of Holmes's sons inherited the property from their mother, Calista Holmes, in 1907. It remained in the Holmes family until the 1970s. Lewis, Lester, and David Holmes each built a house on land adjacent to the homestead. Edgar Holmes moved the old Baptist parsonage on Lincoln Street to the other side of the family homestead.

In 1901, three sons of John Holmes established a cucumber-raising business in seven greenhouses built at the rear of the homestead. Brothers Lewis, David, and Edgar Holmes grew the cucumbers for the New York market. This picture shows Lewis Holmes working in one of the greenhouses. The partnership was dissolved in 1940 and the business was sold to Smith & Simons of New Bedford.

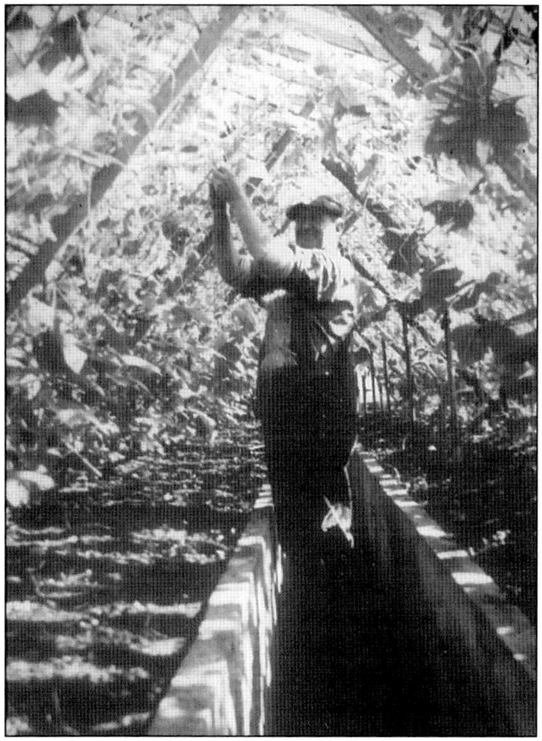

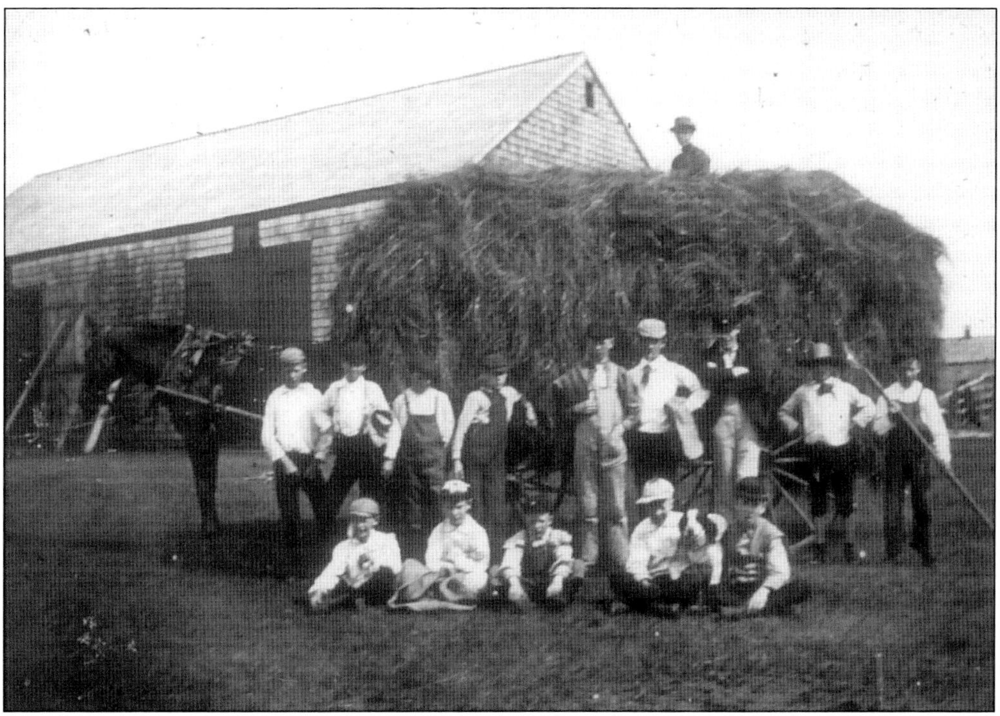

Through the Country Weeks program for Fresh Air Children, young people from Boston spent some summer days at the Holmes Farm. They helped with the farm chores, picked blueberries, and learned to enjoy life on a farm.

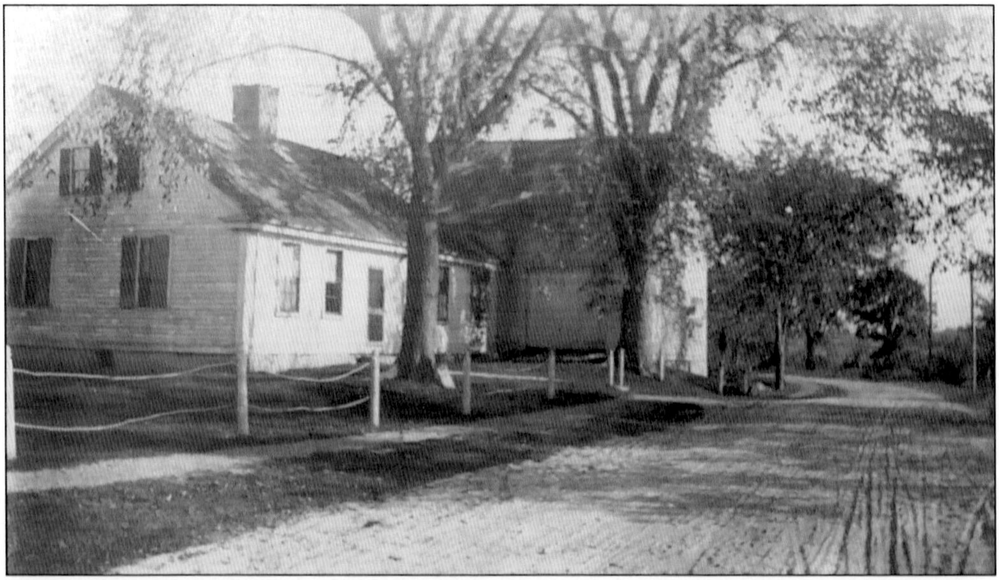

At the turn of the century, the Lincoln, Woodward, and Leonard families settled along Main Street by the Sawmill Curve. Moses Lincoln lived in this early house next to the pond by the curve. He carried on a woodworking business, a shingle mill, and a sawmill powered by the Canoe River. A row of Cape-style, duplex, mill houses were built for the people who worked at these mills. Daniel and Lewis Woodward, direct descendants of Moses Lincoln, inherited the businesses in 1911.

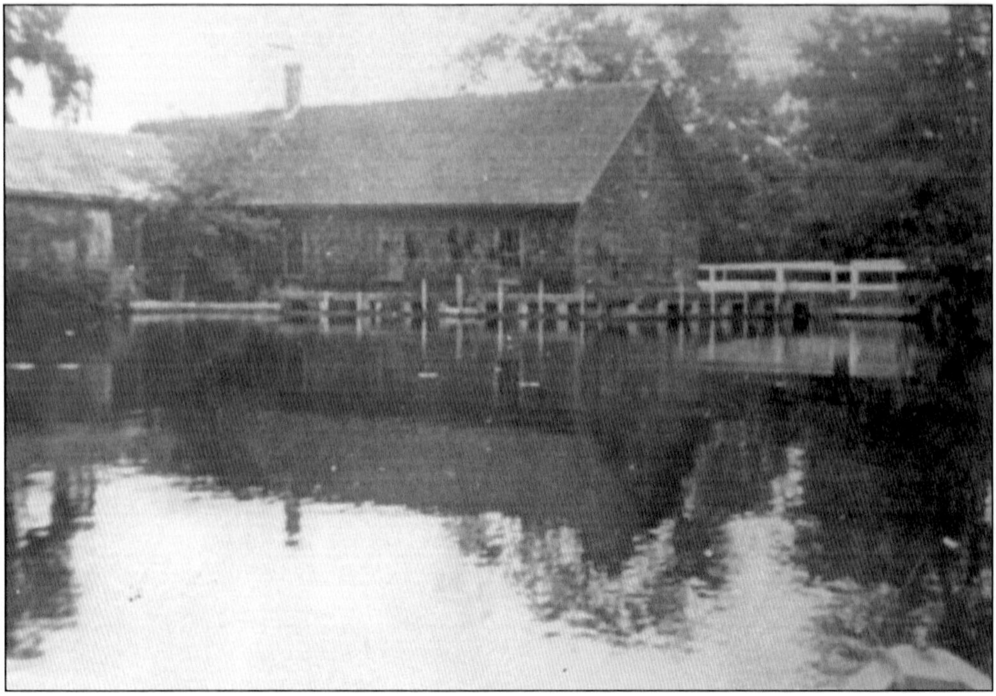

The Woodward brothers ran a shingle mill, gristmill, sawmill, and cider mill at this millpond. In the fall the cider mill was popular with children, who got to watch the process and breathe in the aroma as the apples were pressed to make cider.

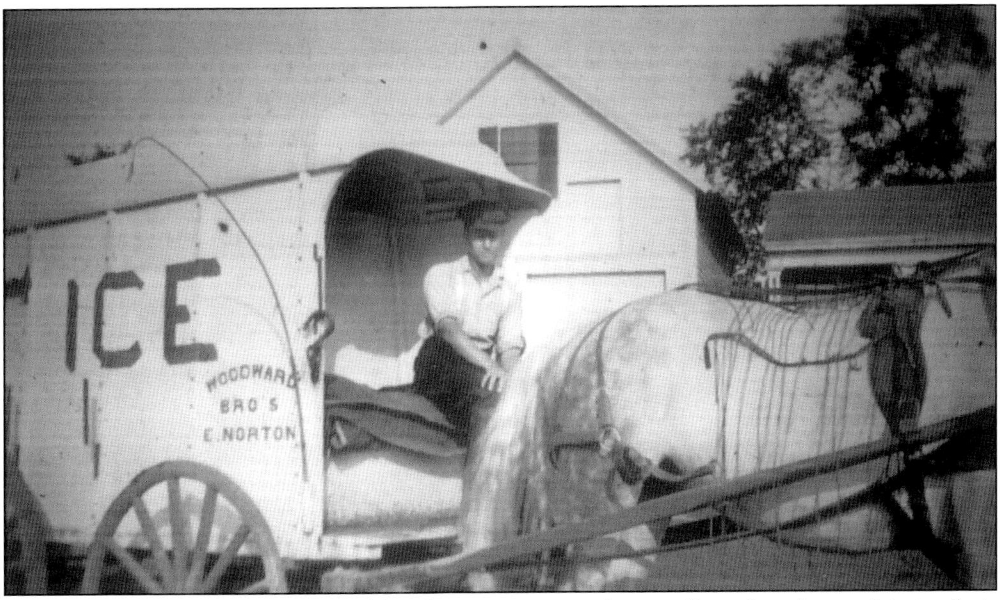

During the winter the Woodward brothers cut ice in their millpond and stored it in their three icehouses. To produce an ice of thicker and better quality, the brothers hired the town fire truck to pump water onto the pond's ice to increase the thickness by about 1.5 inches. Harold Woodward, the son of Daniel Woodward, and his horse Major delivered the ice by wagon to homes throughout the town.

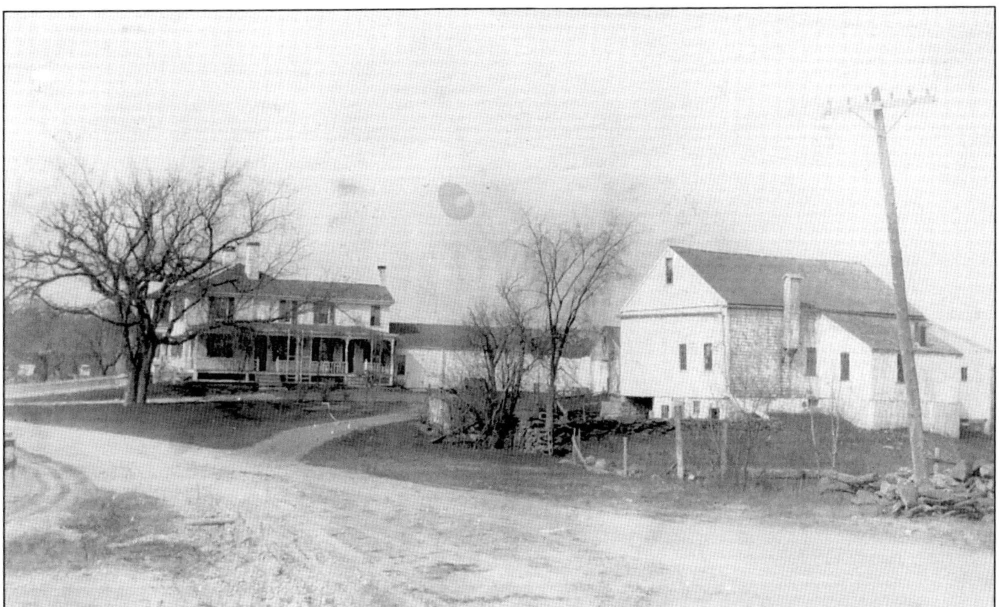

Brothers Everett and Virgil Leonard had farms just beyond Sawmill Curve. This picture shows the farm of Everett Leonard, who ran a meat market in the barn and cured the meat in big barrels behind it. He had two teams on the road six days a week delivering orders. Virgil Leonard and his son Clarence lived in homes across the street. They ran the Leonard Dairy and Poultry Farm.

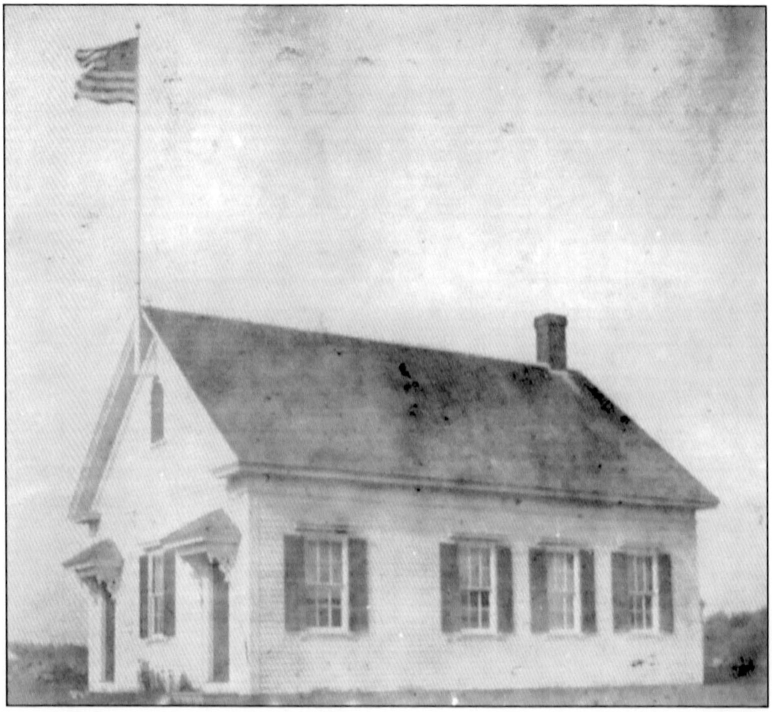

District No. 6 School was located on East Main Street across from Leonard Street. In 1908, this school was closed and the children were transferred to the Center School. The building became the East Norton Community Center, where Saturday night dances were held. The building was destroyed during the fire of 1933.

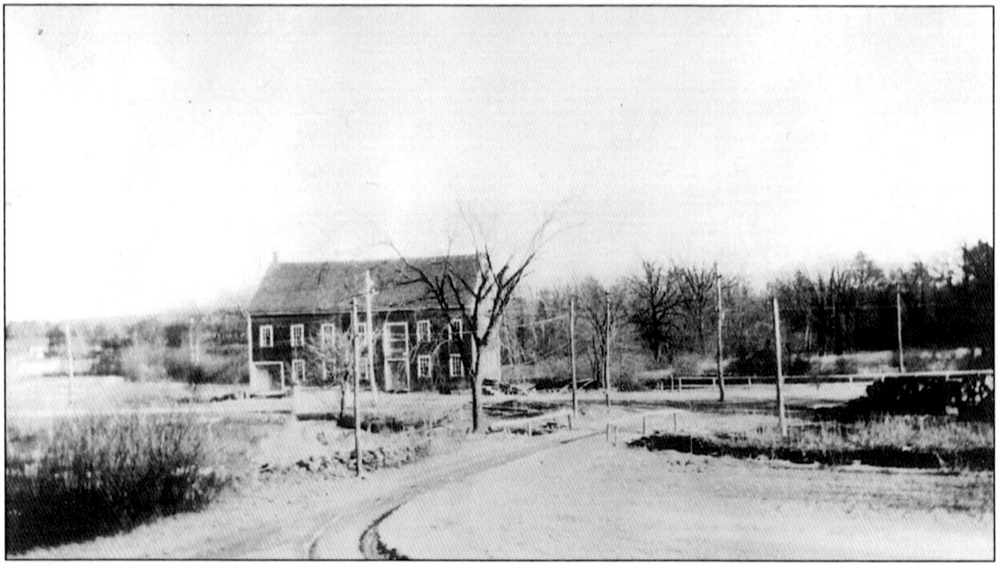

The April 25, 1933 fire caused tragic changes to this neighborhood. It started in the Woodward's planing mill, shown here. The fire spread quickly and destroyed the mill, Virgil Leonard's house and barn, and District No. 6 Schoolhouse. Three other homes and barns were scorched, and fields were burned. Firemen were handicapped for water pressure, as there were no hydrants. Pumpers from Attleboro, Mansfield, and Taunton boosted water from the river. Wheaton College girls and neighbors assisted in saving most of the Leonard furniture. The Woodward's replaced the destroyed mill with a cider mill, and Virgil Leonard rebuilt his house and barn. With the future plan of extending Route 495 through this area of town has come the realization that this neighborhood would be completely lost.

Five

MEADOWBROOK - CRANE'S

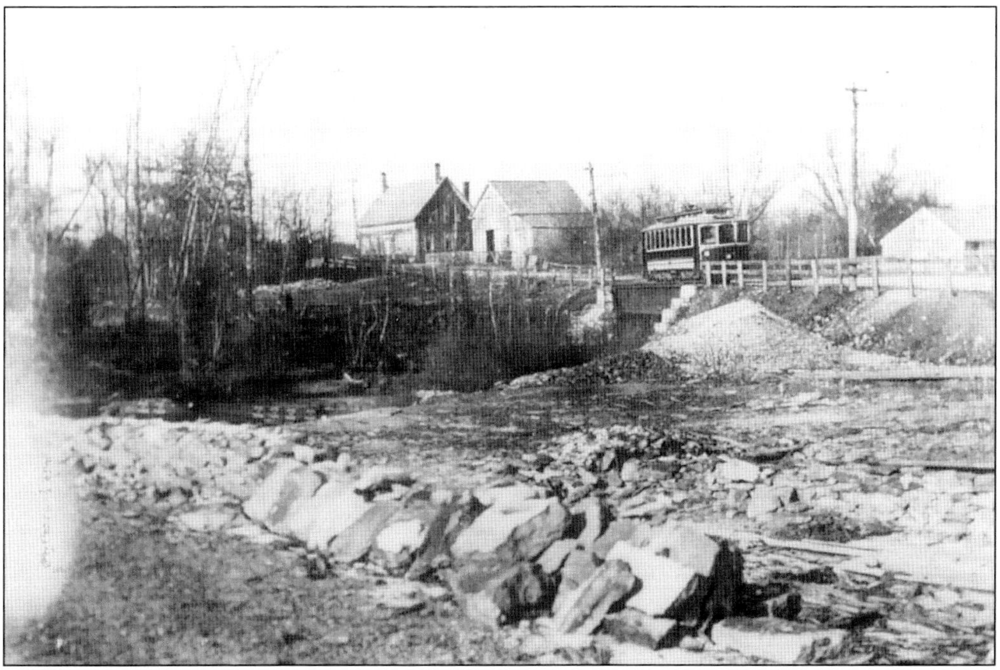

This early view shows a trolley crossing the Wading River by the Copperworks on Taunton Avenue. The Crocker Brothers of Taunton ran a copper-iron smelter and rolling mill that produced finished metal in sheets. Copper large-cent planchets were produced and shipped in wooden kegs to the U.S. Mint to be stamped. Then, the coins were shipped back to the Copperworks, which distributed them to the banks. In 1884, the Crocker Brothers closed their Norton business and moved to their Taunton plant.

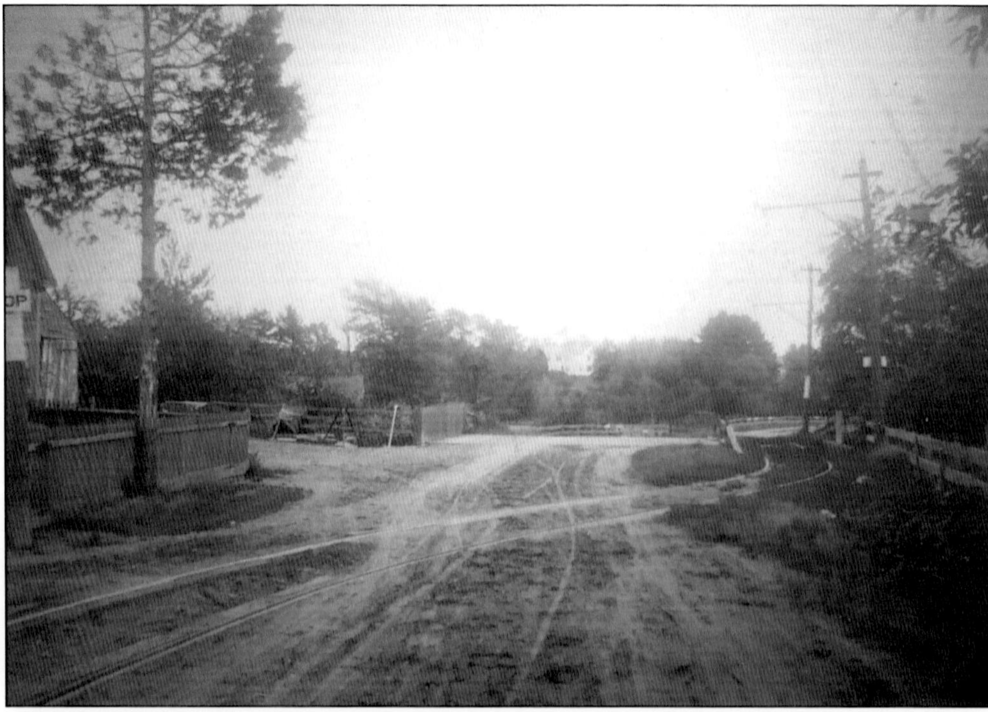

At the Copperworks barn, the trolley had to stop before crossing the road. In the center of this picture is the Josiah Woodward House on the hill.

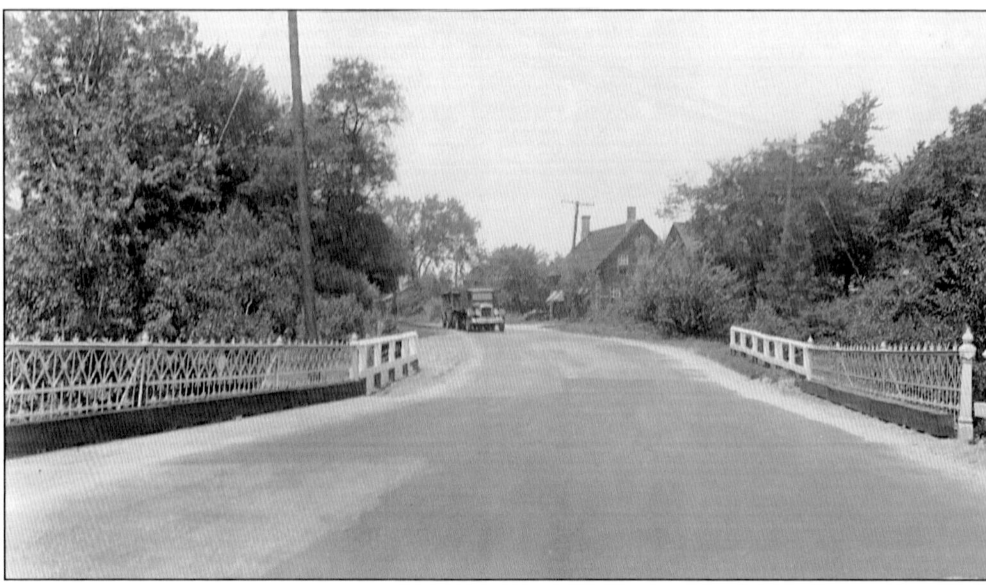

This is a later view of the same area. The trolley tracks have been removed and the road has been widened and paved. The superintendent's house of the Copperworks can be seen. Notice the decorative iron railings on the bridge.

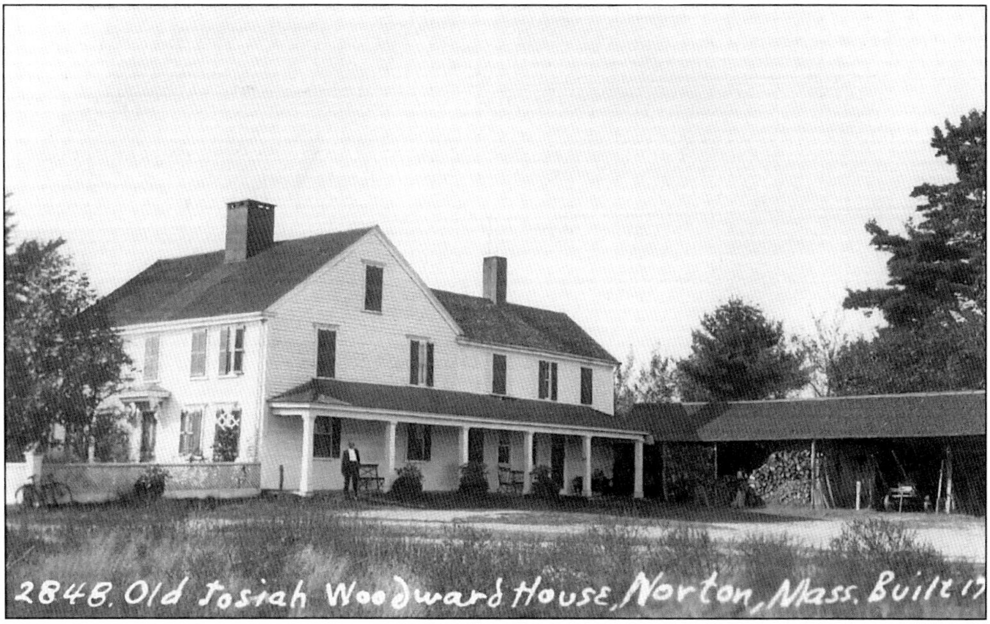

The Josiah Woodward House is at the junction of Taunton and New Taunton Avenues. Frederick Woodward, Josiah's brother, also lived here.

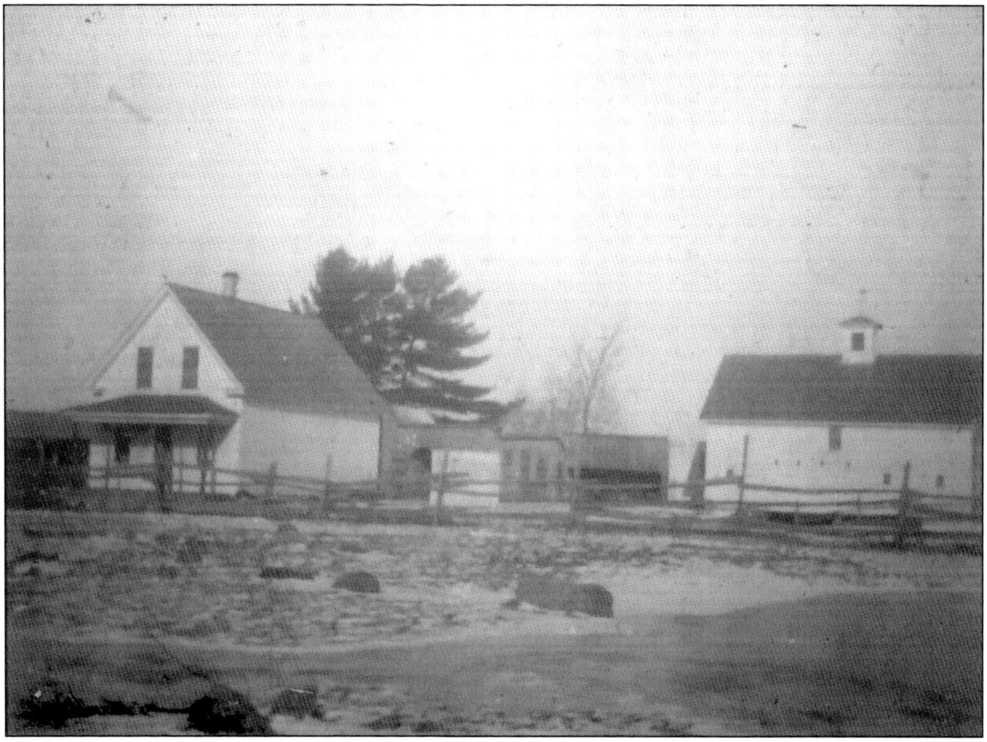

This is the original location of the Woodward Store and farm on Taunton Avenue by Woodward Street. Josiah and Frederick Woodward operated a neighborhood store while running the farm.

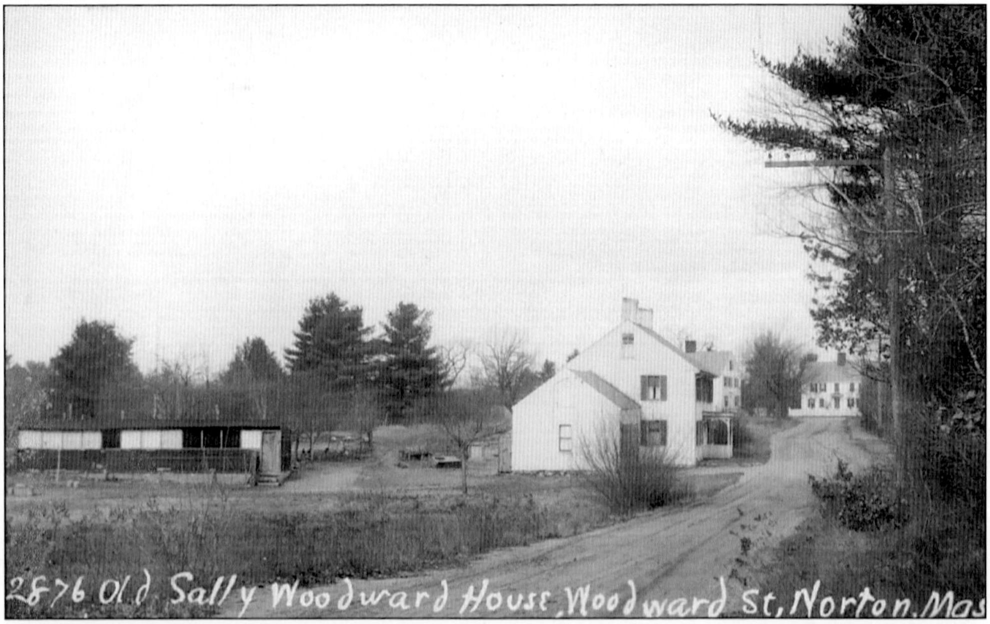

The Sally Woodward House is located on Woodward Street. Many Woodward families lived and farmed in this area. At the foot of the street, the Josiah Woodward house can be seen.

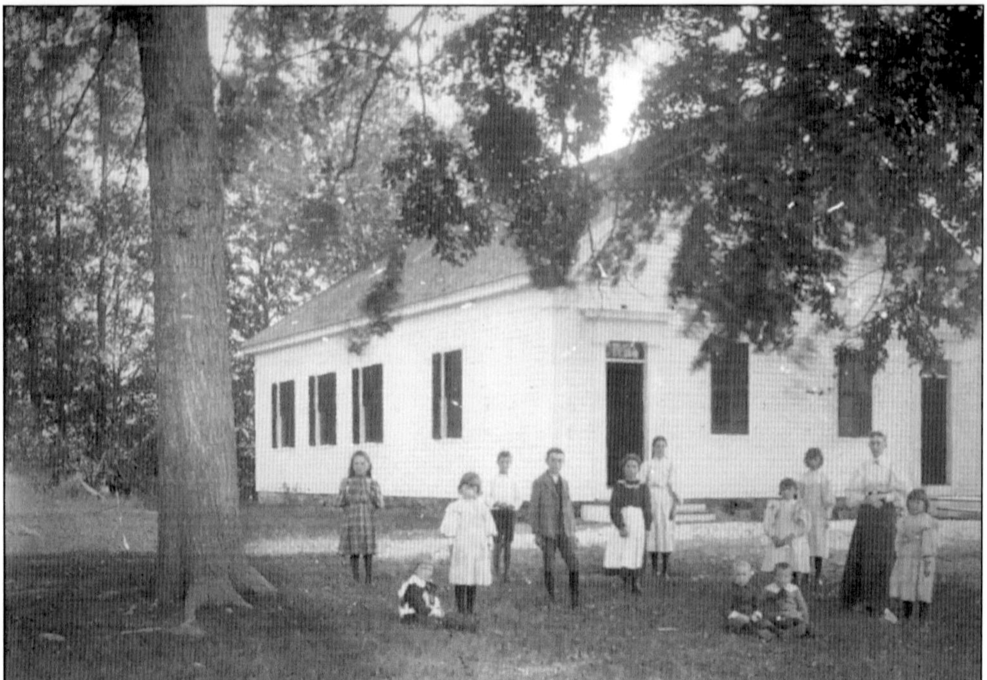
The District No. 3 Schoolhouse was located at the corner of South Worcester and Woodward Street. It is a unique schoolhouse with two rooms and a stairway to the basement, which very few schools had.

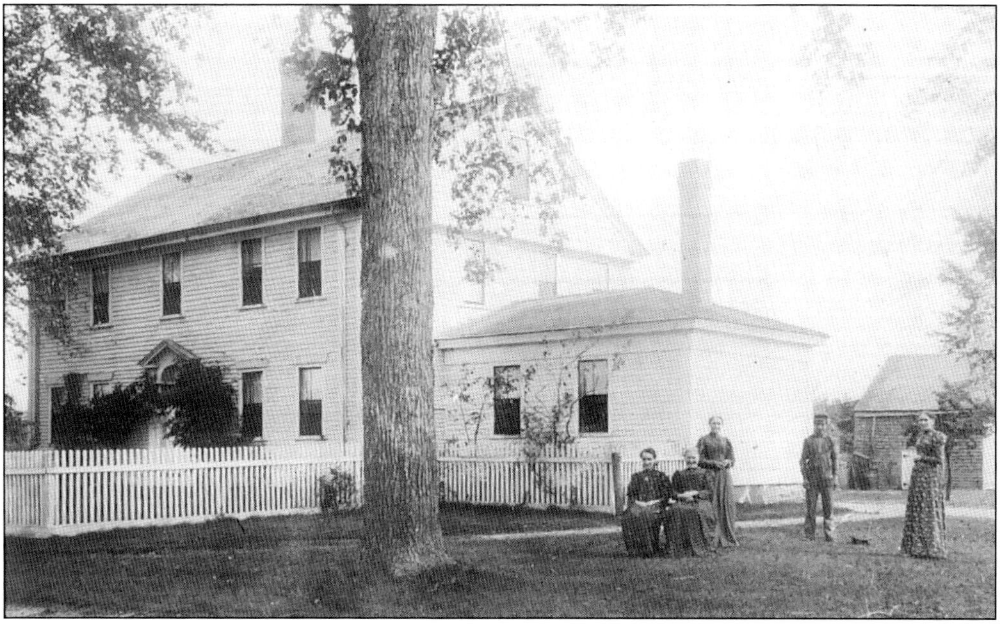

The Seneca Lincoln House was located by Meadowbrook Lane. After the house shown here burned down in 1908, Lincoln built another home at the same location.

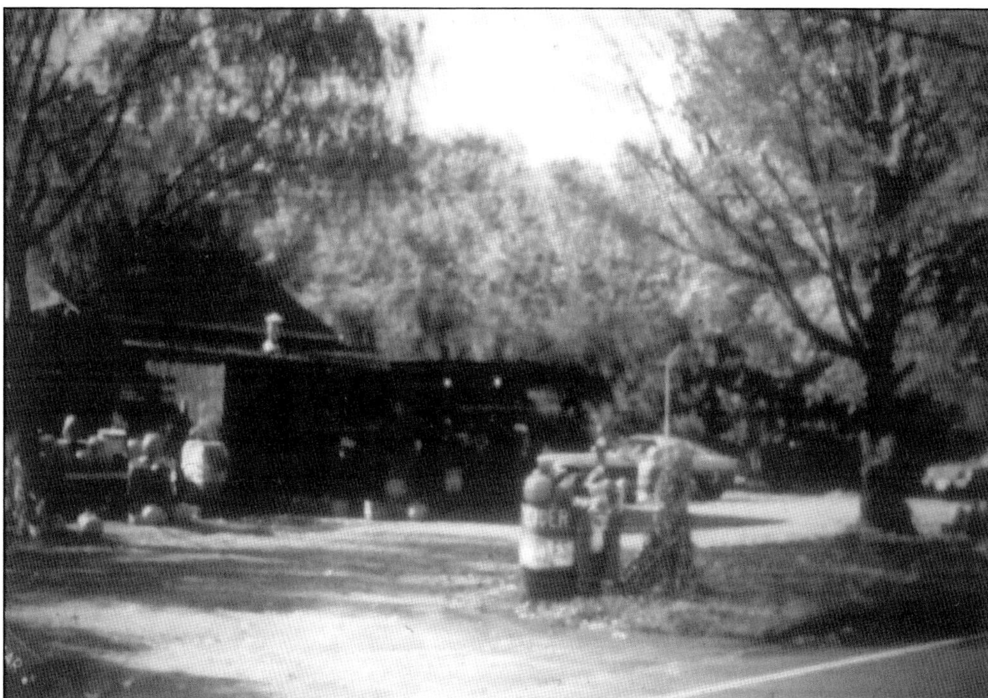

Ed Marvel's cider mill was located on Taunton Avenue near Meadowbrook Pond. In the fall, families were drawn to Marvel's stand by the smell of apples being pressed to make cider and by the fine selection of pumpkins for Halloween.

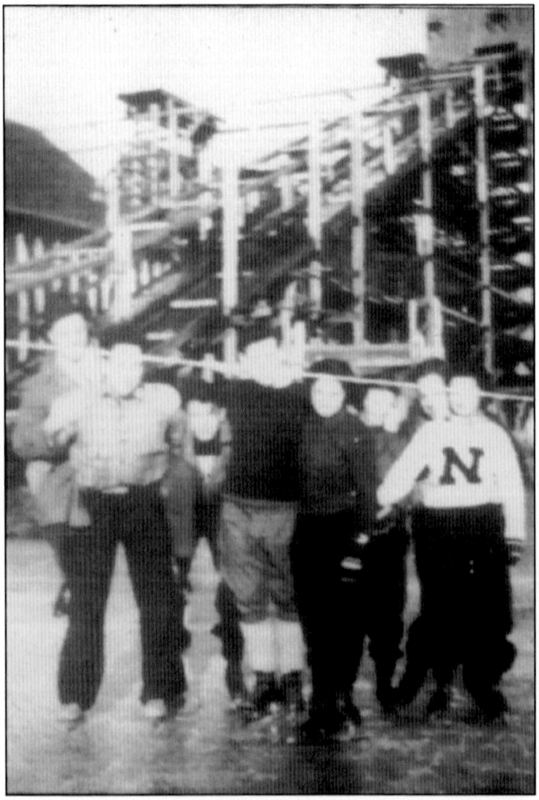

The drive along Taunton Avenue to the Taunton line affords a very picturesque view of Meadowbrook Pond. Over the years, various mills operated there. Until 1941, ice harvesting was done, with the icehouse located by the railroad tracks.

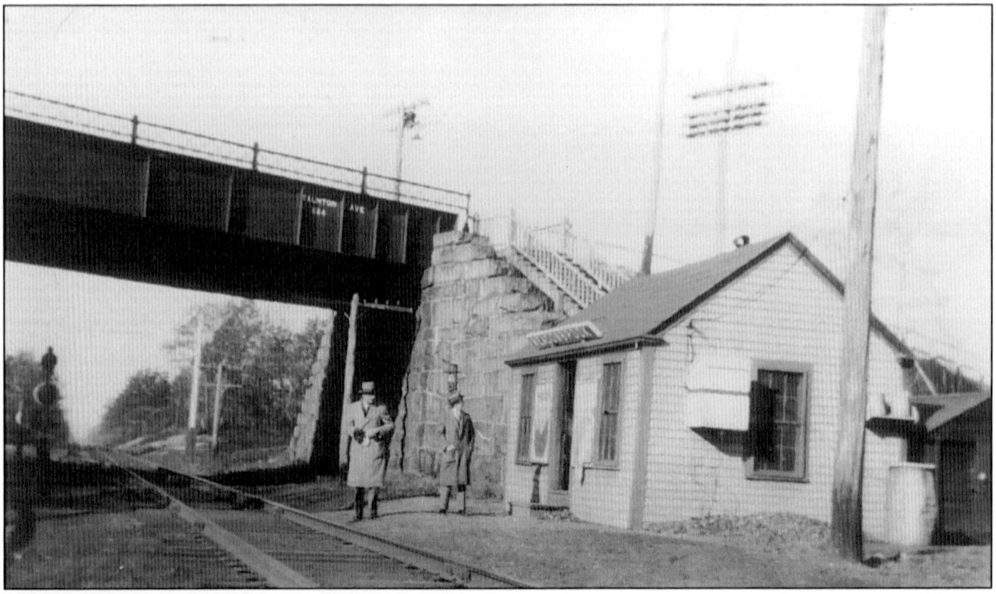

The Meadowbrook Railroad Station was on Route 140 across from Meadowbrook Pond on the Taunton and Attleboro railroad line. This area was called Norton Furnace until the early 1900s, when it became known as Meadowbrook. Lydia Lincoln Austin was the station agent for many years.

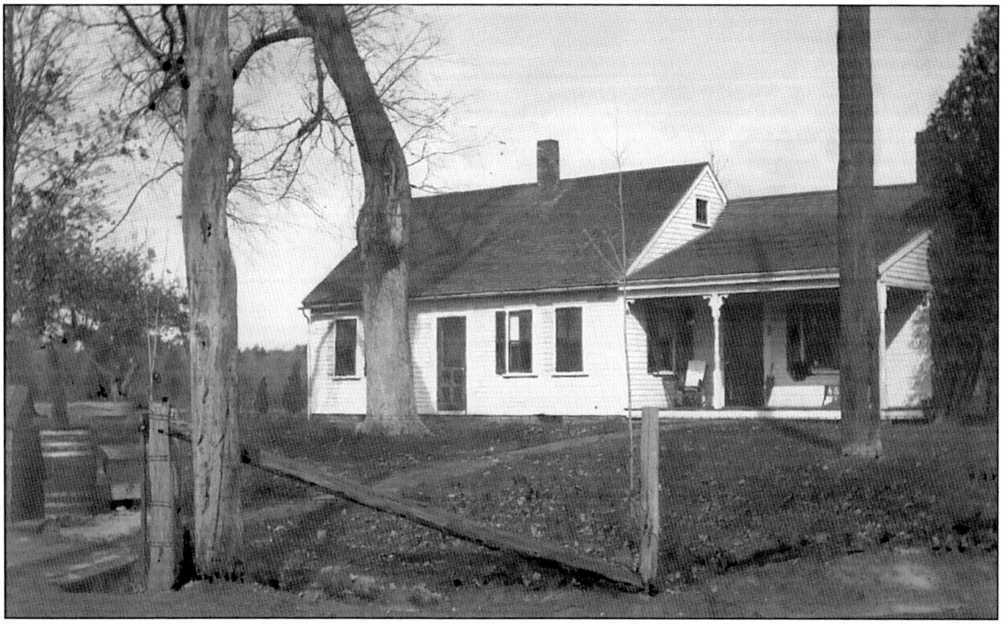

Behind the railroad station was the home of Lydia Austin. The Meadowbrook Post Office was located in her kitchen. She was the first and only postmaster at Meadowbrook. The post office closed in 1912.

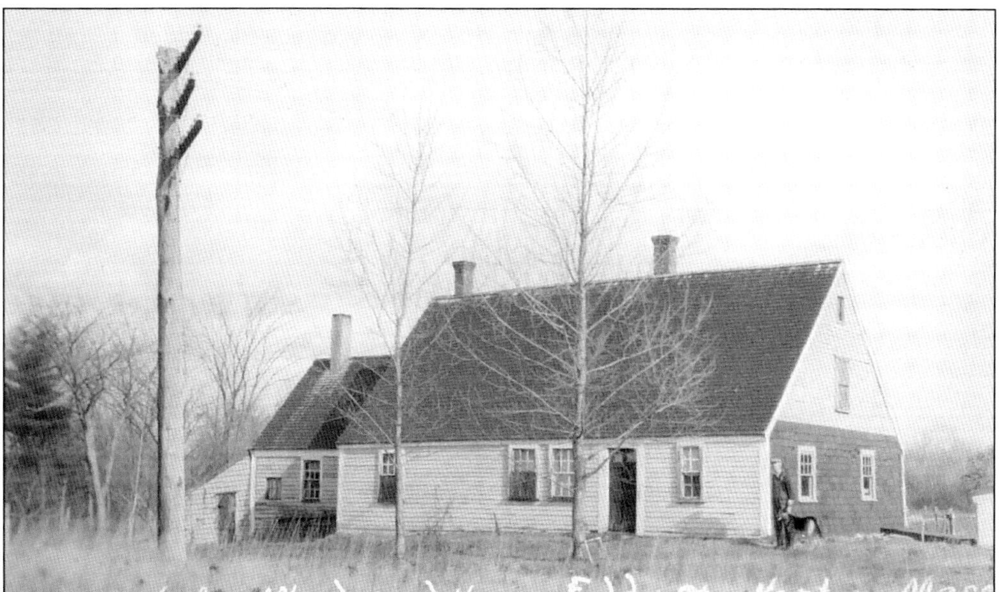

Another Woodward house, which no longer exists, was on Eddy Street. At the entrance of Eddy Street from Taunton Avenue, a milestone tells the distance to Worcester.

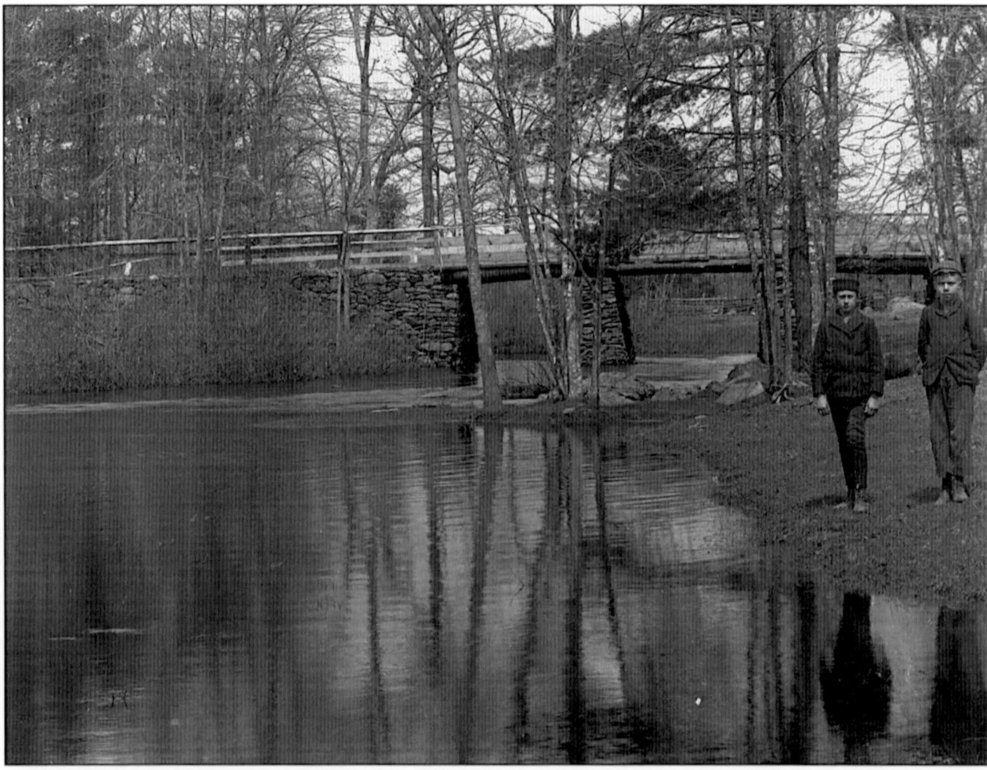

This is Woodward's Spring Bridge just over the town line on Norton Avenue in Taunton. The trolley company built a popular park here. Norton families often took the trolley on Sundays to spend the afternoon at the park.

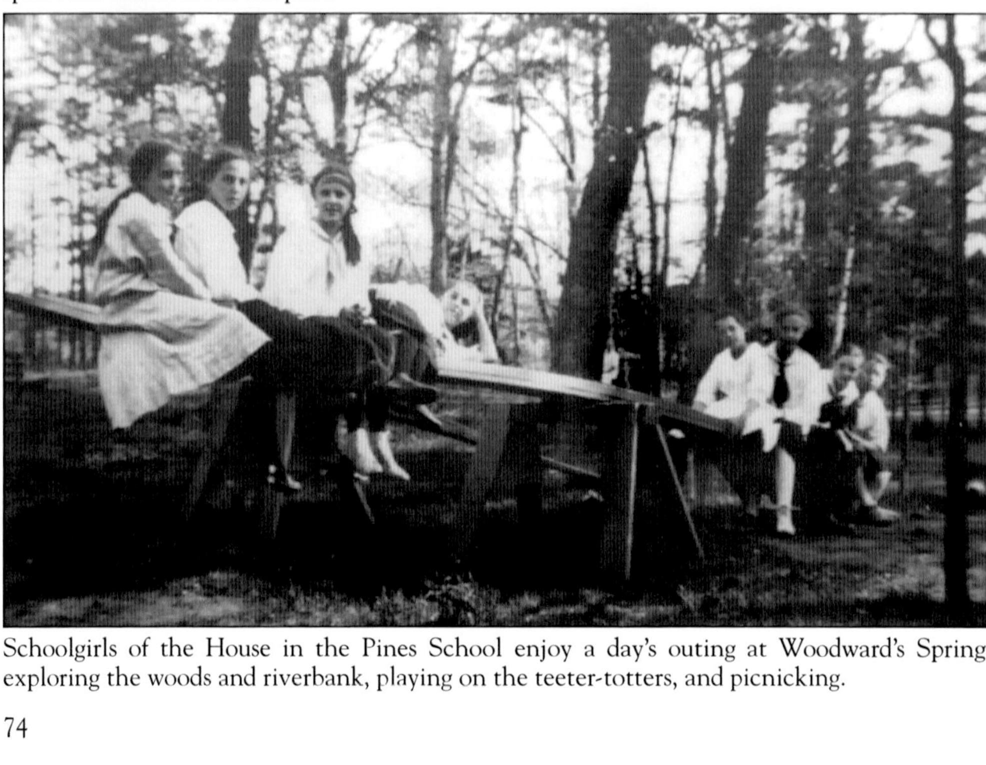

Schoolgirls of the House in the Pines School enjoy a day's outing at Woodward's Spring, exploring the woods and riverbank, playing on the teeter-totters, and picnicking.

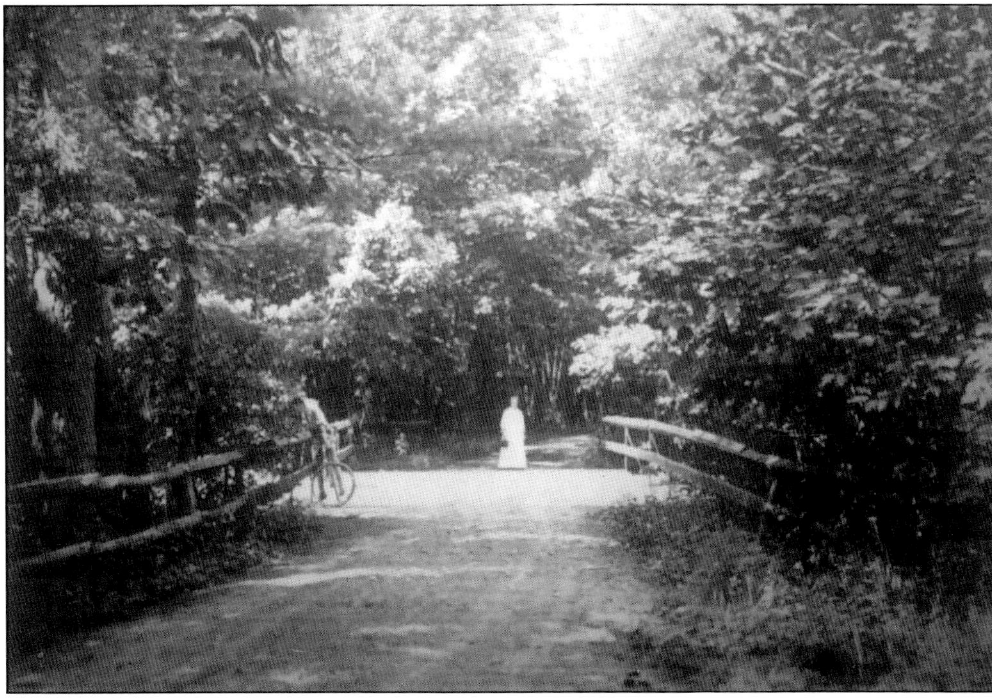

Crane Street has always retained its rural beauty. The Three Mile River flows under the old wooden bridge, with its stone piers. In the woods by the bridge are trails that offer pleasant walks.

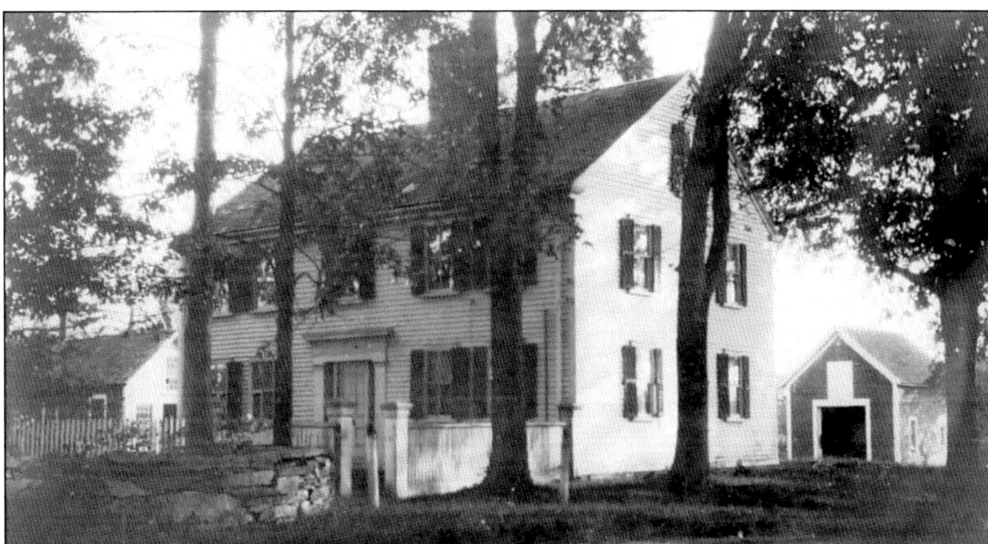

This is the Crane Farmhouse on Crane Street. Capt. John Crane built the house in 1765. The old Crane Farm was originally part of a 130-acre homestead. Crane's descendants have occupied it continuously for seven generations.

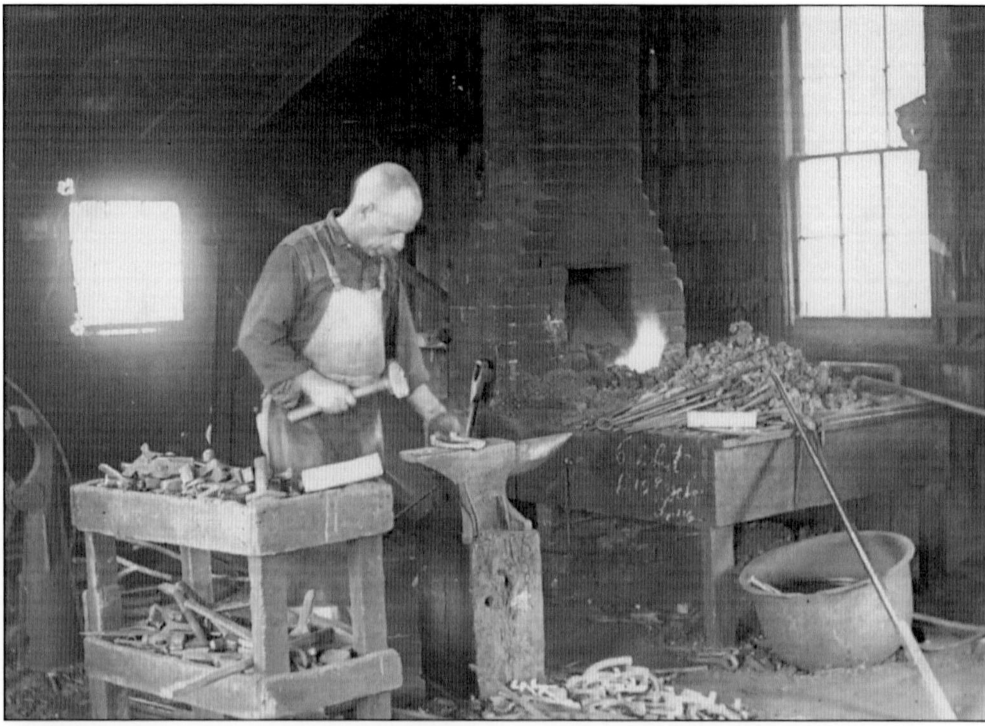

The blacksmith and carriage shops were across the street from the Crane Homestead. Terry Crane was a blacksmith and wheelwright. Frank Crane was the carriage painter.

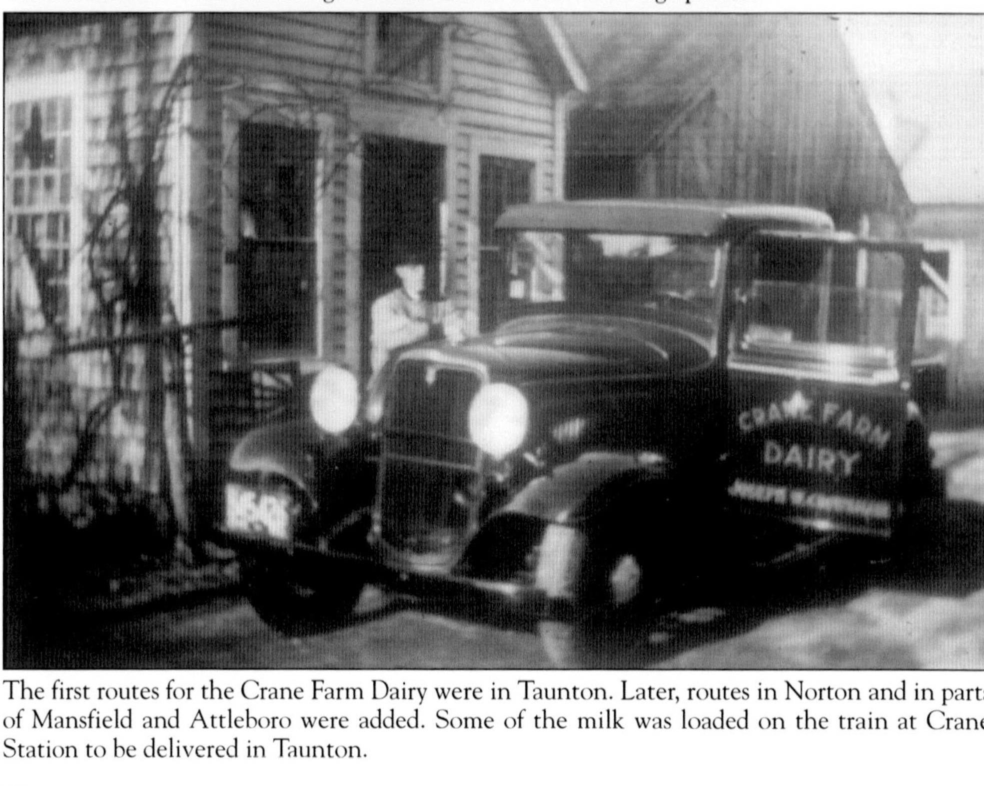

The first routes for the Crane Farm Dairy were in Taunton. Later, routes in Norton and in parts of Mansfield and Attleboro were added. Some of the milk was loaded on the train at Crane Station to be delivered in Taunton.

At one time, Crane Farm was a very busy dairy farm. The family first sold their milk at their barn. The raw milk was bottled in the milk room. The family also produced flavored milk, cream, butter, and eggs. Elwood Spencer and Al Lamontague are standing in the wagon.

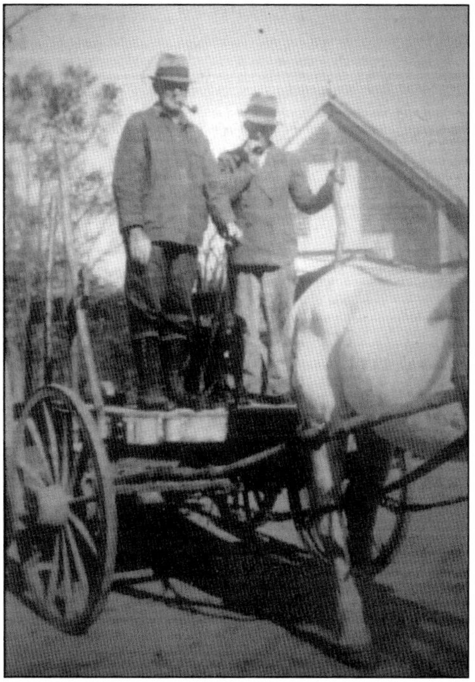

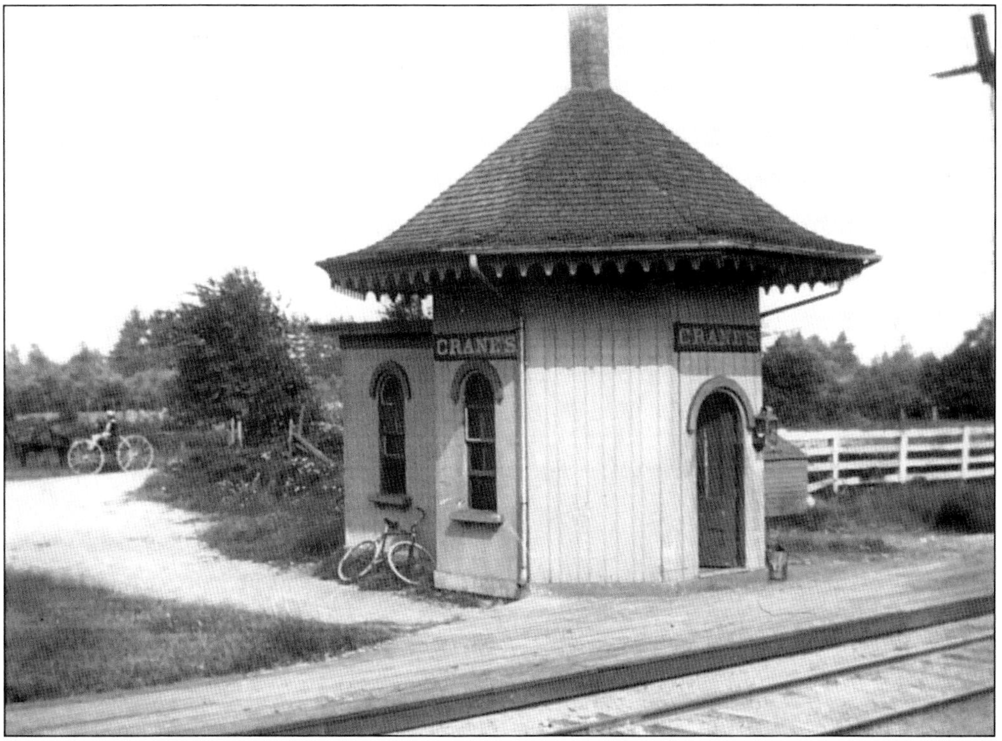

The Crane Railroad Station faced Crane Street near Hill Street. This station had a telegraph and the attendants lived in cottages nearby. Freight trains would stop to deliver grain and hay for the Crane Farm. This station was also a whistle-stop for passengers wanting to get on or off the trains.

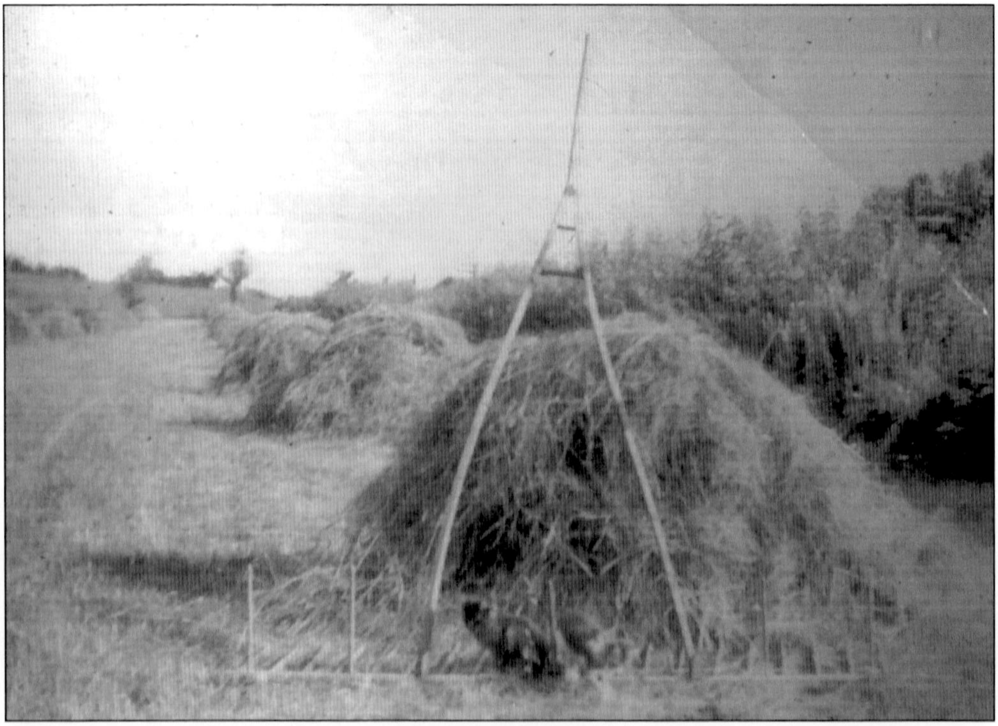

When Norton was more of a farming community, the farmers were busy in the fall cutting their fields. The entire family would help doing this farm chore.

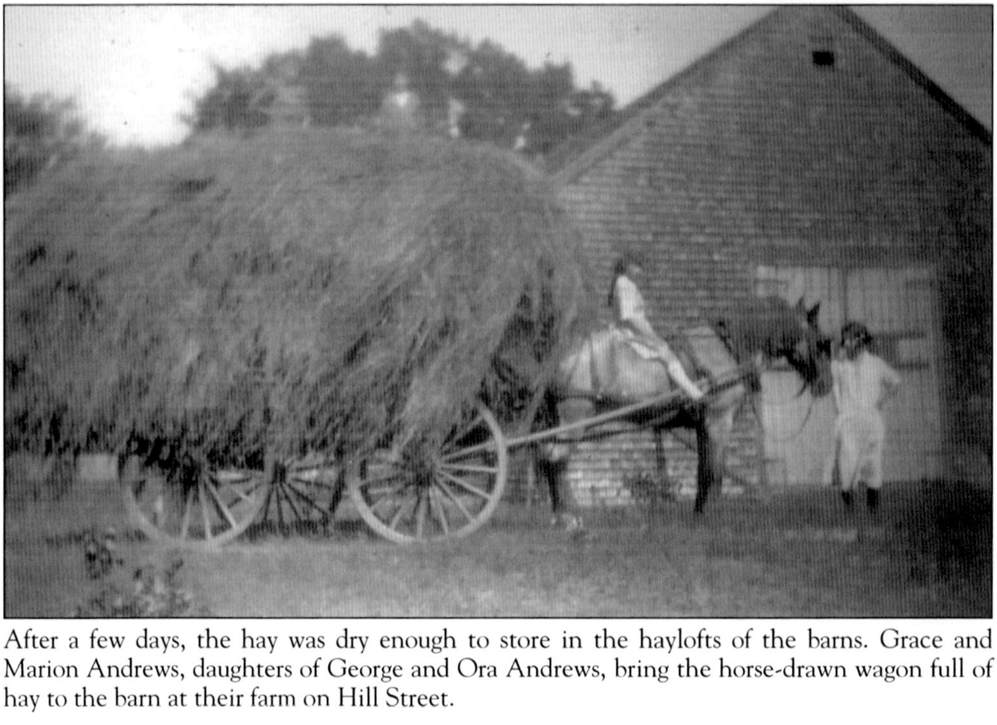

After a few days, the hay was dry enough to store in the haylofts of the barns. Grace and Marion Andrews, daughters of George and Ora Andrews, bring the horse-drawn wagon full of hay to the barn at their farm on Hill Street.

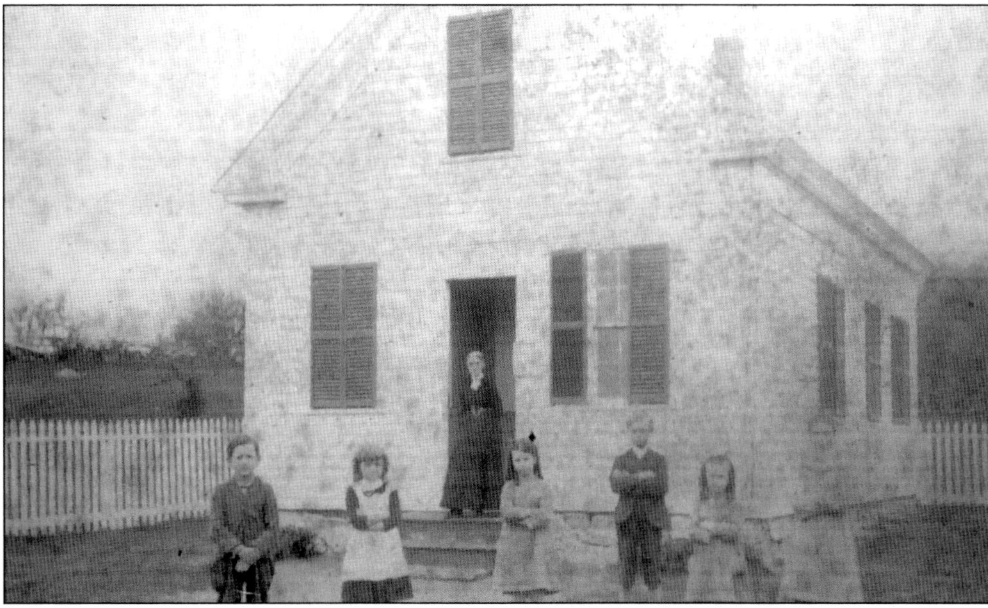

The District No. 7 Schoolhouse was situated on South Washington Street. During some terms, the school was closed because of low enrollment. The children attended either the Crane School in Taunton or the District No. 6 School. Adelaide Austin was the teacher until the school closed in 1904.

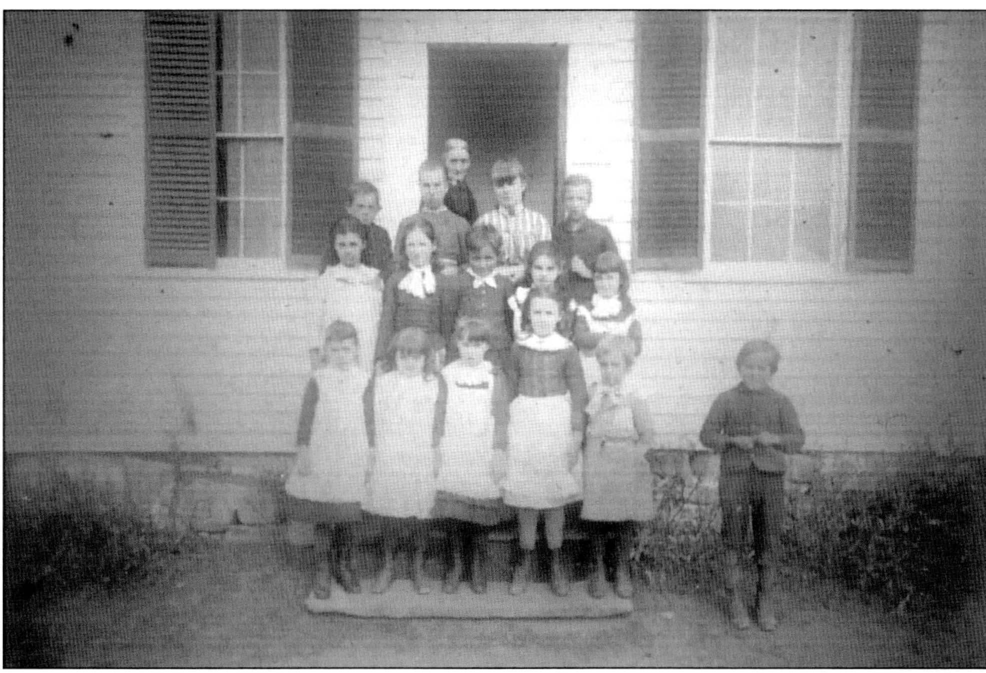

Schoolchildren stand with their teacher on the steps of the District No. 7 Schoolhouse.

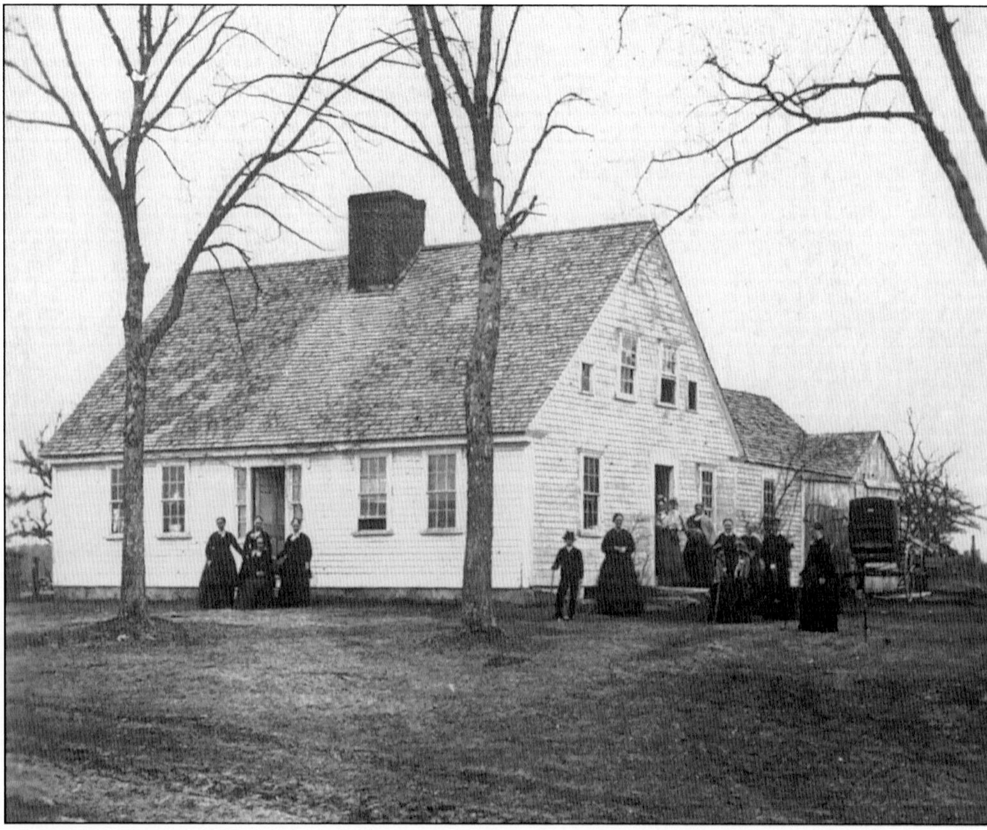

The Laban Lincoln House stood down the street from the District No. 7 Schoolhouse. This photograph was taken *c.* 1875. Family and friends appear to be gathering after a funeral. The Eddy Lincoln Cemetery is next to the house.

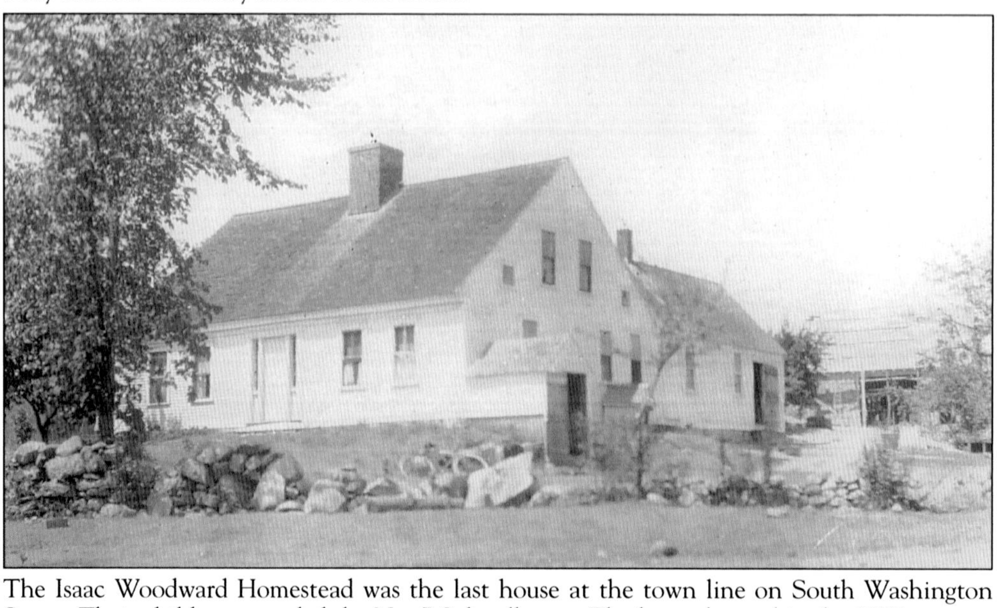

The Isaac Woodward Homestead was the last house at the town line on South Washington Street. Their children attended the No. 7 Schoolhouse. The house burned in the 1970s.

Six

Norton Reservoir

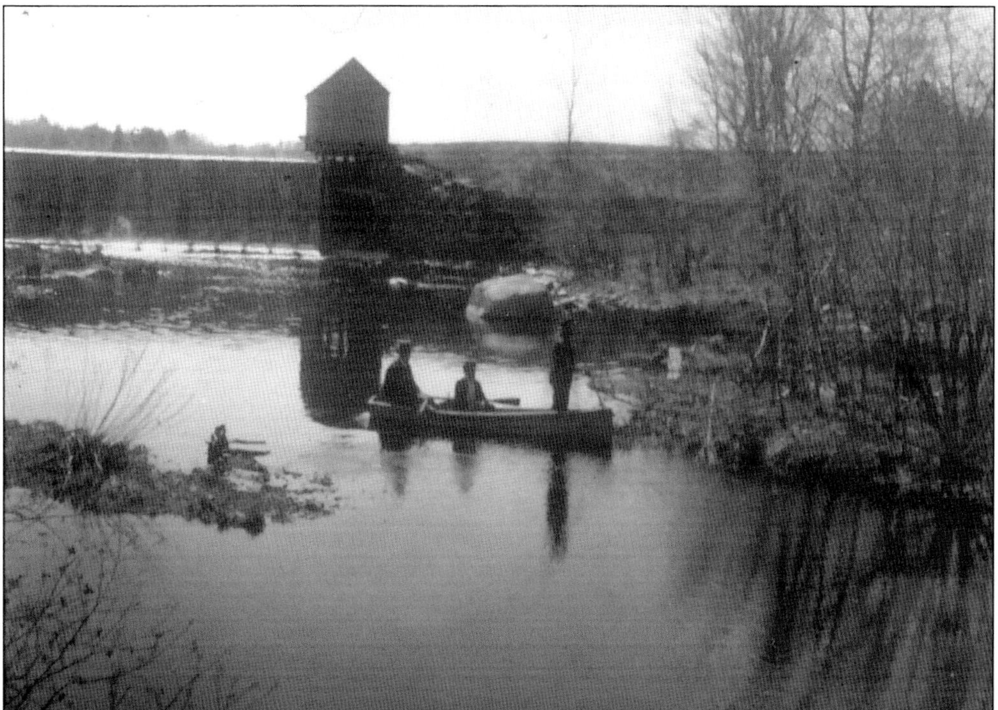

During the early years, the Rumford River meandered along the northeastern side of Norton from Mansfield. It passed under Twenty-first Street (Reservoir Street) near Twentieth Street (Cobb Street). The river continued its journey south, meeting the Wading River where the two rivers formed the Three Mile River. This river continued into Dighton, where its water was used for power at the Mount Hope Finishing Company. In 1868, because this factory needed more waterpower, the company began the process of building a dam on the Rumford River in Norton.

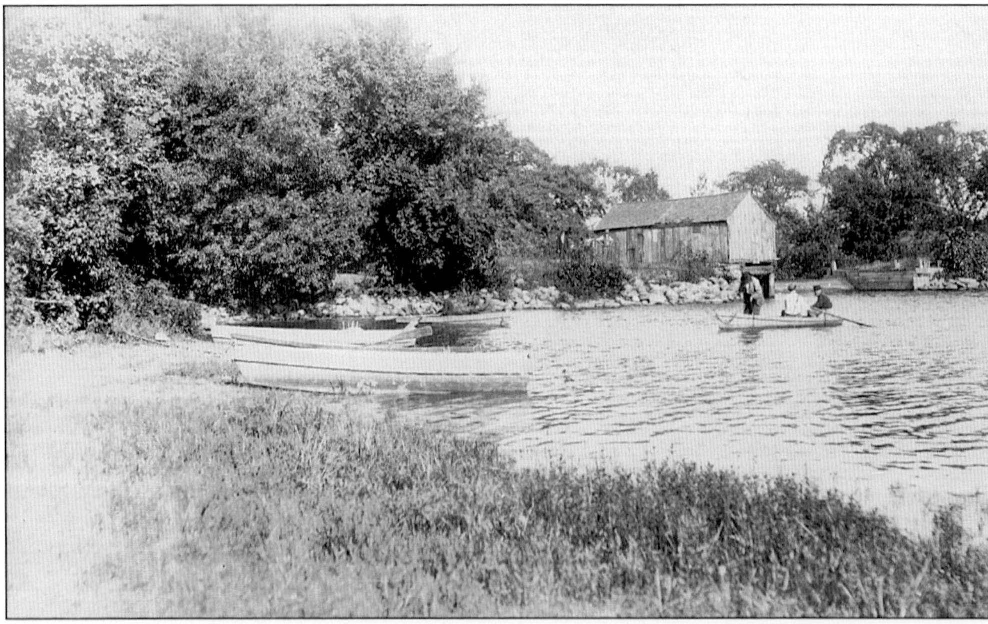

The Wading River Reservoir Company bought over 400 acres of land from the farmers in this area. A dam was built, forming a body of water called the Norton Reservoir. The company regulated the flow of the water by lowering or raising the gates at the dam. The controls for the dam were located in the gatehouse. During the 1890s, James Goff rented boats by the dam.

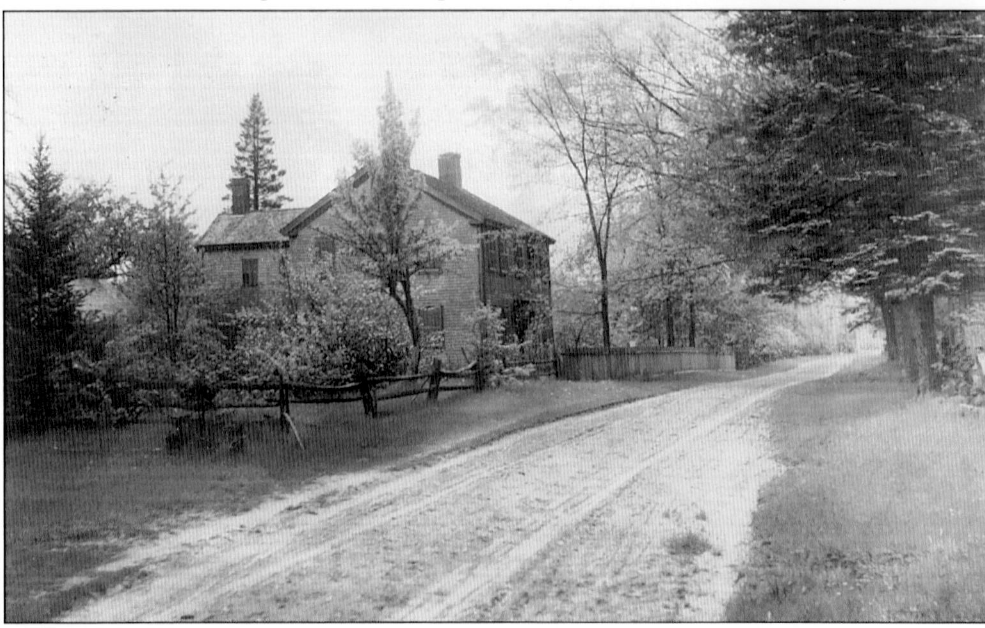

In the early days, streets did not have names but were numbered. Streets were given names by the town in 1902. Twentieth Street was named Cobb Street after the Cobb Family, whose homestead is found on this road. Daniel Cobb lived on Twenty-first Street (Reservoir Street). After he married, he bought Daniel Smith's farm on Twentieth Street, which his son Silas Smith inherited. It is written that Silas Smith bought one apple pie a week and worked out a cardboard pattern to cut that pie into exactly seven pieces, one for each dinner.

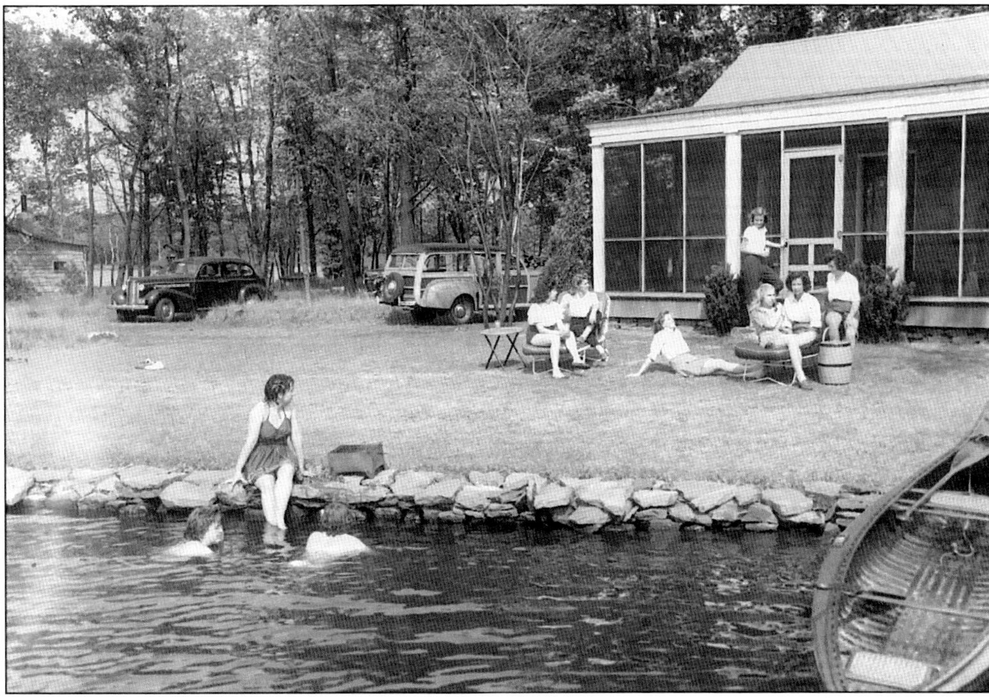

Gertrude Cornish, headmistress of the House in the Pines School, owned this place on the reservoir, where she and her students enjoyed relaxing hours by the water. Located off Reservoir Street at the end of a narrow dirt road, the house was hidden from view on the road side by tall trees.

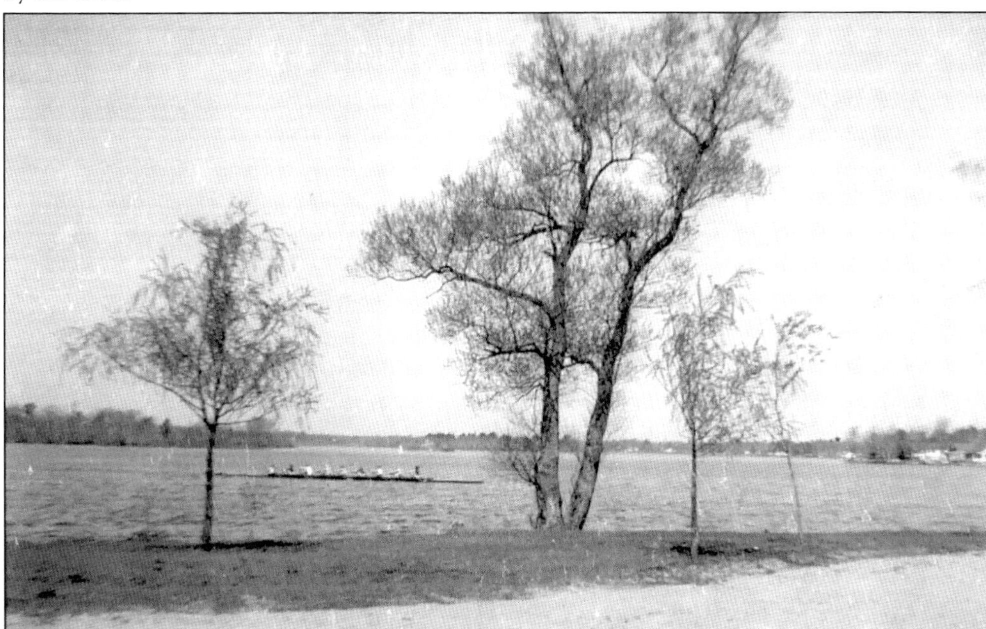

Headmistress Gertrude Cornish had a boathouse where the House in the Pines School kept canoes and sculls. Students practiced their crewing skills on the smooth, clear waters of the reservoir.

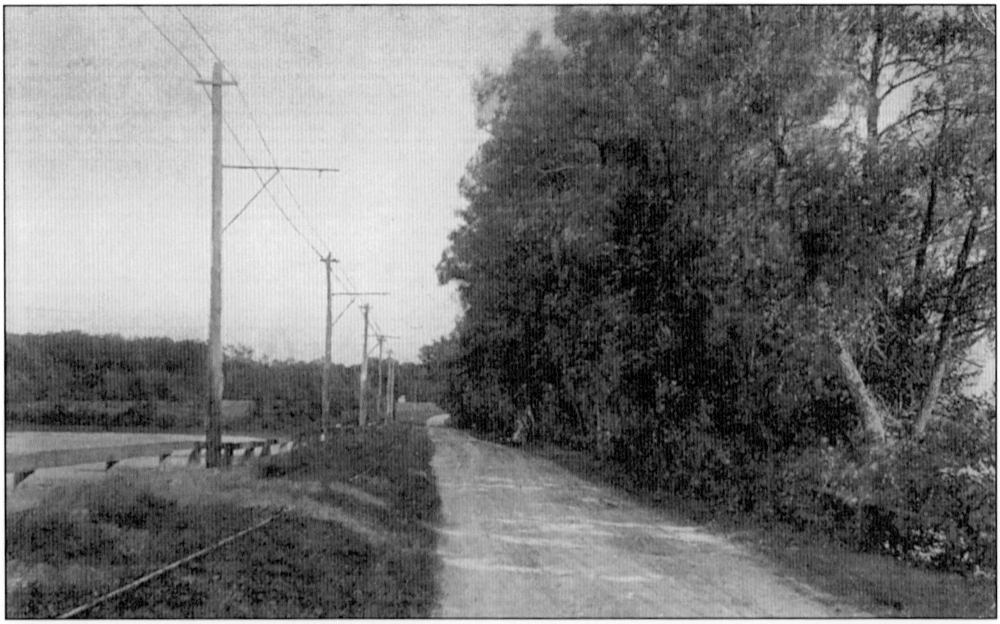

This early view shows Mansfield Avenue as it passes by the Norton Reservoir. At the left the trolley tracks can be seen. When Mansfield Avenue was reconstructed in 1929, the new part became part of Mansfield Avenue and the old part was named Smith Street.

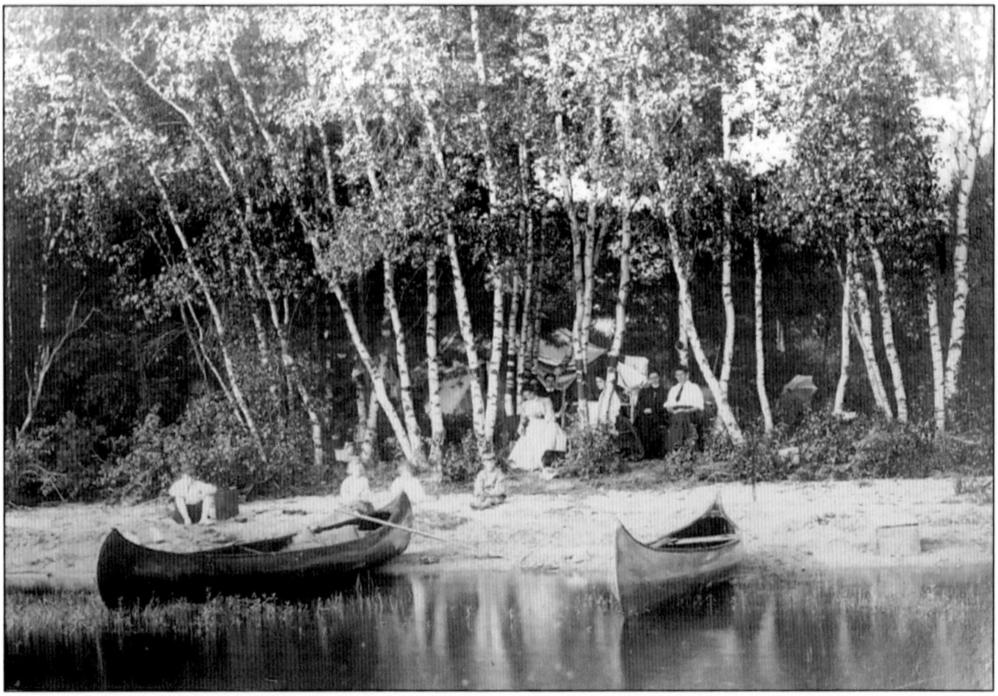

Many islands are found on the reservoir. Some of the larger islands were popular camping spots. Families from the city came to Norton, rented rowboats and canoes, and spent a day on one of the islands, such as Birch Island. Some of them pitched tents and enjoyed a leisure summertime stay.

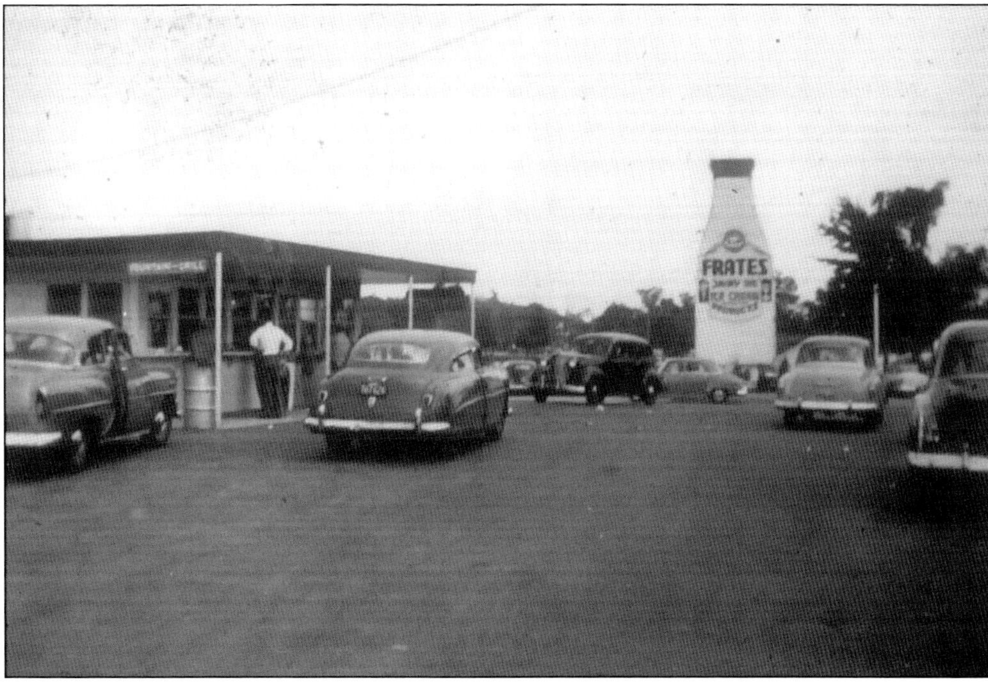

Frates Dairy was a very popular eating place in the 1950s at the beach by the reservoir along Mansfield Avenue. Notice the milk bottle sign. On warm summer days, people enjoyed swimming and boating.

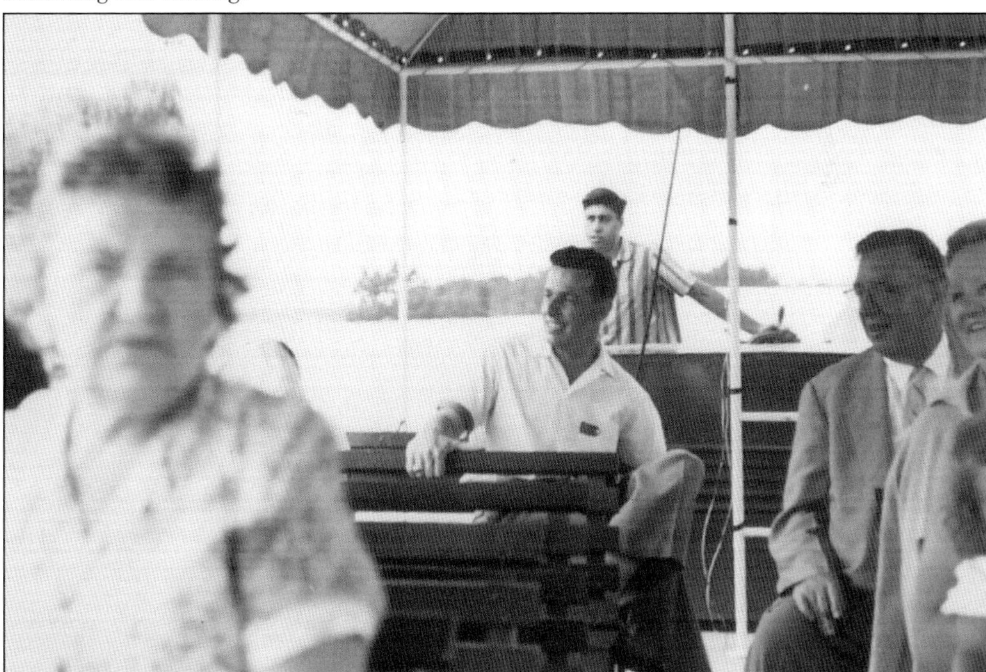

When the Ribeiro brothers ran Frates Dairy, they had a boathouse and landing place by the lagoon. From there they took people on swan boat cruises around the reservoir. Boaters were able to put small motorboats in the water at this landing for a day's fishing or boating.

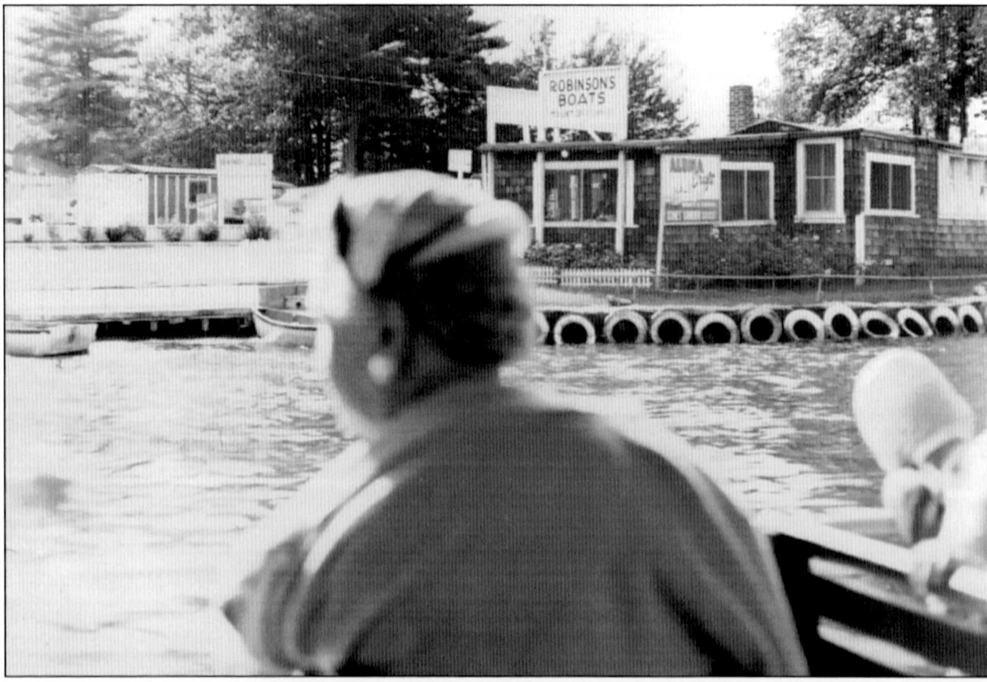

Off Mansfield Avenue is Robinson Lane, which goes to the Robinson family boathouse overlooking the reservoir. George Robinson built the first house at the end of the lane. He and his son Raymond Robinson rented canoes and boats. The family also had camps there, which they rented. Each camp bore the name of a bird.

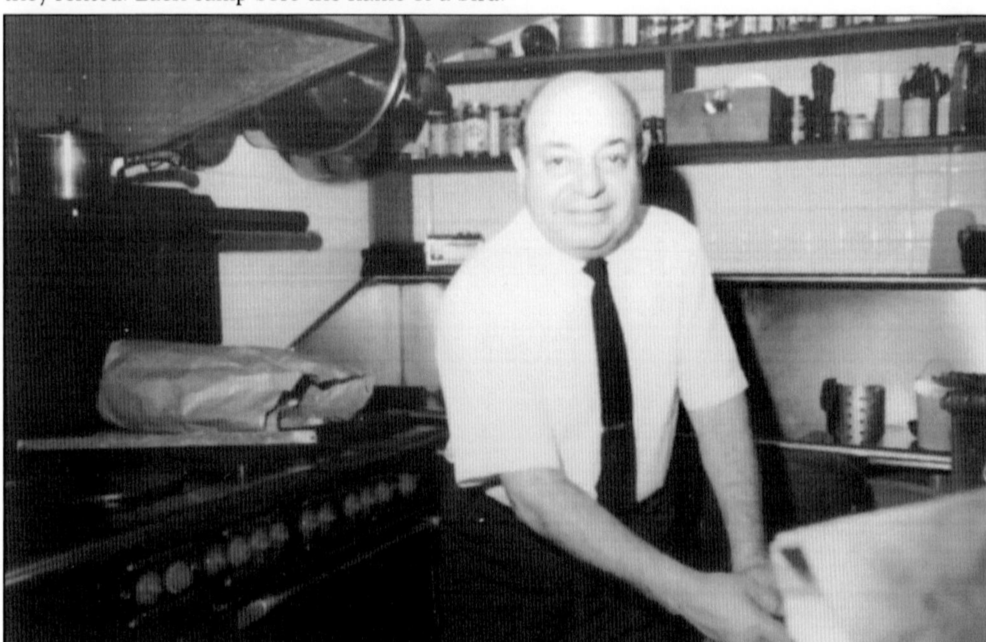

For many years Charles Pino owned and operated the Victory Club Restaurant. Overlooking the reservoir on Mansfield Avenue by Smith Street, the restaurant was well patronized because of Pino's delicious steaks and congenial atmosphere.

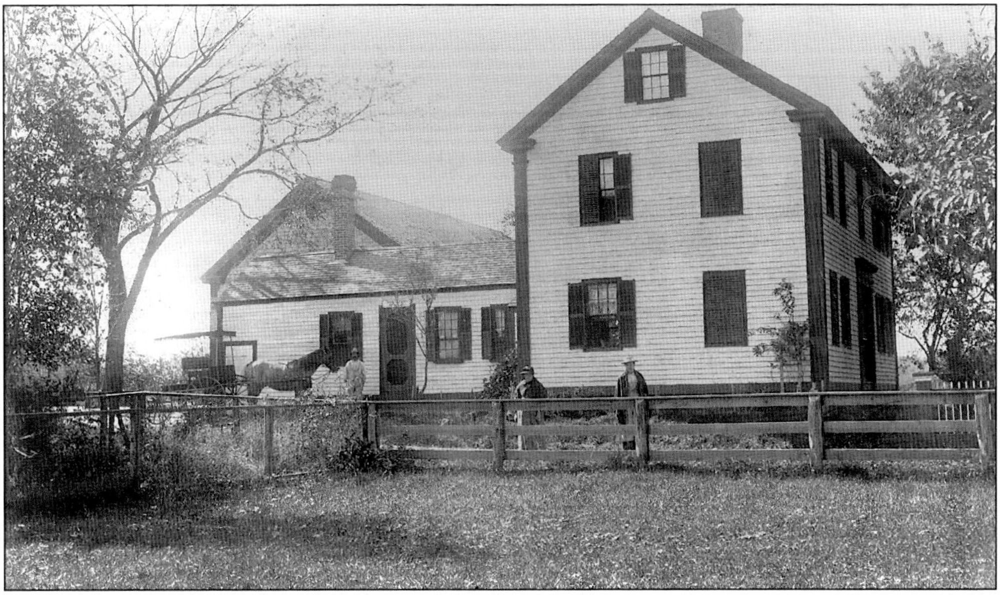

This house on Smith Street was part of a farm owned by Jacob Leonard. The farmland extended to Freeman Street and along both sides of Mansfield Avenue. Some of Leonard's land was flooded when the Norton Reservoir was formed. Leonard is pictured standing by the house, with his mother and his sister Etta at the fence.

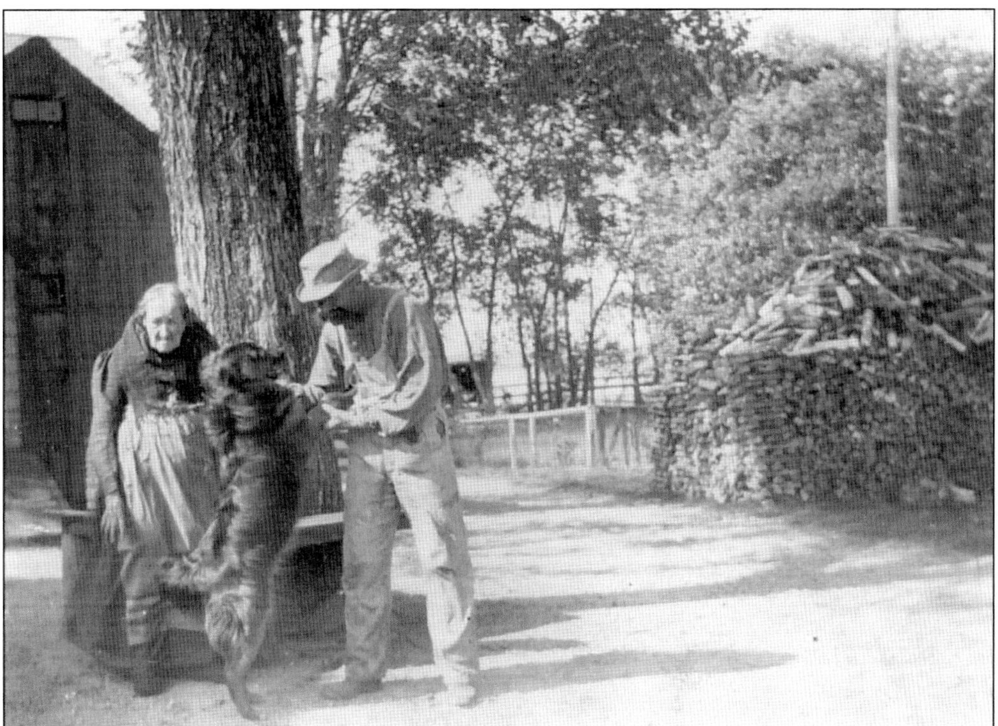

Out by one of the barns with the dog are Jacob Leonard and his mother, Eunice Wetherell Leonard. Notice the neatly stacked, split wood. Leonard was the town clerk and treasurer for 28 years and was a justice of peace for 38 years.

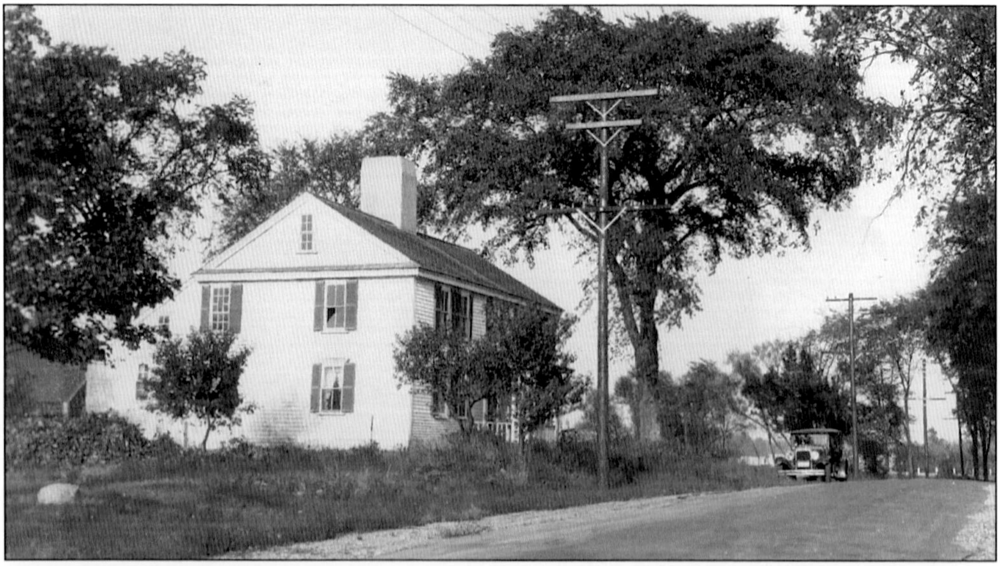

The Cromwell Leonard House is located across the street from the Leonard farm. Generations of Leonards owned this house until Etta Leonard died. The house was then sold to Alden Walker, who rented it to the construction company that built the new Route 140, *c.* 1929. In later years, there was a tearoom in the house.

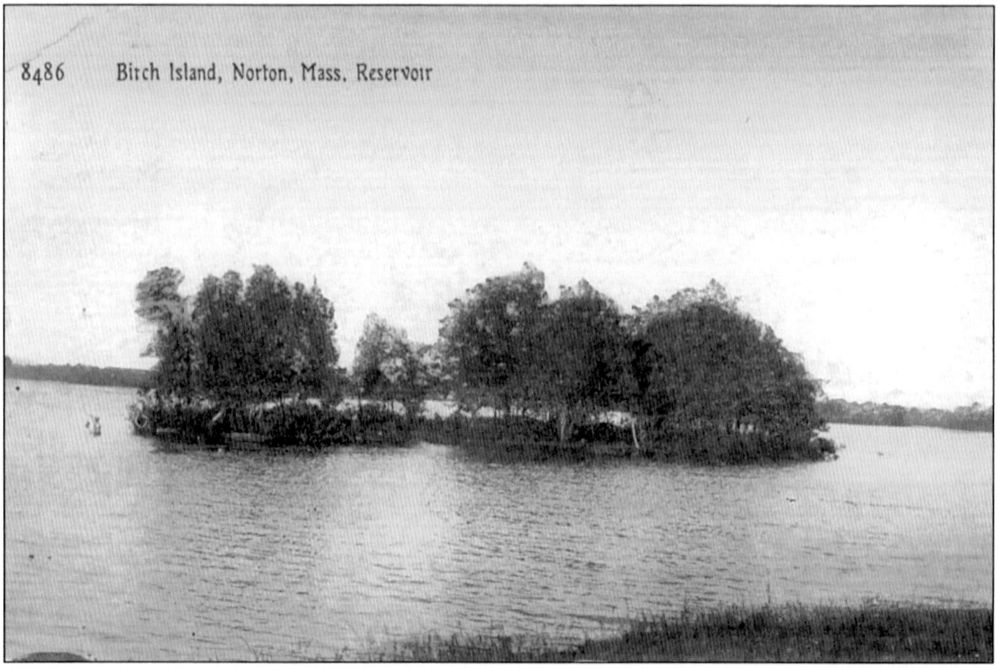

There is a story that identifies the Cromwell Leonard House as part of the Underground Railroad, which helped runaway slaves reach safety in the North. Under the main cellar of the house is a hidden subcellar that is said to have been connected to an escape tunnel leading out to the island pictured here.

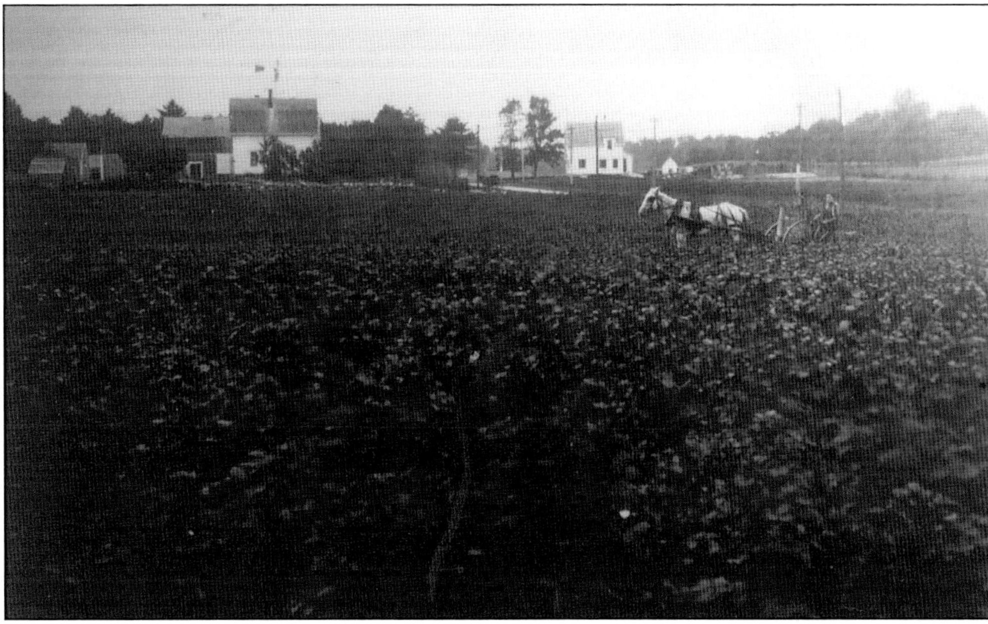

On Mansfield Avenue by Smith Street was Edgewood Farm. Alden Walker had fields of potatoes on both sides of Mansfield Avenue. In later years his fields became the site of the Country Haven Nursing Home. His fields across the street became the site of Pino's Driving Range and, in later years, the Norton Flea Market.

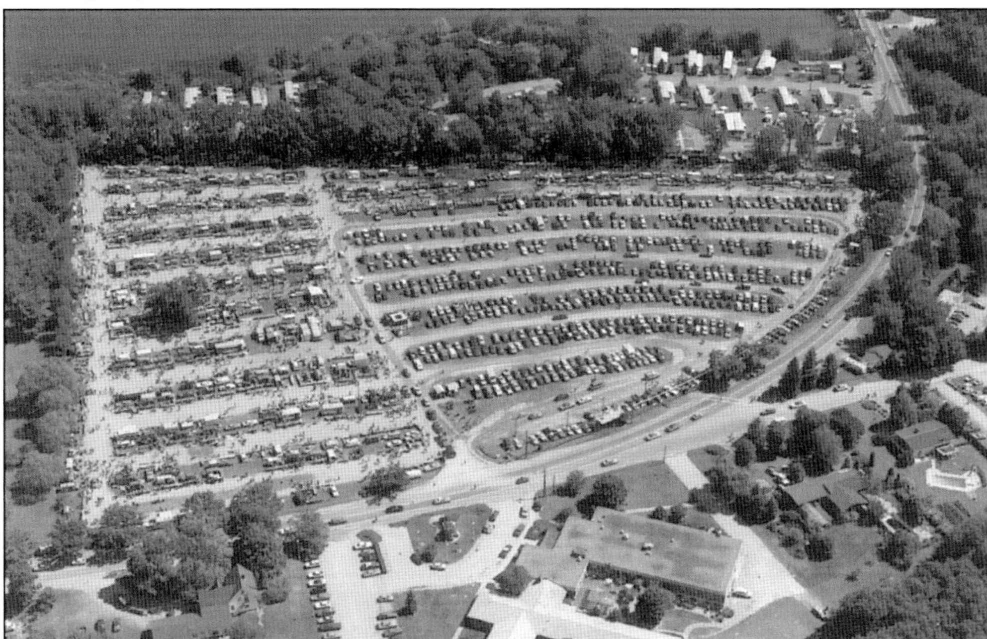

For several years, Norton was known throughout the region as the town with the largest weekly flea market in New England. The huge Norton Flea Market and Antique Sales was held on Charles Pino's land on Mansfield Avenue by the Norton Reservoir. This busy flea market, run by Richard Pino and George Bernheimer, brought people from far and near to browse, buy, sell, seek bargains, or be entertained.

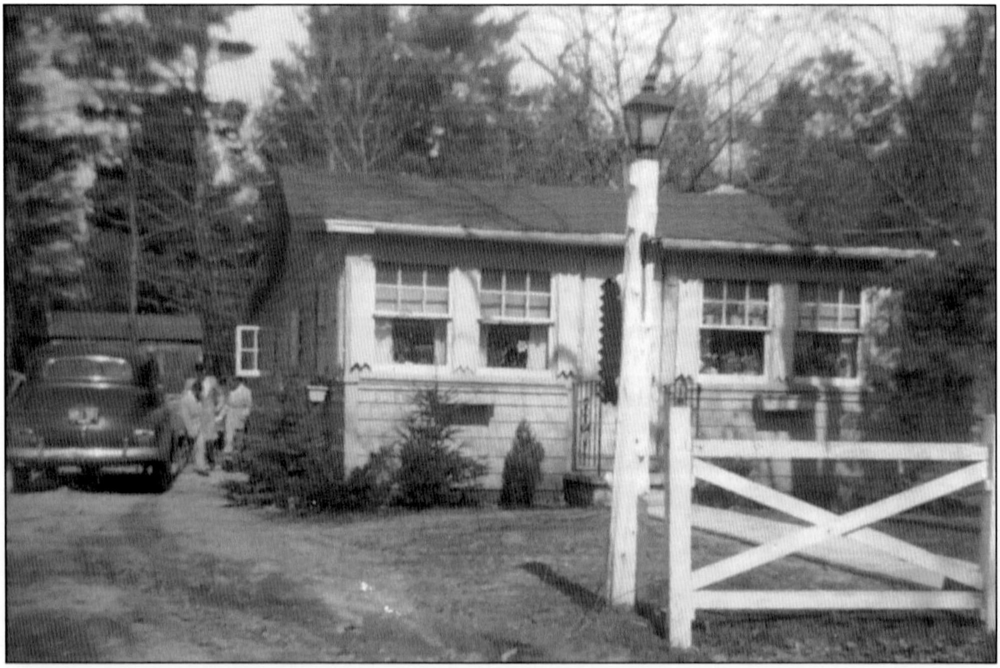

In the late 1930s, Fred and Ethel Kroker bought several hundred acres of land on both sides of Reservoir and Cobb Streets. The land was divided into lots of less than a quarter acre. Summer camps were built on the lots, and people from cities, such as Boston, Brockton, Providence, and Pawtucket, bought them. The area became known as Norton Grove because of the beautiful, tall pine trees.

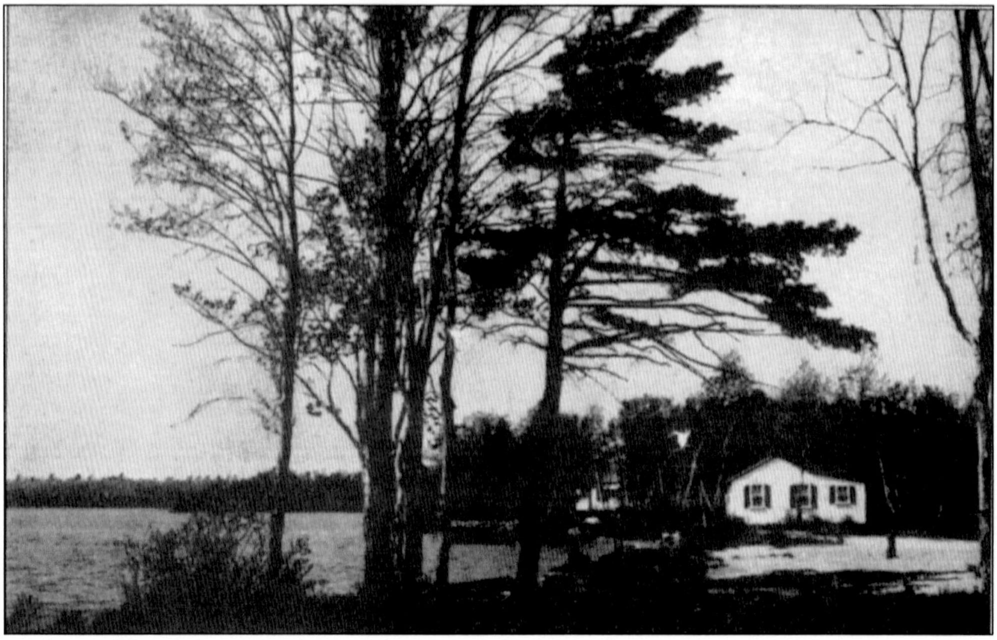

By the middle of the 1940s, hundreds of camps had been built and sold to families for summer vacation cottages. Juniper and Evergreen Beaches were popular swimming and gathering spots for the young folk.

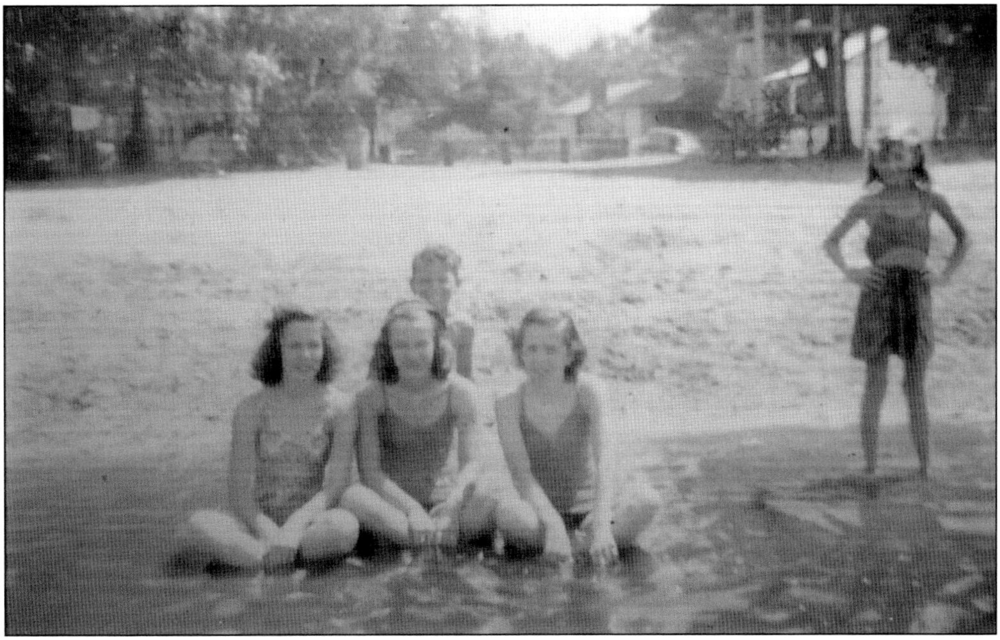

Both Juniper and Evergreen Beaches were private. To be able to go on the beaches, people had to belong to the Norton Grove Association. Bathers wore tags, which cost 25¢ a season. John Ferguson patrolled the two beaches to check for tags.

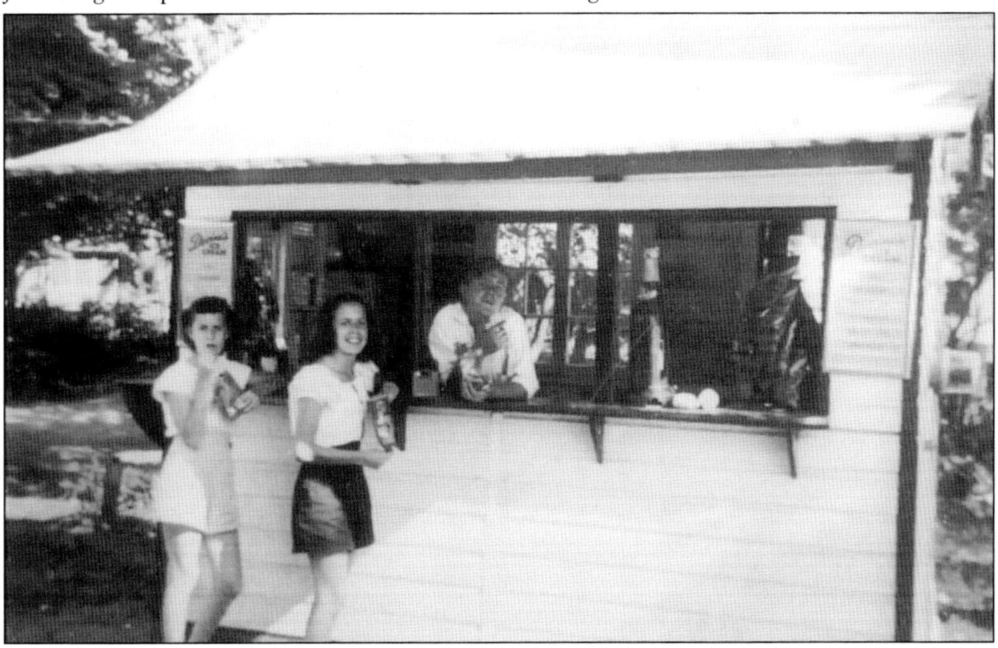

Bill and Mary Rogers owned the Rogers Friendly Store at the corner of Reservoir and Cobb Streets. Behind the store, on Saturday nights, outdoor movies were shown. During intermission, children ran into the store to buy candy, soda, or ice cream. There were two other neighborhood stores in the Grove area on Reservoir Street: Masse's General Store and Barber Shop by Highland Road and Thorton's at the town line. Shown here is the little refreshment stand at Evergreen Beach that the Rogers family ran.

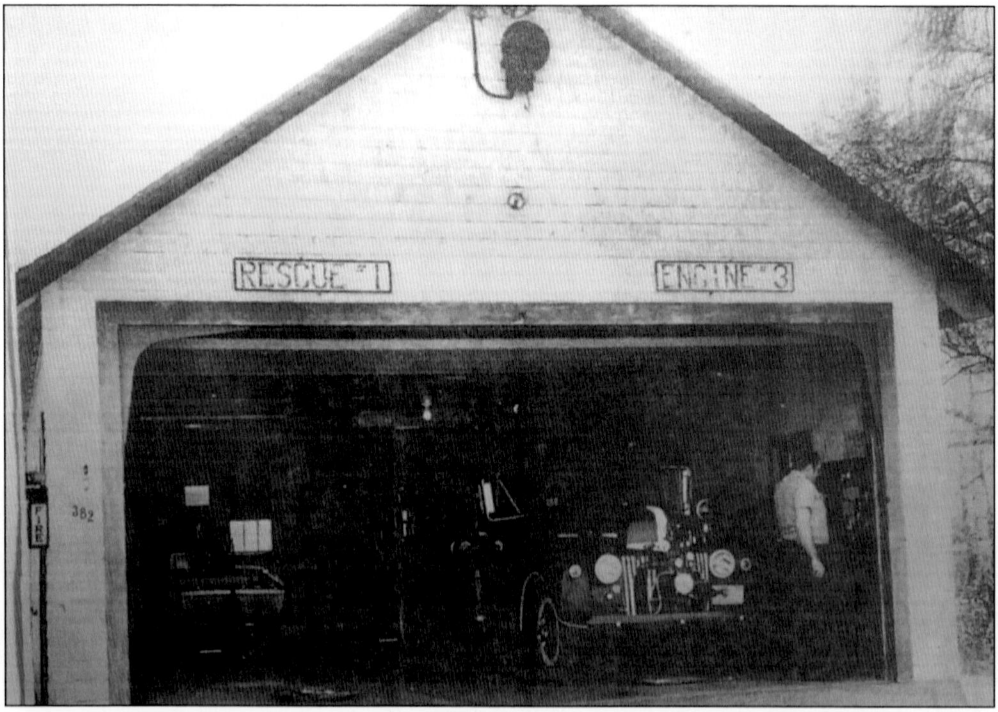

In 1944, the Norton Grove Association offered to build a fire station, install a siren for an alarm, and heat and care for the building if the town would furnish a fire truck. The members raised money by holding barbecues, penny sales, and field days. In 1958, the firemen of Company No. 3 raised money on their own to buy a 1946 Ford V-8 Walk-in Truck and made it into a rescue truck. Howard Ferguson was the first captain of the rescue squad.

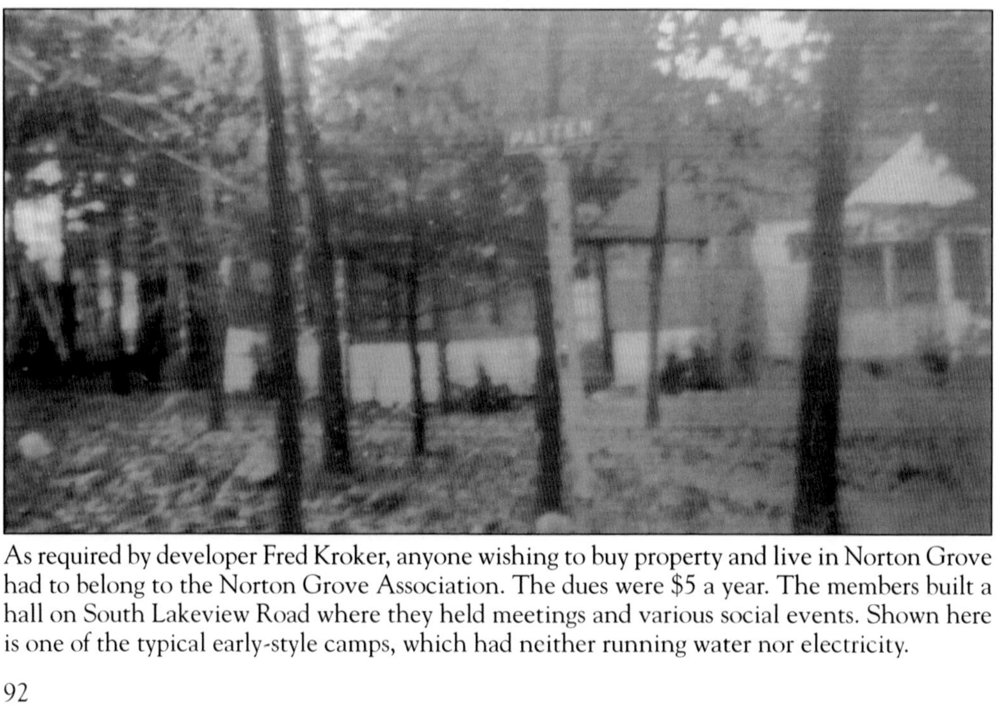
As required by developer Fred Kroker, anyone wishing to buy property and live in Norton Grove had to belong to the Norton Grove Association. The dues were $5 a year. The members built a hall on South Lakeview Road where they held meetings and various social events. Shown here is one of the typical early-style camps, which had neither running water nor electricity.

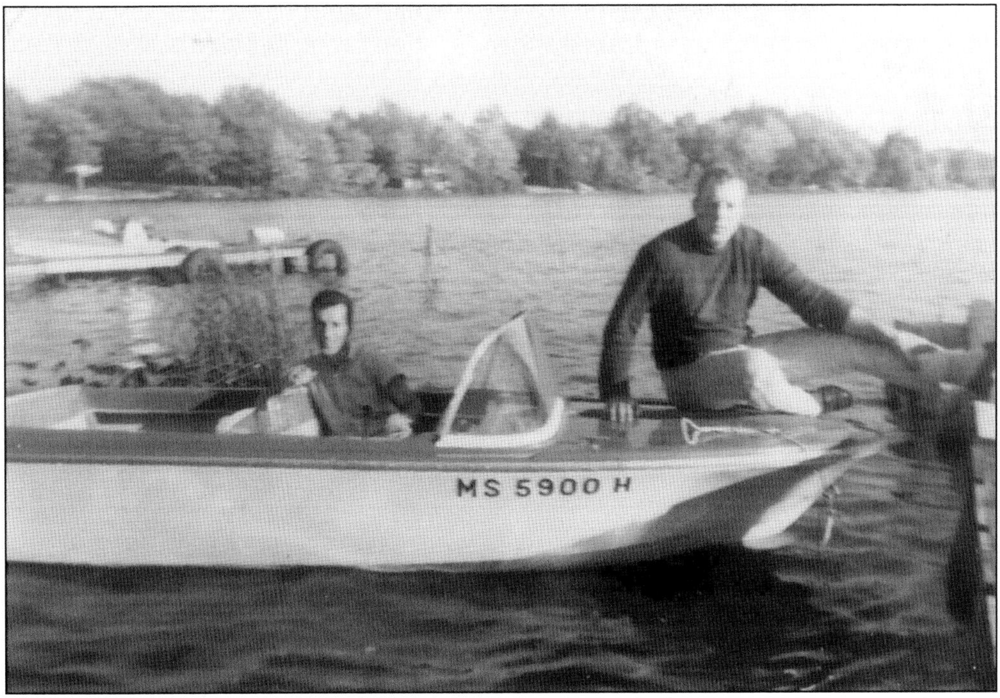

Norton Reservoir became a very active recreational area with the influx of summer residents at Norton Grove. People enjoyed boating, canoeing, and water-skiing.

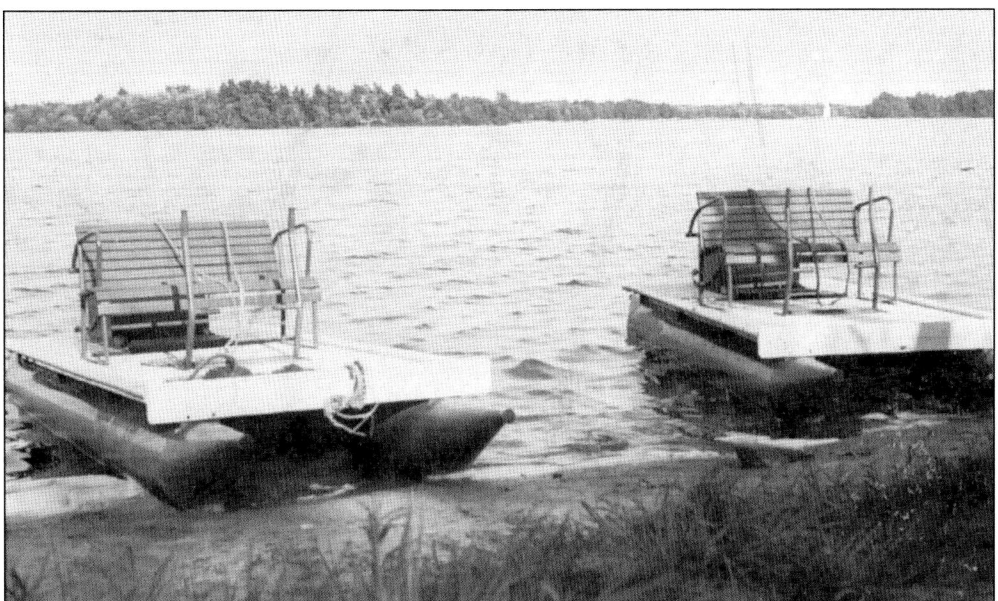

Fishing for largemouth bass and horned pout was a popular pastime, either by standing along the shoreline or cruising in a boat. Some of the bass caught weighed as much as 5 pounds.

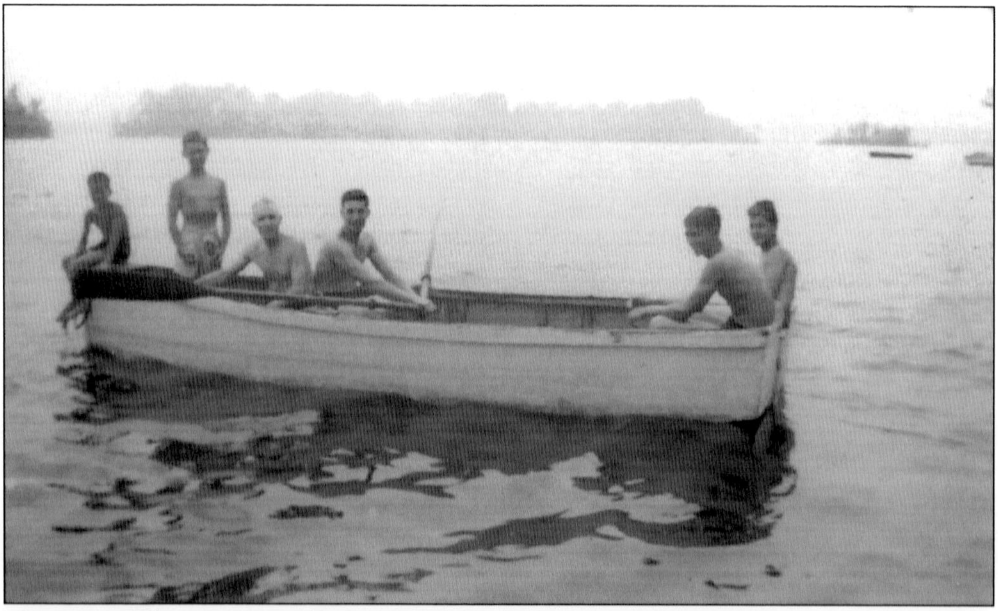

The young folk spent many happy summers on the water. They rowed out to the islands to camp. Boy Scouts also camped on the islands. Norton Grove organized a Boy Scout troop with John Ferguson as the first leader. Later leaders were Howard Ferguson and Steve MacCaffrie. Kevin MacCaffrie was the troop's first Eagle Scout.

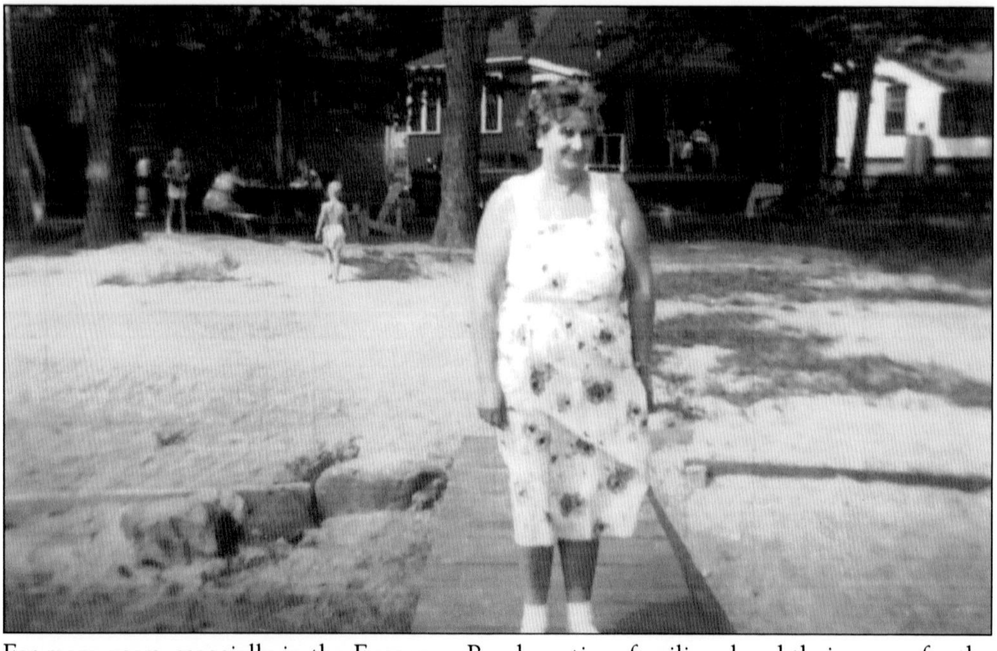

For many years, especially in the Evergreen Beach section, families closed their camps for the winter after Labor Day and returned to their homes until the following summer. After electricity and town water were installed in this area, people began to winterize their camps so that they could live there year-round. Among those who did so were Geraldine O'Reilly, shown here, and her husband, who converted their summer cottage on Alder Road and became permanent residents of the town.

Seven

WINNECUNNET

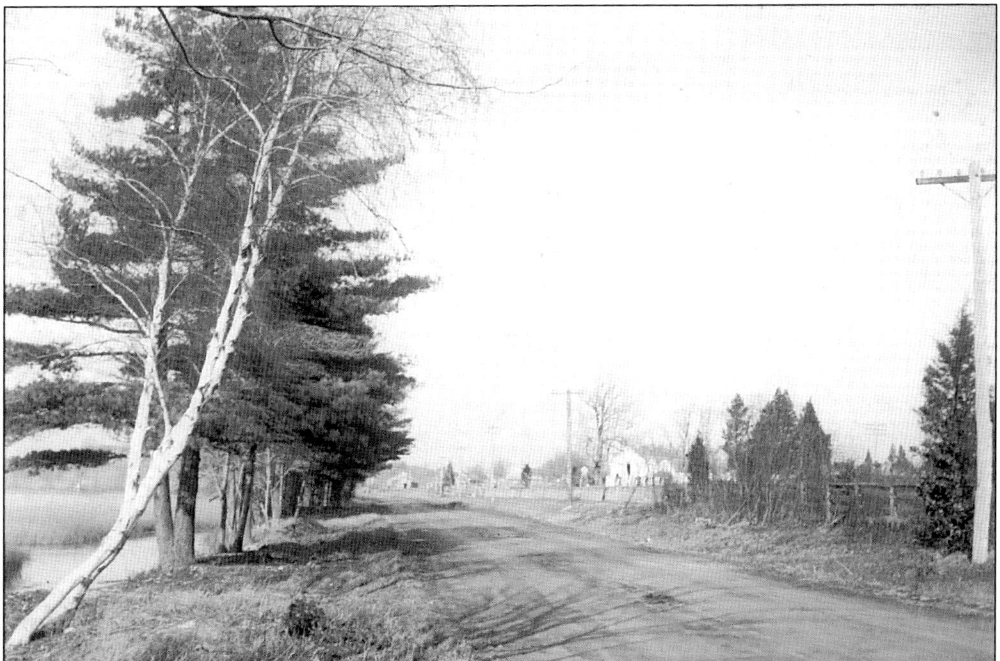

Winnecunnet Village is about 3 miles east of Norton Center. This village has grown more slowly than the rest of the town. Lake Winnecunnet is the only good-sized, natural body of water in the town. It is said that Winnecunnet is a Native American word for "the place of black geese." Old Bay Road extends from Boston Bay to Taunton, passing through Winnecunnet. Originally a Native American trail, it was later used by the early settlers. It became a postal route and stage road. Bay Road was made a scenic road by the town in 1974, and the entire byway is a national historic highway.

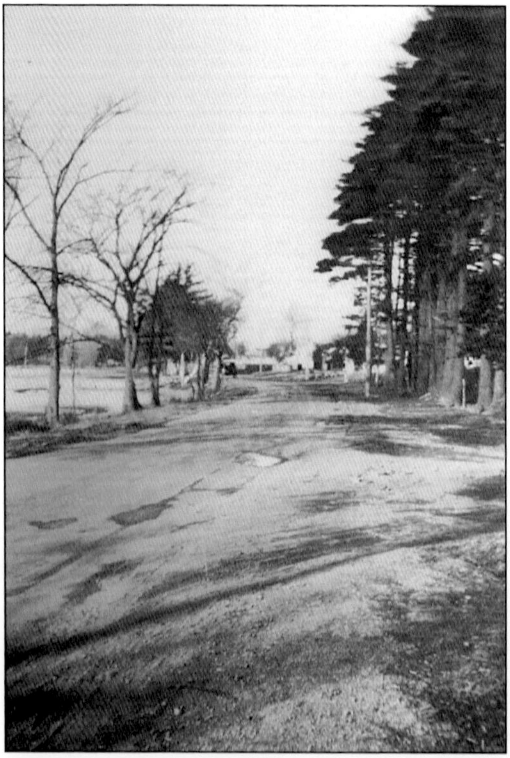

After the Battles of Lexington and Concord signaled the start of the American Revolution, hundreds of men from area towns began marching along Bay Road to Boston to fight in the war.

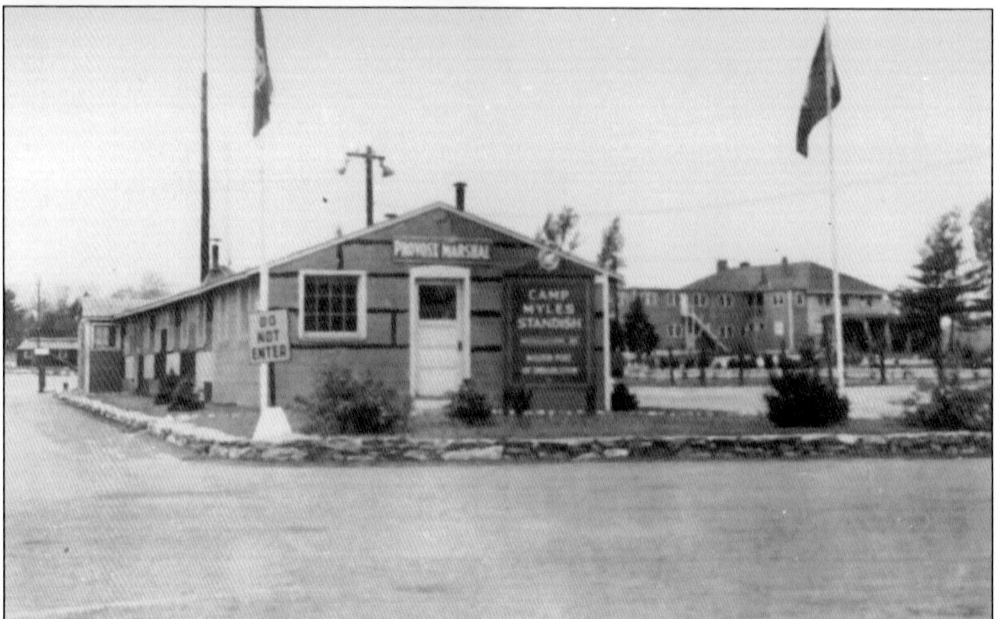

Bay Road remained well traveled until the state built Route 138. The new road, which ran from Boston to Taunton, roughly paralleled Old Bay Road; thus, Bay Road became a quieter byway. No major changes, other than paving, were made along Bay Road until 1943. At the beginning of World War II, the U.S. Army built Camp Myles Standish along Bay Road. Parts of the road had to be reconstructed to accommodate the increased traffic from the army camp.

Just across the Snake River is the site of the first house in Norton, marked by a large slab of blue slate. This monument was erected for the 250th anniversary of Taunton. William Witherell ran a tavern at this site. He lived there with his wife, his three sons, and a daughter. As a sergeant, he took an active part in the King Philip War. Behind this marker is the location of the first burying ground in the town, which was used by the early members of the Witherell, Dean, and Lincoln families.

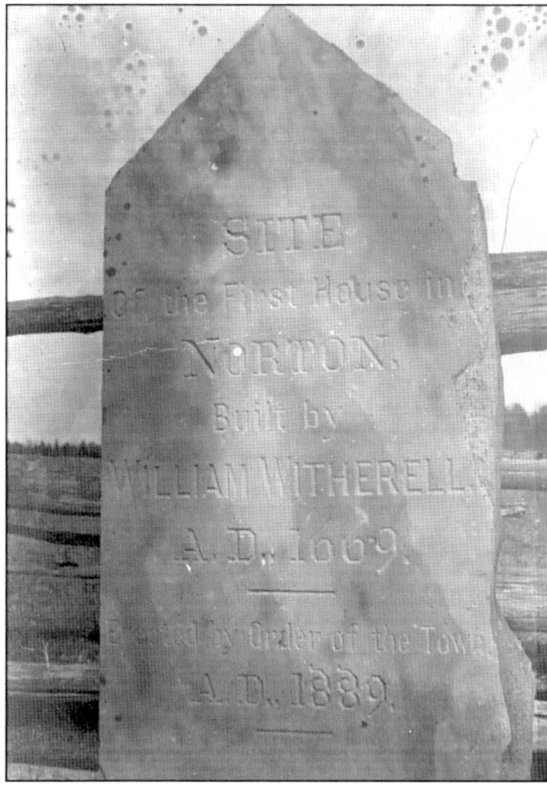

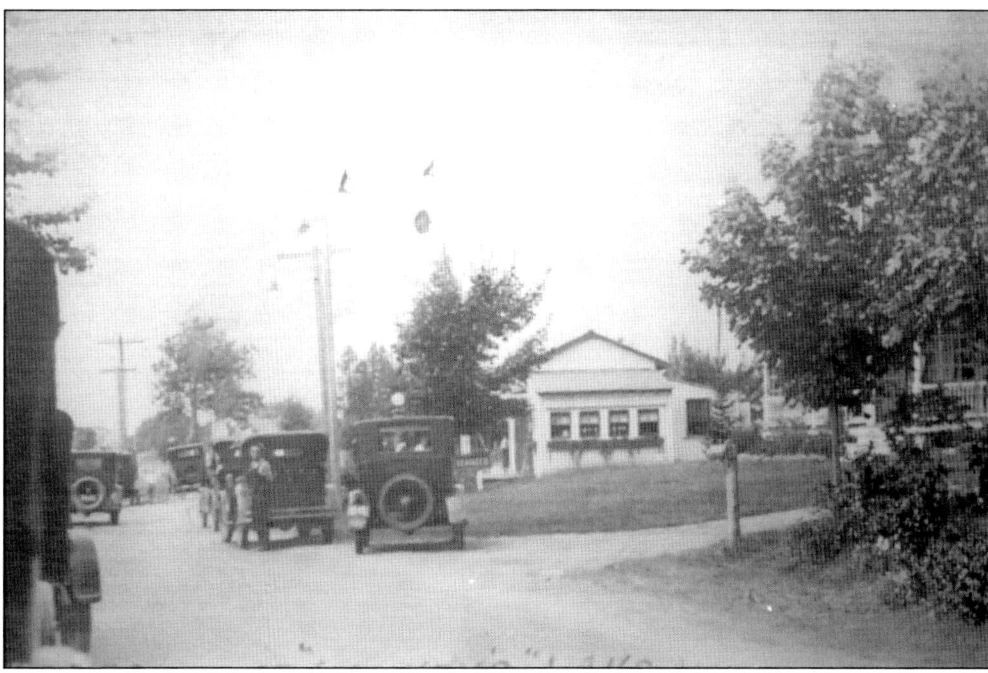

Lanky Reinhard opened a sandwich and ice-cream stand by the family house across from the lake on Bay Road. He and his family made a bathing beach on the lake. During the summer, Lanky's Beach was crowded with city people enjoying a day's outing.

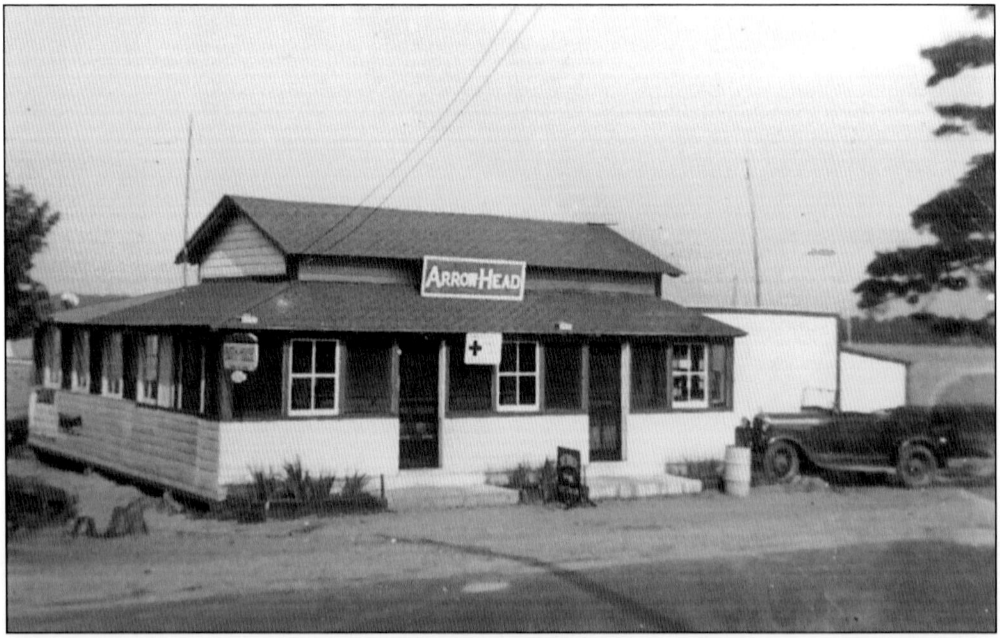

After a few years, Lawrence "Lanky" Reinhard moved his stand across the street onto the waterfront and renamed it the Arrowhead. An addition was added to this building for the Winnecunnet Yacht Club. Reinhard formed the club to encourage and promote sailboat racing.

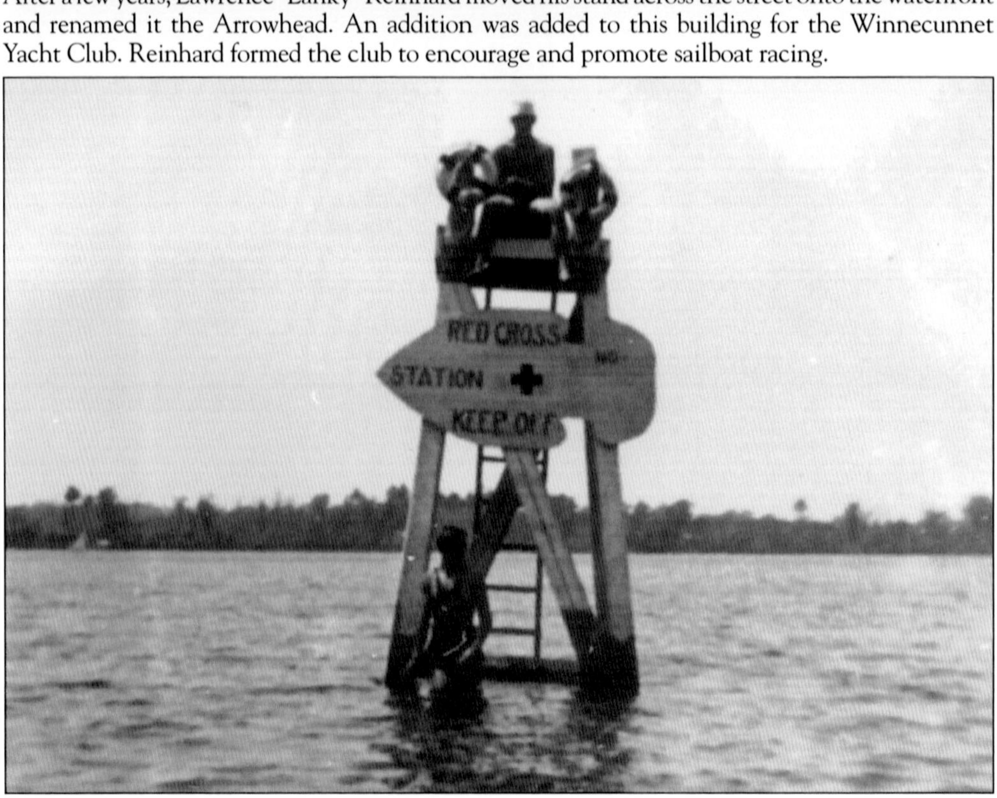

At the Winnecunnet Yacht Club, there was a Red Cross station. The troop of Sea Scouts held its training meetings at the club. The American Red Cross gave junior and senior swimming classes and lifesaving courses at Arrowhead Beach.

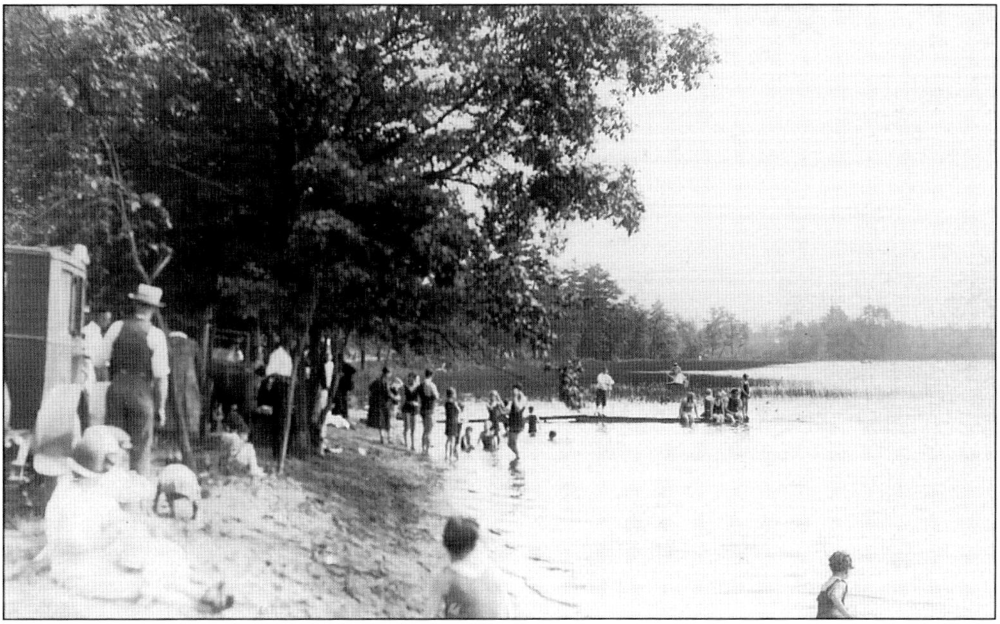

During the summers of the 1930s and 1940s, Winnecunnet Lake was a popular area. City families came to spend the day swimming and boating. The road was usually lined on both sides with parked cars. Along the roadside there was not only the Arrowhead but also a tearoom and a trading post.

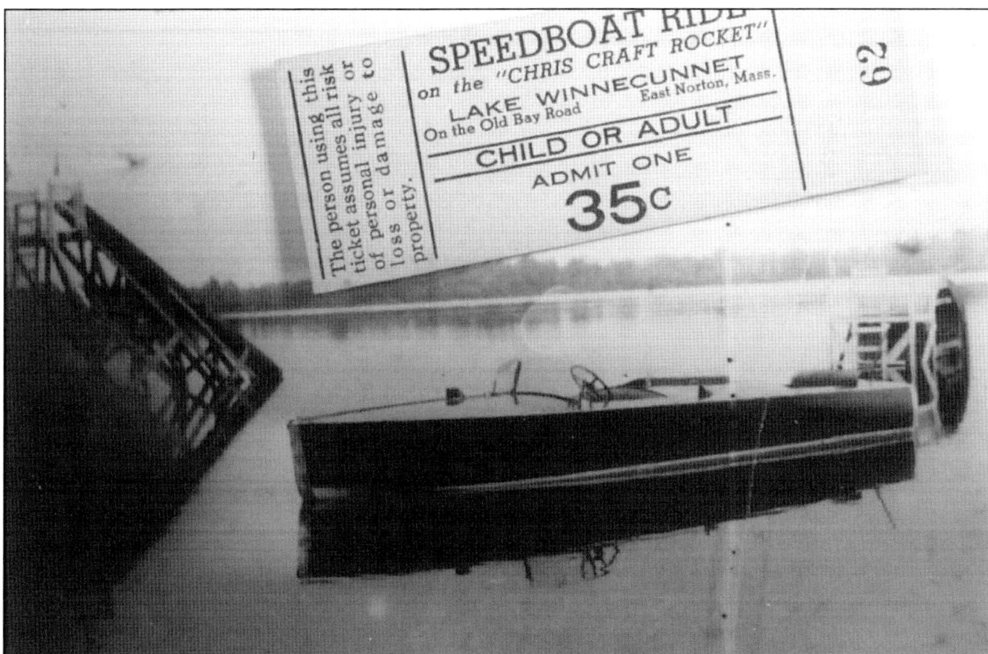

Lawrence "Lanky" Reinhard enlarged his ice-cream business with a boat shed and dock, boathouses, and a waterwheel. With a 35¢ ticket, a person could have a ride on Lake Winnecunnet in the *Rocket*.

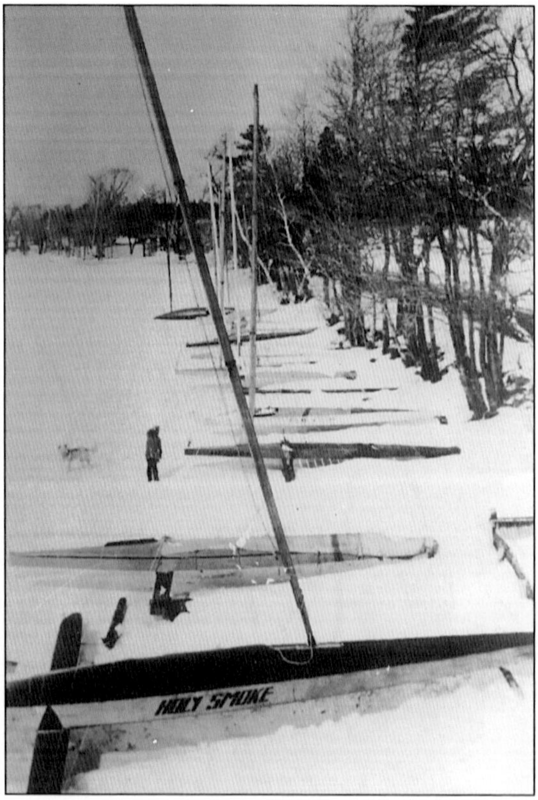

Lanky Reinhard, an iceboat enthusiast, formed a club for the winter sport on the Lake Winnecunnet. Iceboating became very popular; the lake's shore was often lined with these early iceboats, which often had interesting names. The lake had exceptionally smooth ice for the sport. Don Kent, a former WBZ weatherman, often brought his iceboat to Winnecunnet.

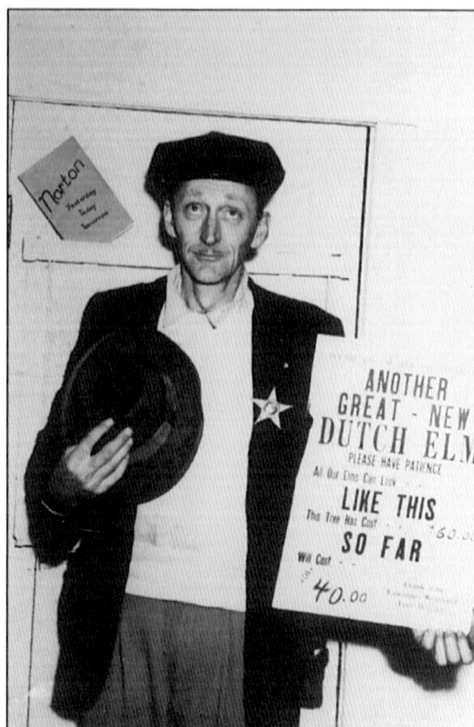

Lanky Reinhard was regarded by many townspeople as mayor of Norton. He served as the town's tree warden for 25 years. When receiving each year's town report, people would eagerly read his humorous tree warden report. With wit and Yankee wisdom, he "wrote 'em as he saw 'em."

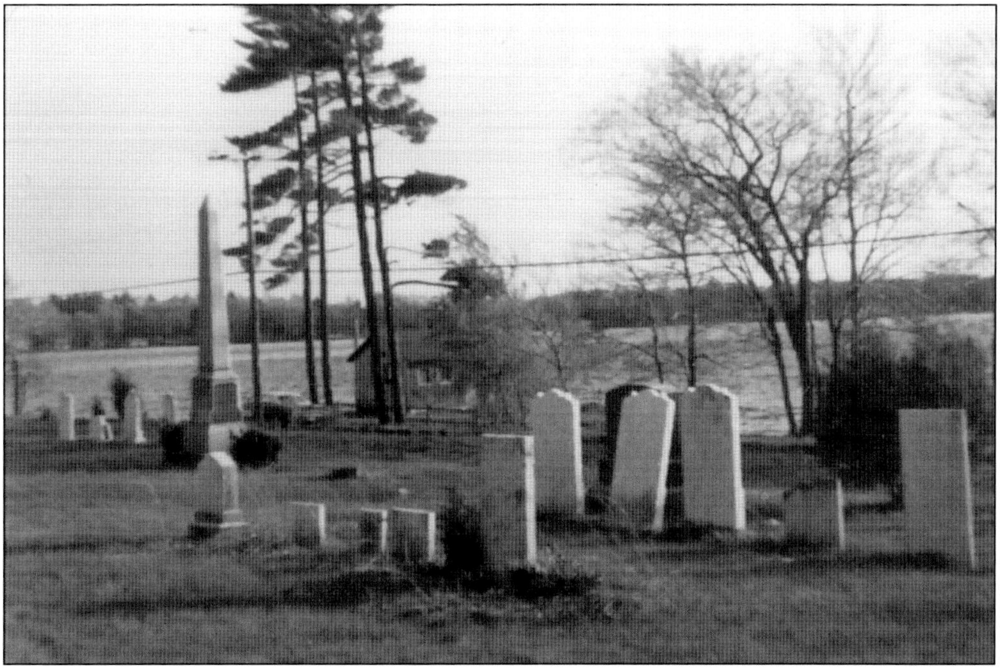

Winnecunnet Cemetery overlooks the lake. The land was originally an open field on the farm of Silas W. Lincoln. Lincoln gave the land to the town *c.* 1862 to be used as a cemetery. Among the old gravestones can be found a stone for John Griggsly, a slave who died in Norton at age 54.

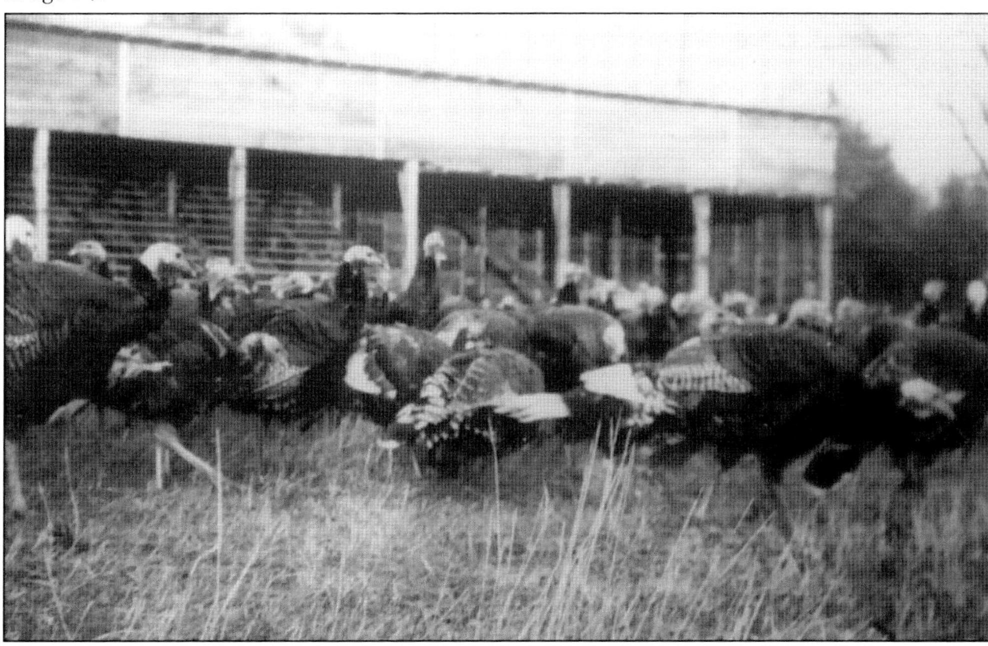

The Winnecunnet Turkey Farm was located off Bay Road behind the Winnecunnet Cemetery. There, Diedrick Runge raised some 40,000 turkeys to be sold to markets for Thanksgiving and Christmas dinners; also, local people came to the farm and chose their holiday turkeys. The birds roosted in the sheds or in trees at night.

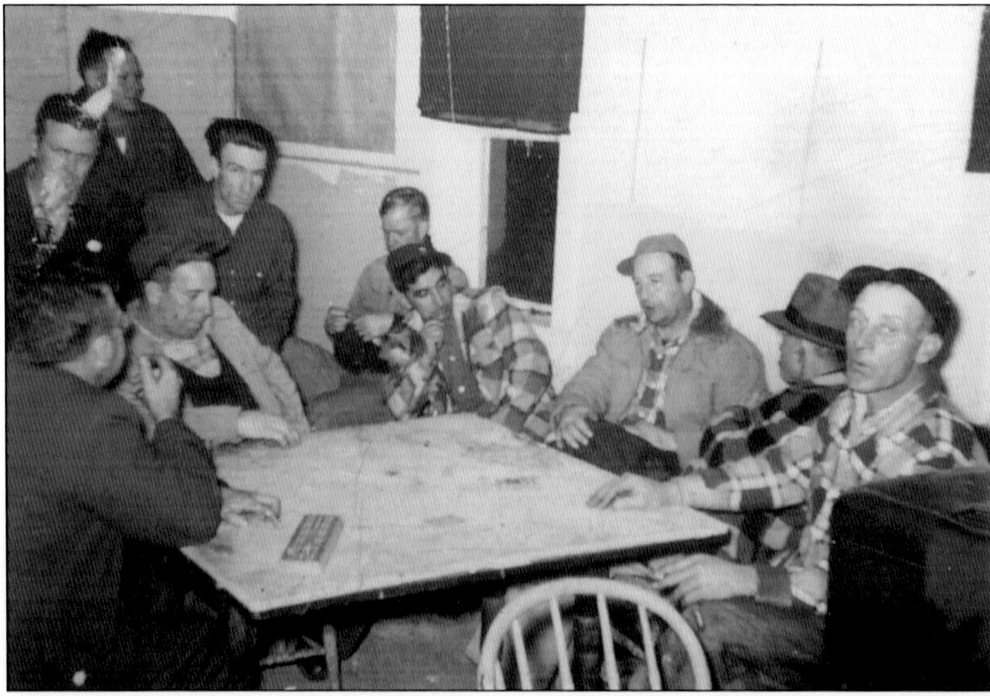

This is the crew of Engine No. 4 at the Winnecunnet Fire Station. Among this volunteer group are Cy Becker, Fred Lemare, LeRoy Stearns, Dick Owen, and Charlie Graney.

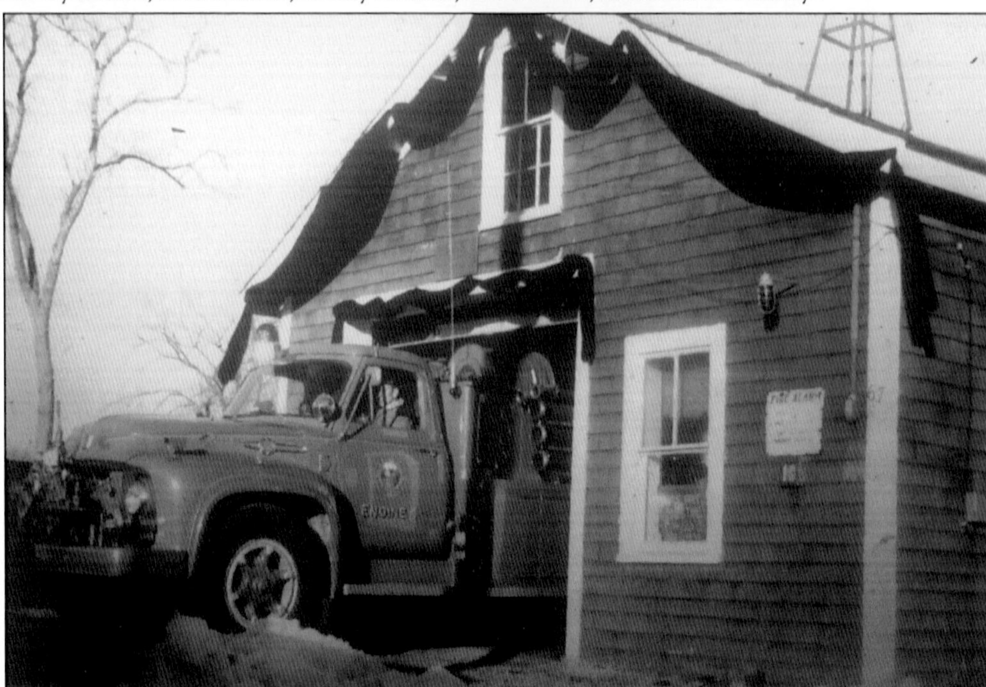

This photograph shows old Engine No. 4 at the first fire station on Bay Road. The station was draped in memory of Fire Capt. Fred Lemaire. The building was originally Morris Casey's barn. It was rebuilt as a fire barn and in 1965, replaced by a new station.

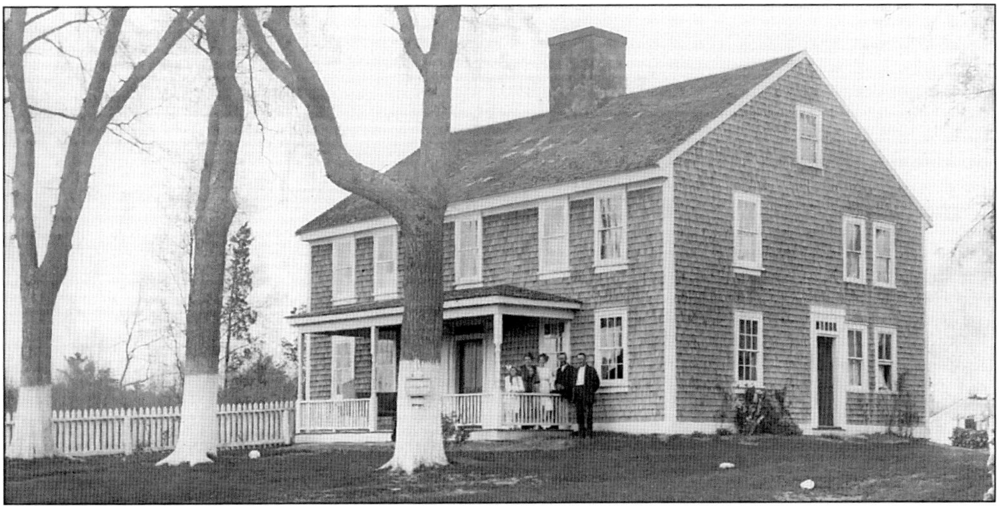

One of the oldest houses on Bay Road is the Joseph White House. Deed transfer records show that it was built before 1715. The house retains six working fireplaces and nearly all of its original paneling and flooring.

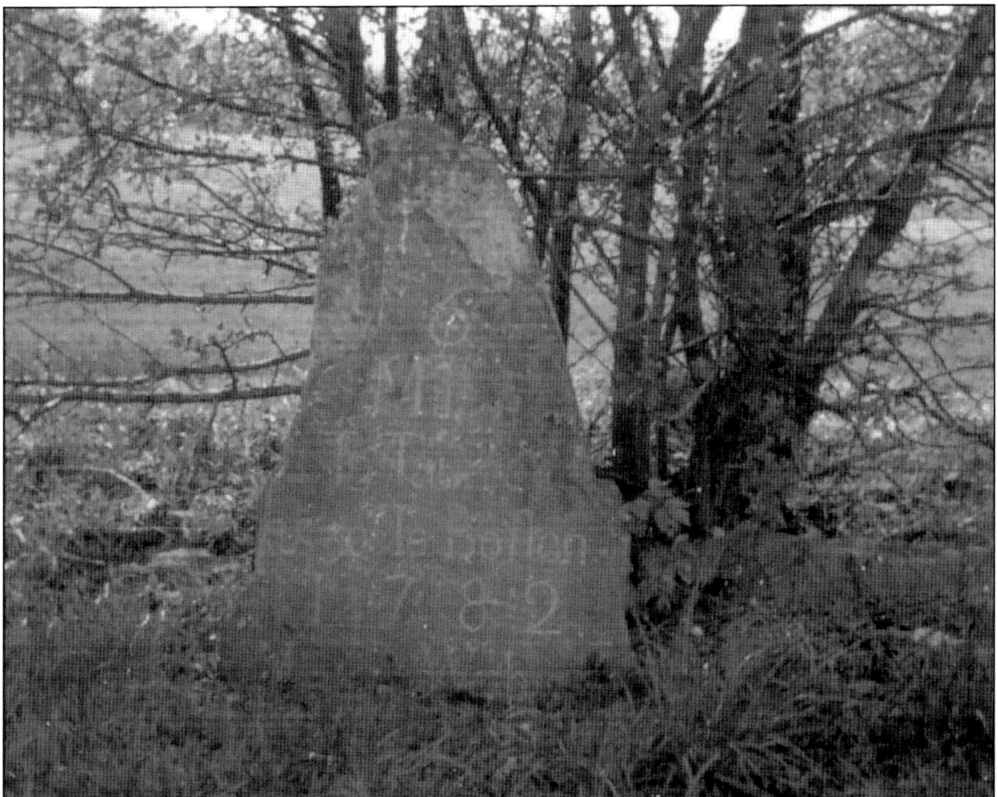

Along Bay Road are milestones that were erected by the post office department in 1767. When the road was declared a postal route, these stones were placed every mile along the road. In those days, mail was paid by weight and mileage, and the stones were used for figuring the latter. Norton has two milestones along Bay Road.

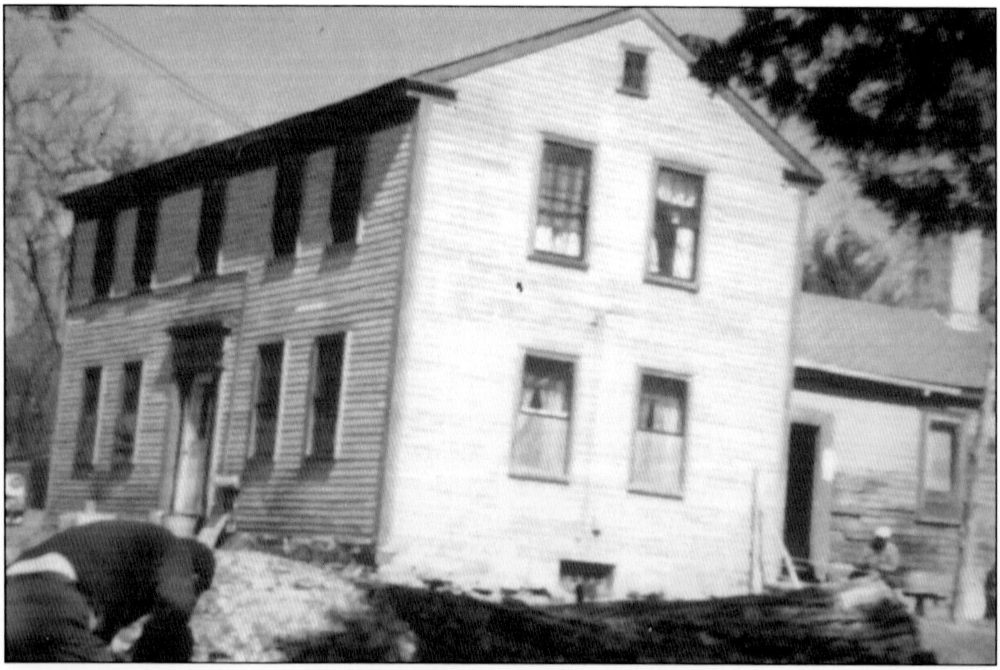

Cranberry bogs are found on Bay Road along the Norton and Easton town line. Bog workers lived in this house during the fall harvesttime. Before modern machinery, the pickers, in a bending position, used wooden scoops with steel teeth. The cranberry vines were pulled apart and the berries rolled out.

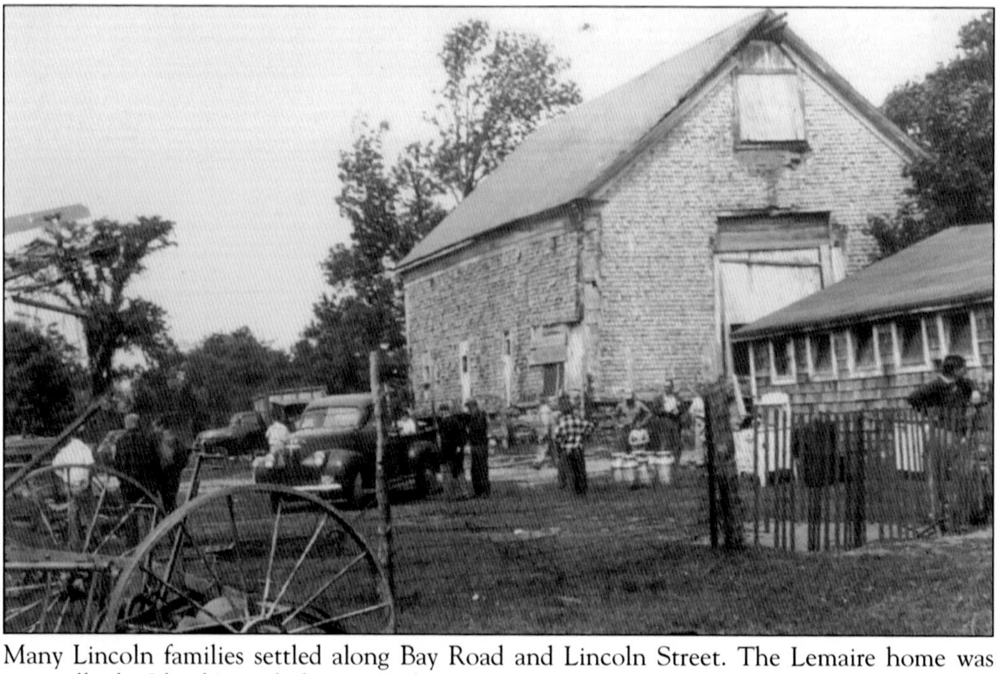

Many Lincoln families settled along Bay Road and Lincoln Street. The Lemaire home was originally the Llyod Lincoln house. In the 1890s, a village post office was located in the house. Fred Lemaire ran a dairy farm here for many years, where a huge barn housed the cows and the milking shed.

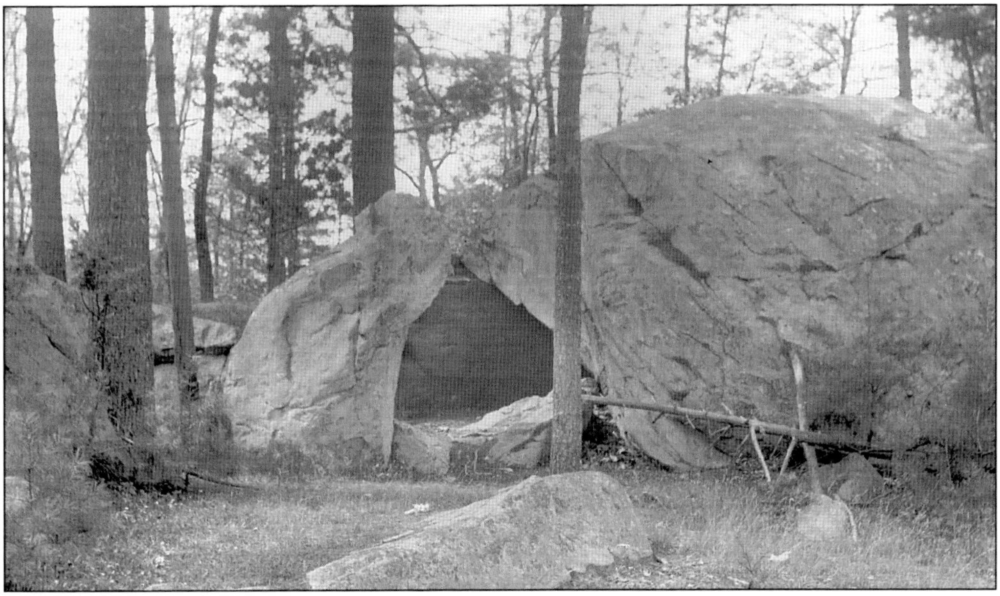

From Plain Street, a path leads to Great Rocky Hill where King Philip's Cave is located. It is said that King Philip, also known as Metacomet, stayed in this cave during his hunting and fishing trips in this area. Scout and school groups enjoy visiting this rock formation.

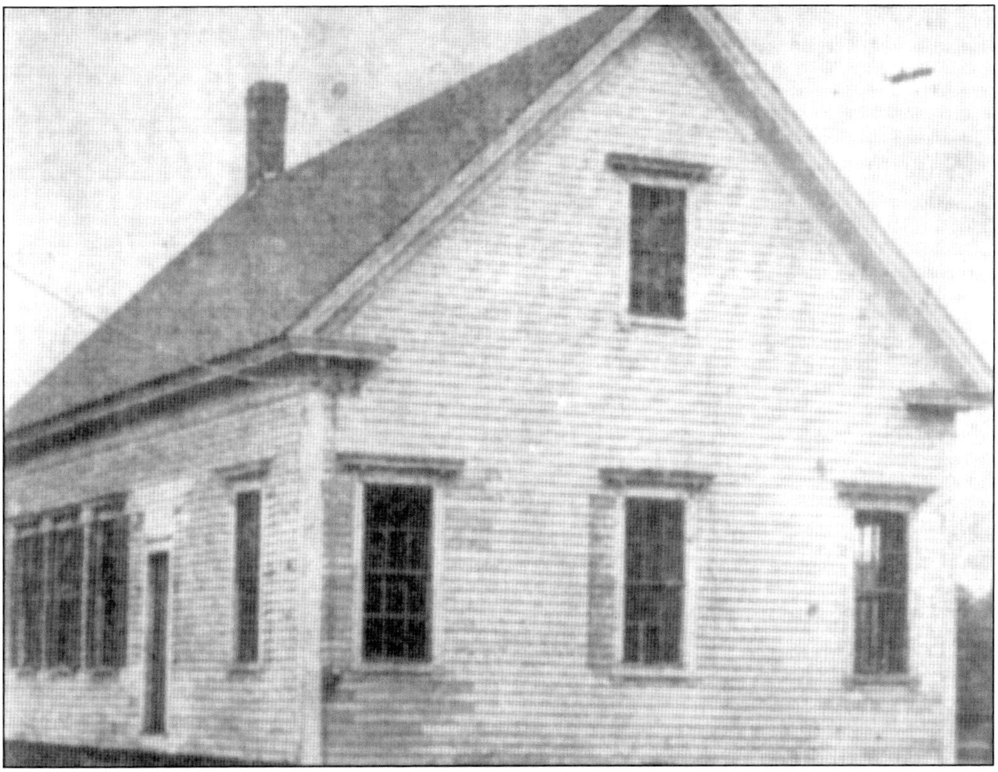

The District No. 8 Schoolhouse was located on Plain Street by Bay Road. It was the last district schoolhouse to close in town. When it closed in 1943, the children attended the Center School.

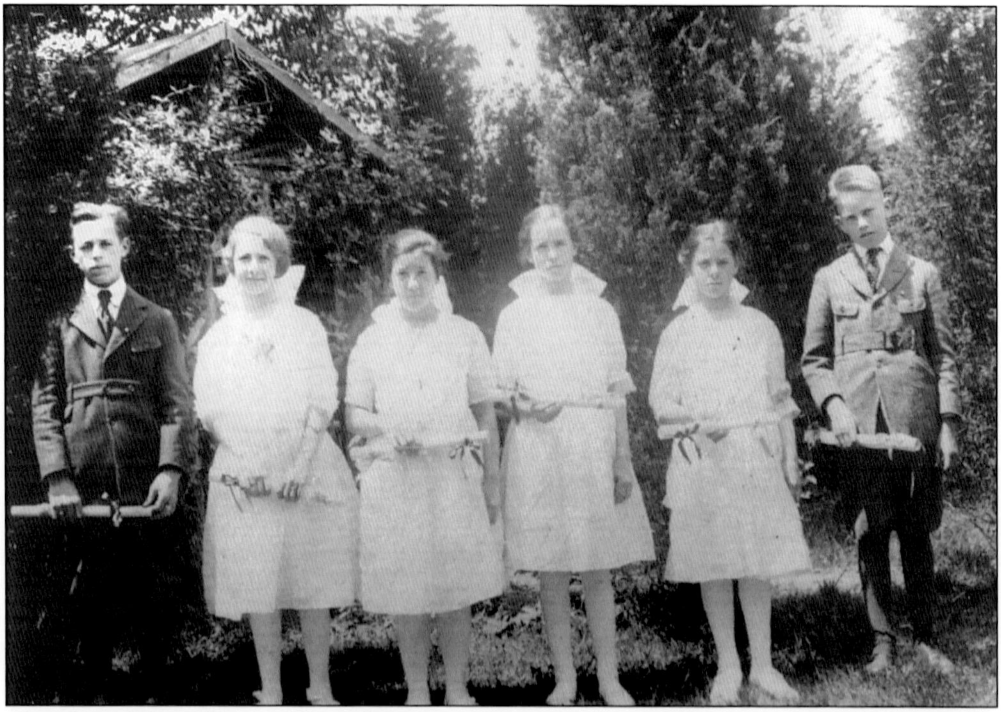

This class graduated in 1921 from the District No. 8 Schoolhouse. Holding their diplomas, from left to right, are Richard Stanley, Doris Campbell, Marjorie Becker, Elsie Lincoln, Alice Becker, and Paul Runge.

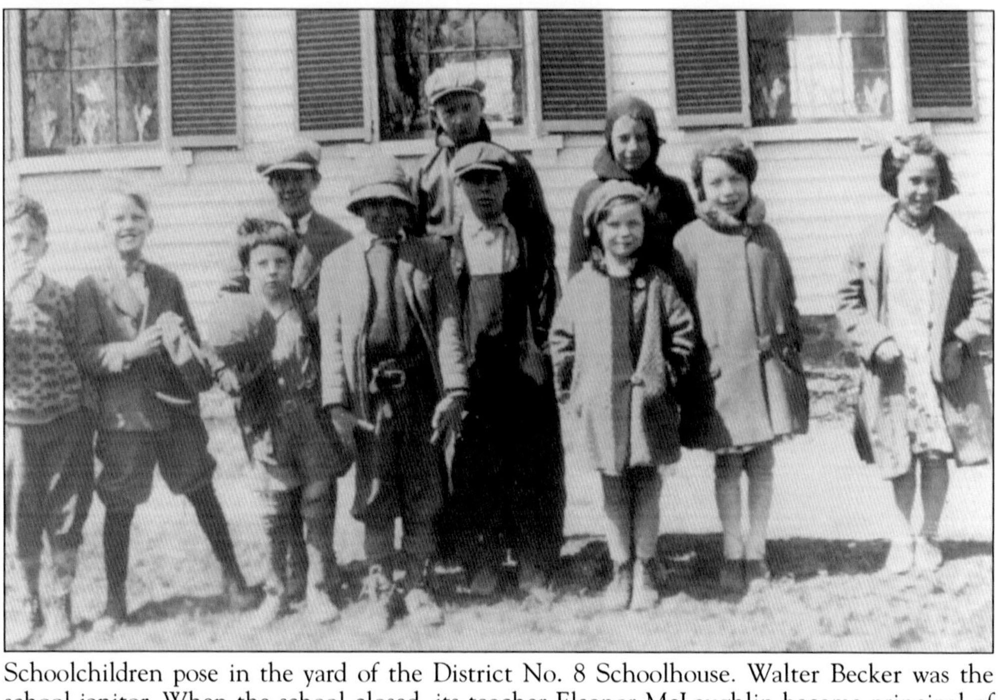

Schoolchildren pose in the yard of the District No. 8 Schoolhouse. Walter Becker was the school janitor. When the school closed, its teacher Eleanor McLaughlin became principal of the Barrowsville School.

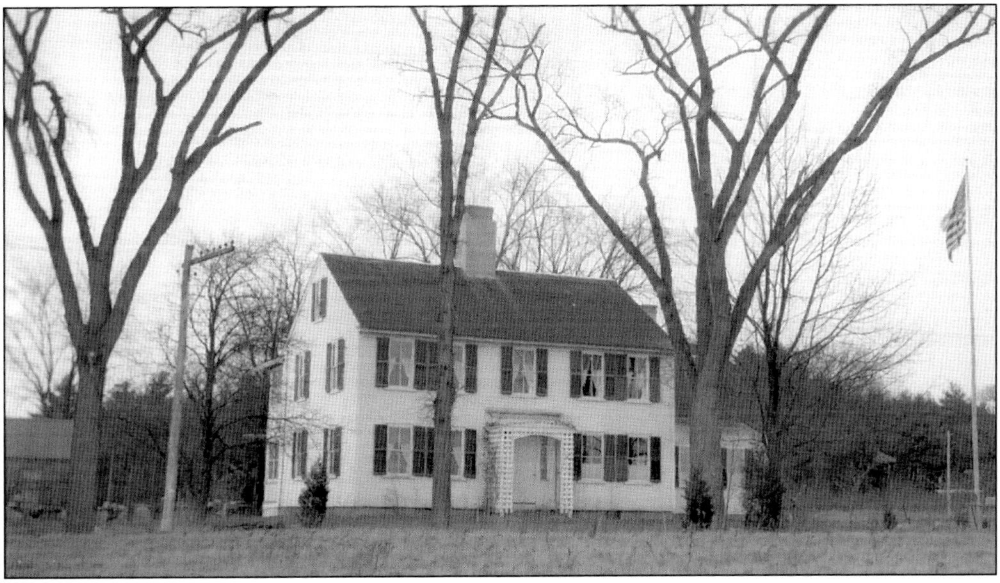

The Thomas Copeland House is located on Plain Street by Mulberry Brook. Benjamin Copeland built it in 1749. In the ell, "T. C. Copeland, age 32, 1820" is carved in a cellar beam.

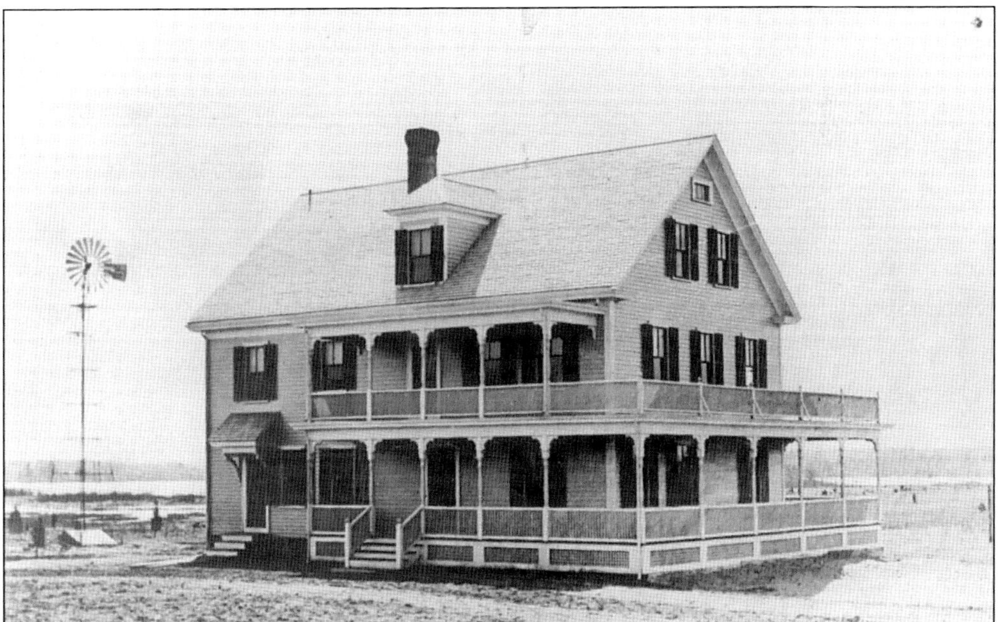

The Winnecunnet House, located on Plain Street, overlooks Winnecunnet Lake. This was an inn run by the Pike family for many years before it became a residence. In 1931, fire destroyed the house.

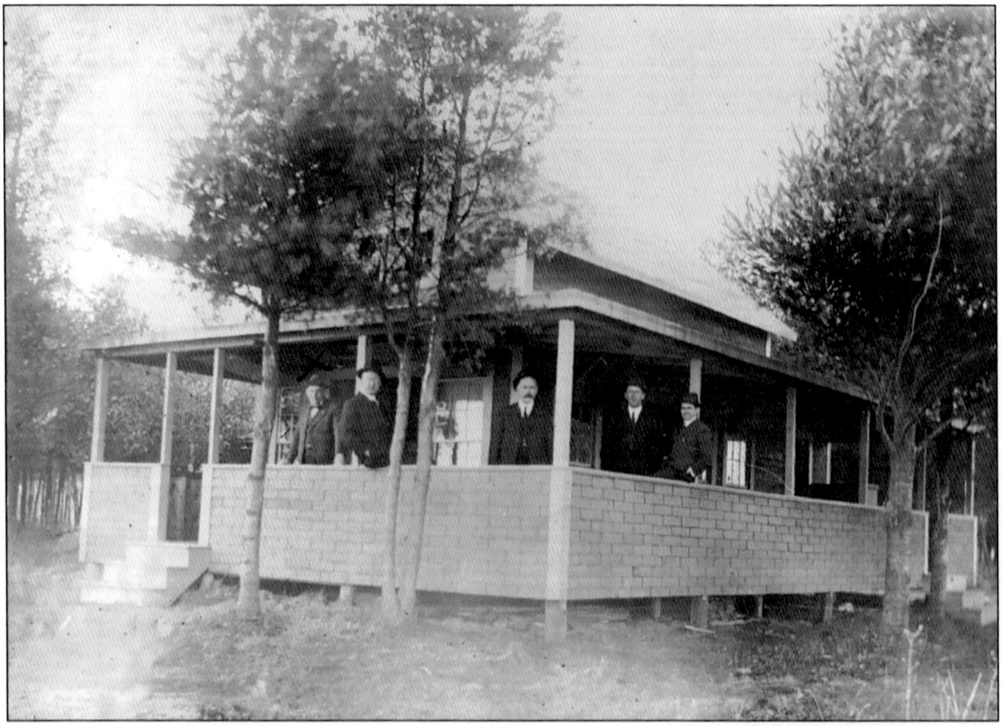

This is a typical early camp found along the back side of the lake. A group of Attleboro men pose on the front porch.

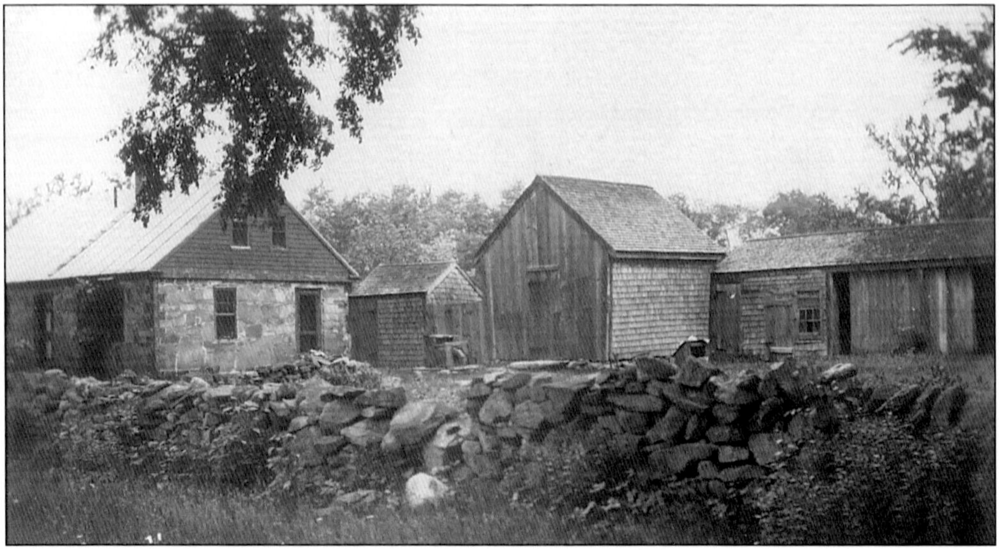

On the far end of Lincoln Street is a stone house that was the home of Solomon Lathrop. Possibly because the house was made of stone, it became known as Solomon's Temple. There was a Calvinist-Baptist church on Lincoln Street at one time.

Eight

WHEATON COLLEGE

That they may have life and have it abundantly.

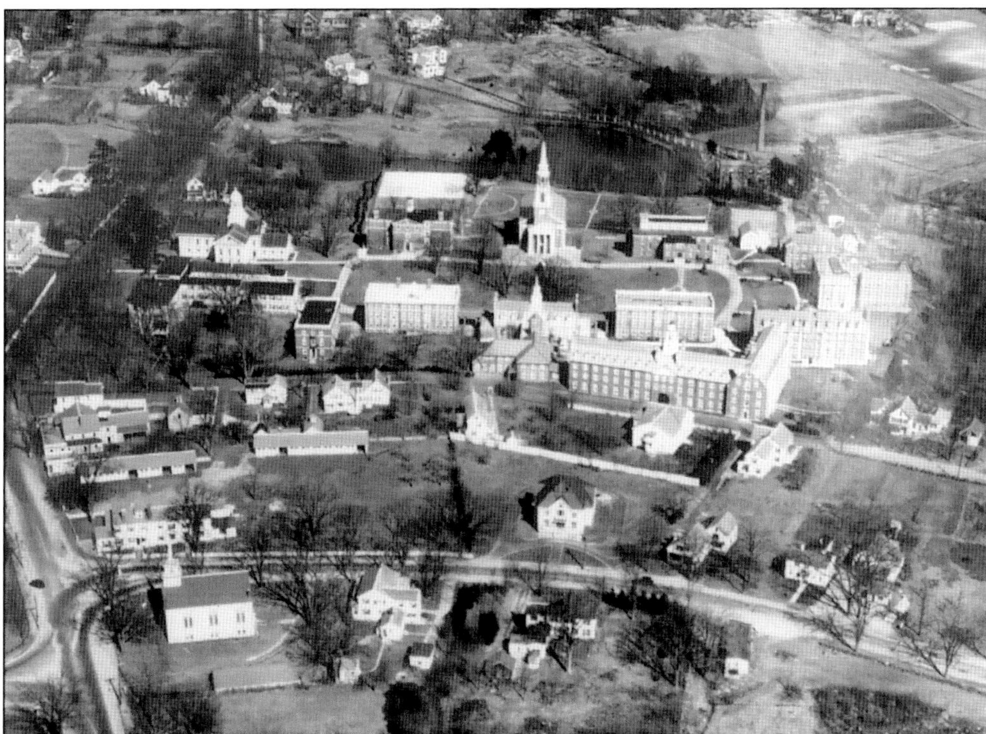

Wheaton College is situated in the central area of the town. The seminary opened in 1835 and became a college in 1912. The old campus resembles a traditional New England common. The president's house serves as the focal point with the buildings grouped around the Dimple, an outdoor amphitheater. As enrollment increased, a lower campus with additional dormitories, a dining hall, and classroom buildings was developed on the east side.

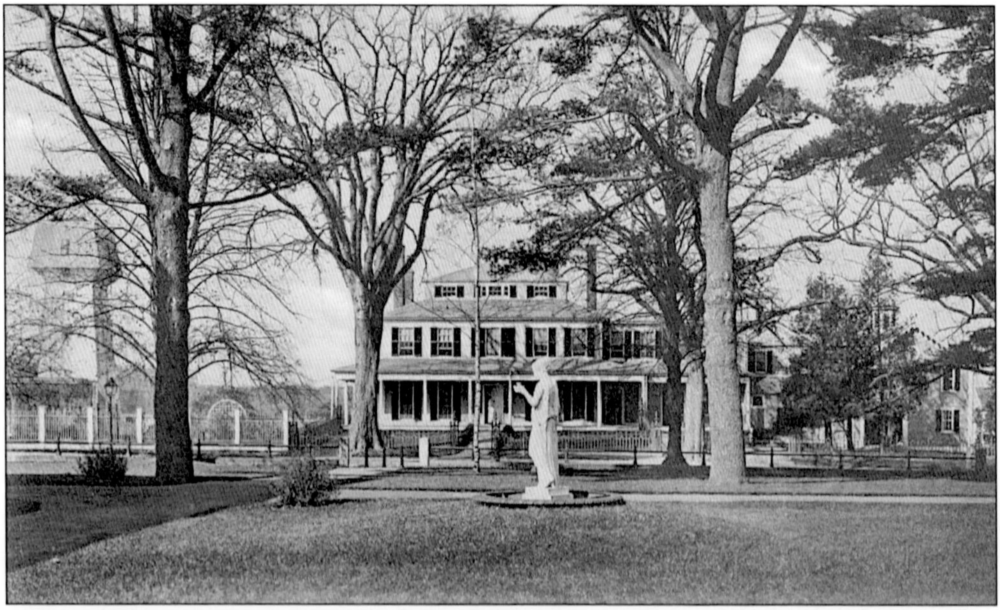

The president's house was built in 1829 by Laban Morey Wheaton as a wedding gift for his bride, Eliza Baylies Chapin Wheaton, who lived there for 76 years and gave the statue of Hebe to the seminary for its 50th anniversary in 1884. From the time of her death to the present, it has been the home of the presidents of Wheaton.

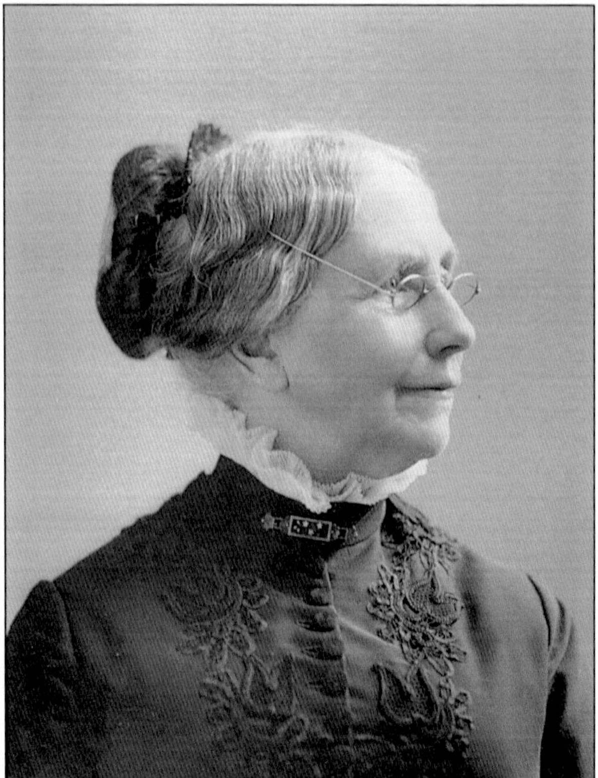

A staunch supporter of education for women, Eliza Baylies Chapin Wheaton committed her life to providing high-quality education for the students of Wheaton Seminary. She is recognized as the founding mother of the seminary. She was the daughter-in-law of Judge Laban Wheaton, and it was at her suggestion that he founded the female seminary as a living memorial for his deceased daughter, Eliza.

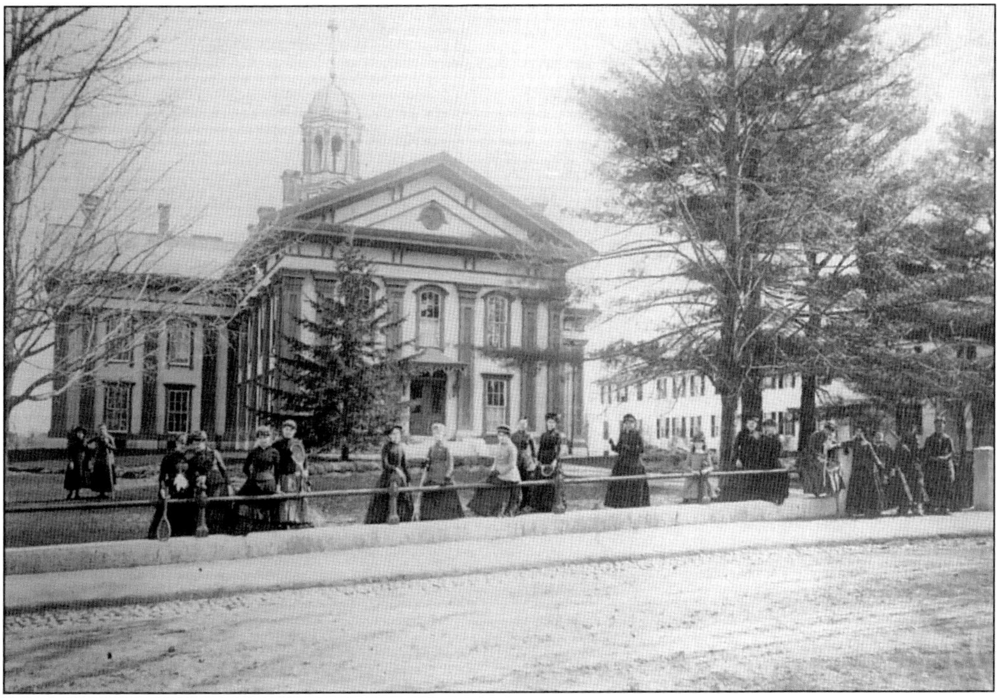

Built in 1849, Seminary Hall was renamed in 1910 for educational pioneer Mary Lyon, who served as a consultant to the Wheaton family at the founding of the seminary and established its curriculum. In 1878, the wooden Greek-Revival building was enlarged to include a science wing, a library, a gymnasium, and more classrooms.

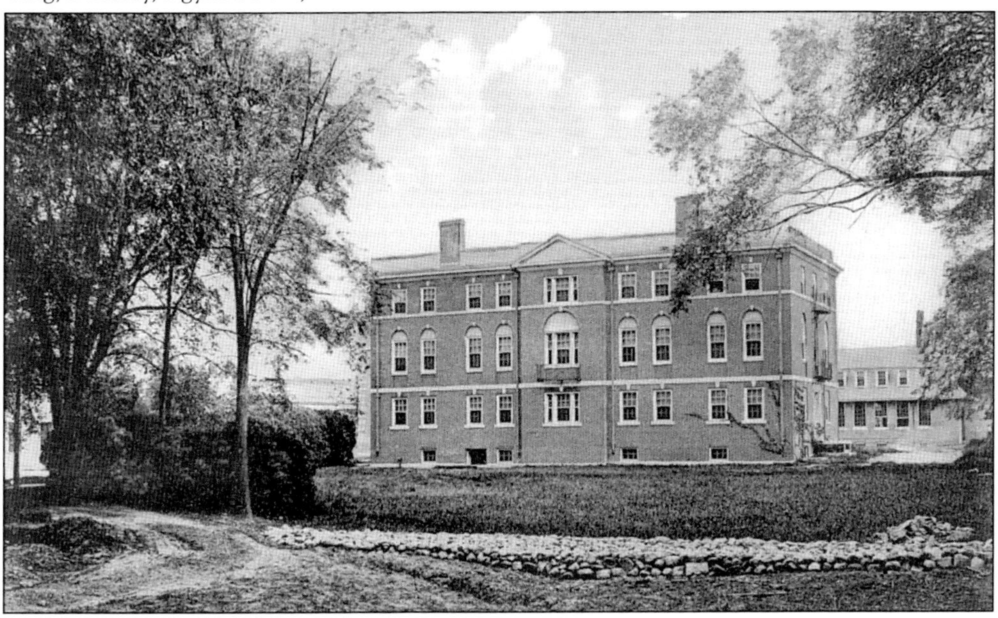

Chapin Hall was Wheaton's first brick building, constructed in 1901. It was named for Samuel Austin Chapin, brother of Eliza Wheaton. After he and his wife came to Norton to reside with his sister, Chapin became a staunch friend of the seminary and befriended the needy of the town.

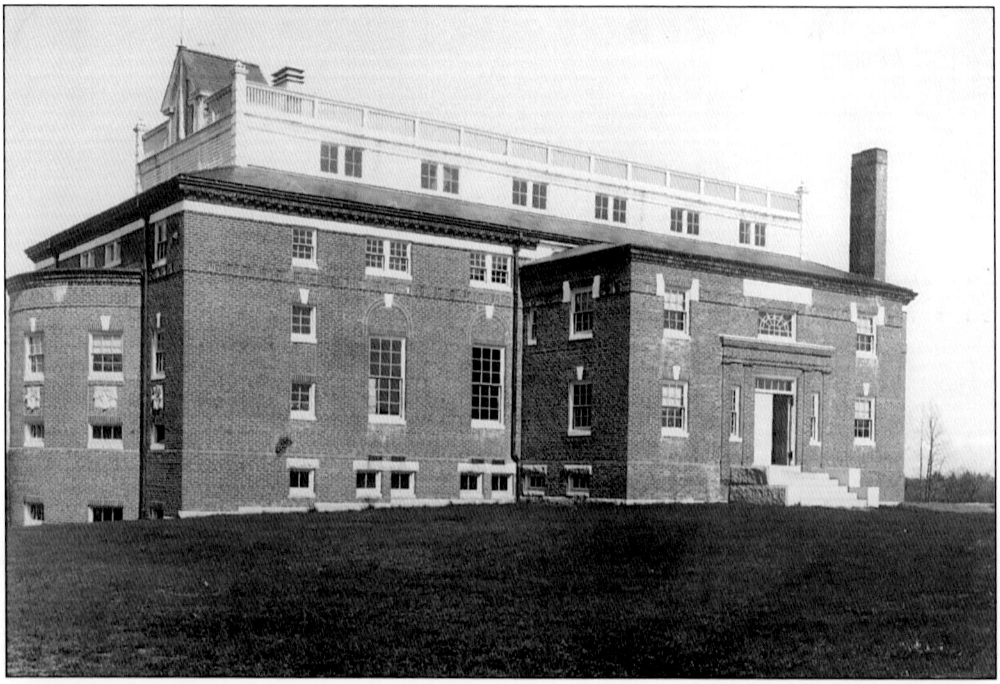

In 1903, this gymnasium designed by George Tilden was built. Dr. Dudley Sargent of Harvard University, a leading expert on physical education, served as consultant. The first swimming tank was in the basement. Then, in 1936, a new swimming pool wing was built. For many years Norton grammar and high school graduation ceremonies and proms were held in this gym.

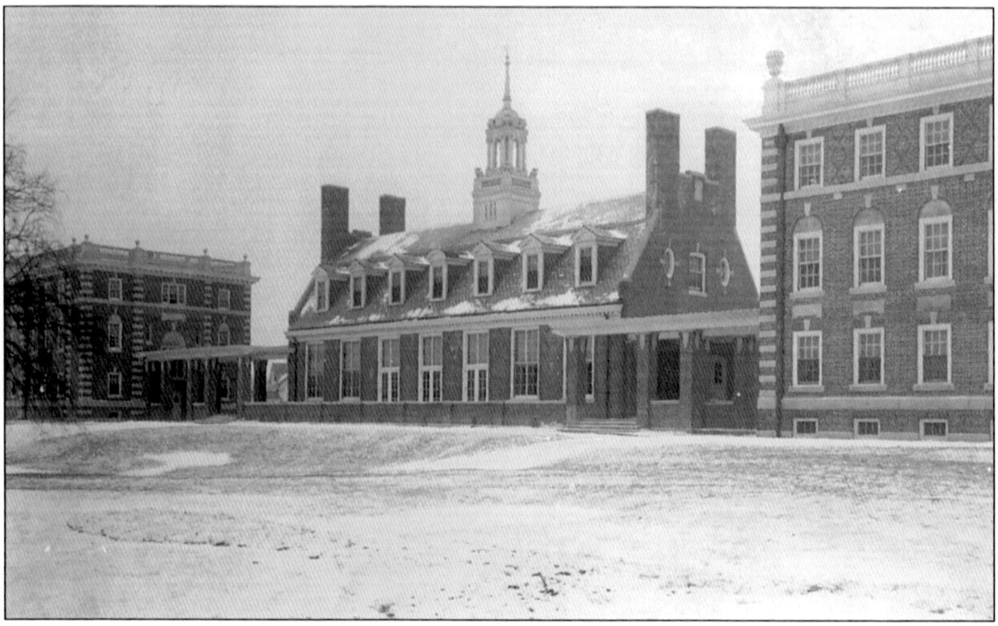

Emerson Dining Hall is situated on the west side of the campus quadrangle. Built in 1908, it was named in honor of the Emerson family. Alfred Emerson was a trustee and treasurer of the seminary. His wife, Martha Vose Emerson, was the school's principal from 1840 to 1842. Two of their daughters graduated from the Wheaton Seminary and later taught there.

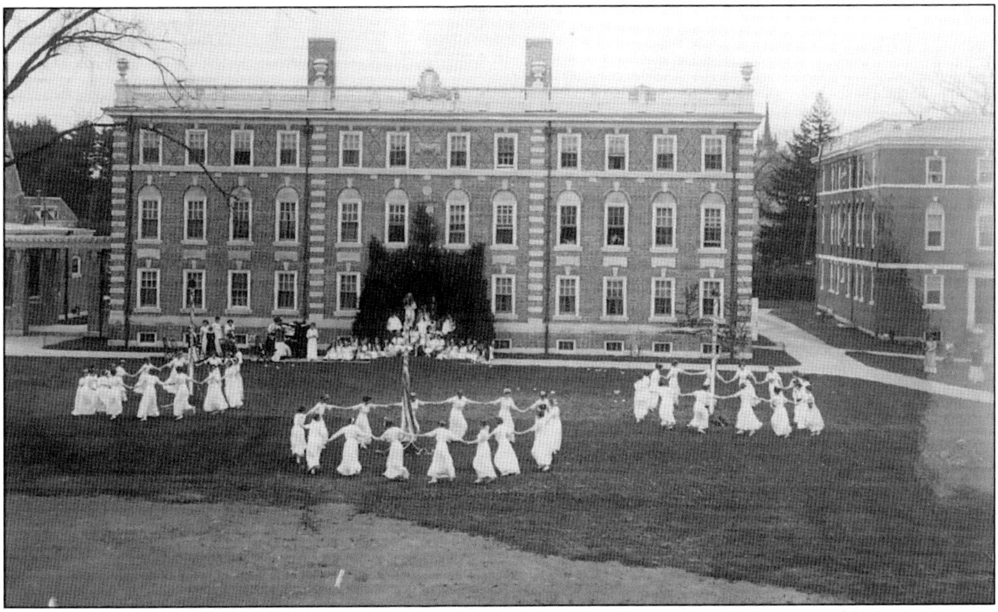

This dormitory is named for Lucy Larcom, who established the study of English literature at Wheaton Seminary. In 1855, she founded *Rushlight*, the student literary magazine, which continues to this day. During her youth, she worked in the Lowell textile mills; later, she became a close friend of poet John Greenleaf Whittier. This photograph shows the May queen and her court on the Larcom steps during May Day festivities.

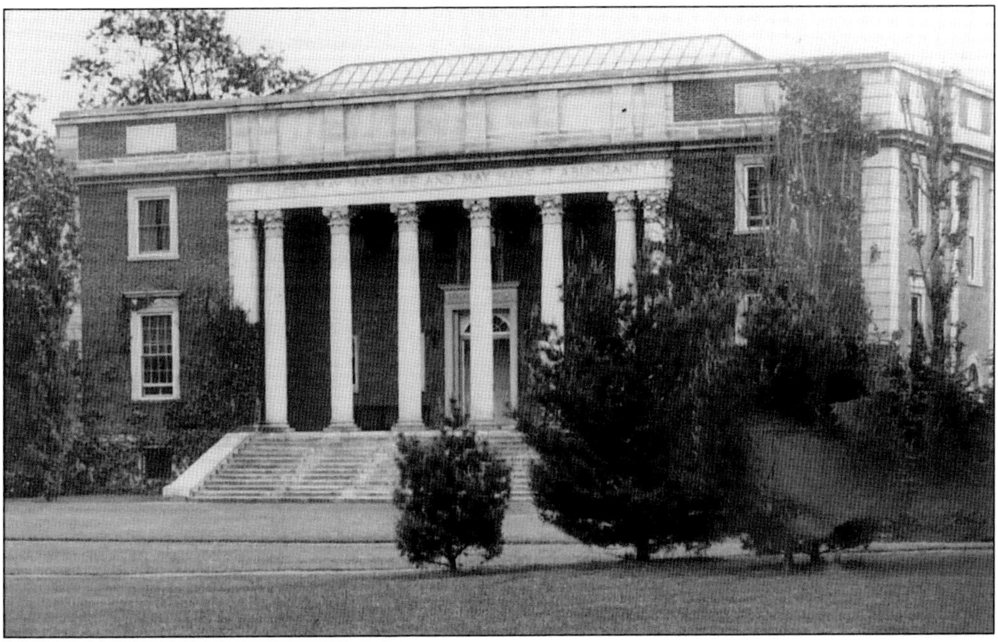

Wheaton's library began in a room in Old Metcalf Hall. It was moved into another small building before being housed in Mary Lyon Hall. Needing more space, it was moved to the chapel basement in 1918, where it remained until this building was opened in 1923 at the southern end of the campus. The Jackson Wing was added in 1941; the periodicals wing was built in 1961.

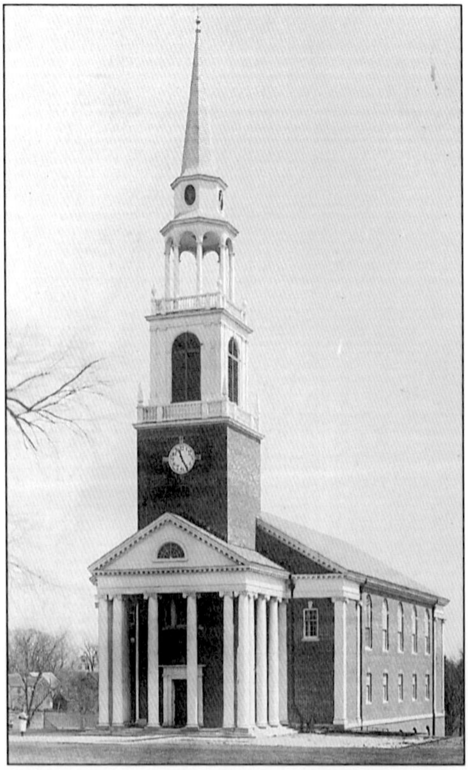

The beautiful white spire seen in the skyline upon approaching the Wheaton College campus belongs to the Cole Memorial Chapel. Designed by Ralph Adams Cram and built by L.M. Witherell & Sons of Taunton, the chapel was dedicated in 1926 in honor of the Reverend Samuel Valentine Cole, Wheaton's president from 1897 until his death in 1925.

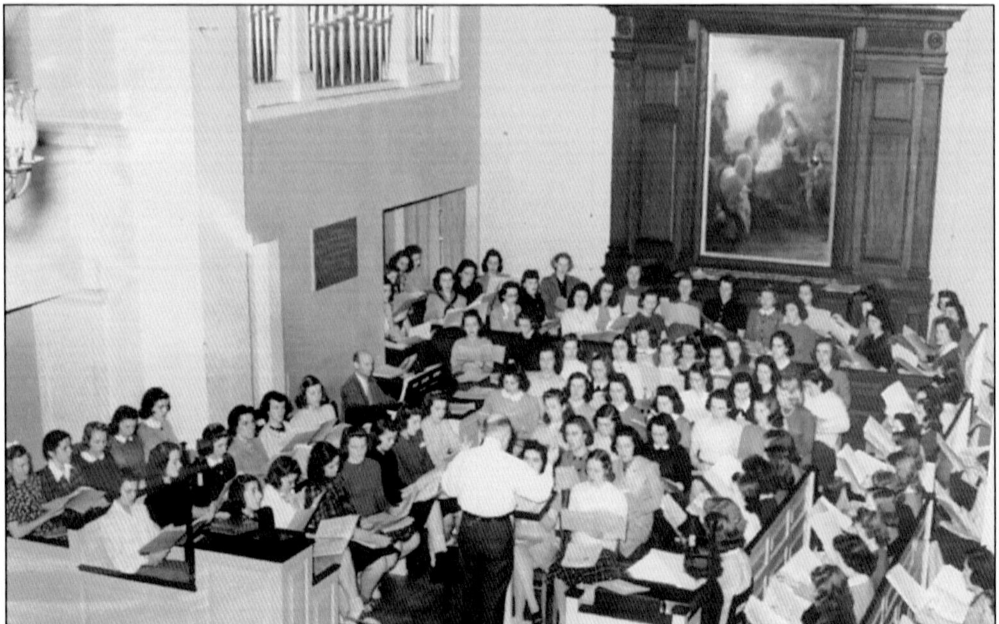

For many years, Dr. Carl Garabedian was the choir director at Wheaton College. Prof. Frank Ramseyer was assistant director and organist. The choir sang at Sunday services and also performed at Christmas Vespers and other concerts during the year. In 1950, the choir performed three Bach concerts commemorating the 250th anniversary of the composer's death.

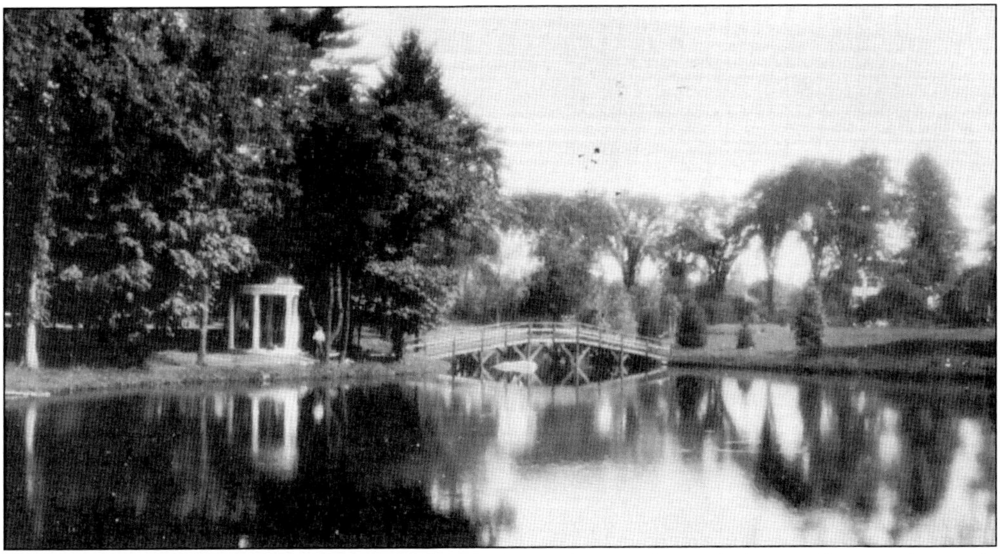

In 1929, marshland was excavated and transformed into Peacock Pond. During the early years, the pond was busy with swimmers, boaters, skaters, and children peering at the huge goldfish. The pond received its name from the weathervane of the Cole Chapel that reflected on its waters. The Greek temple by the pond was built in 1935, using pillars from the porch of Old Metcalf Hall.

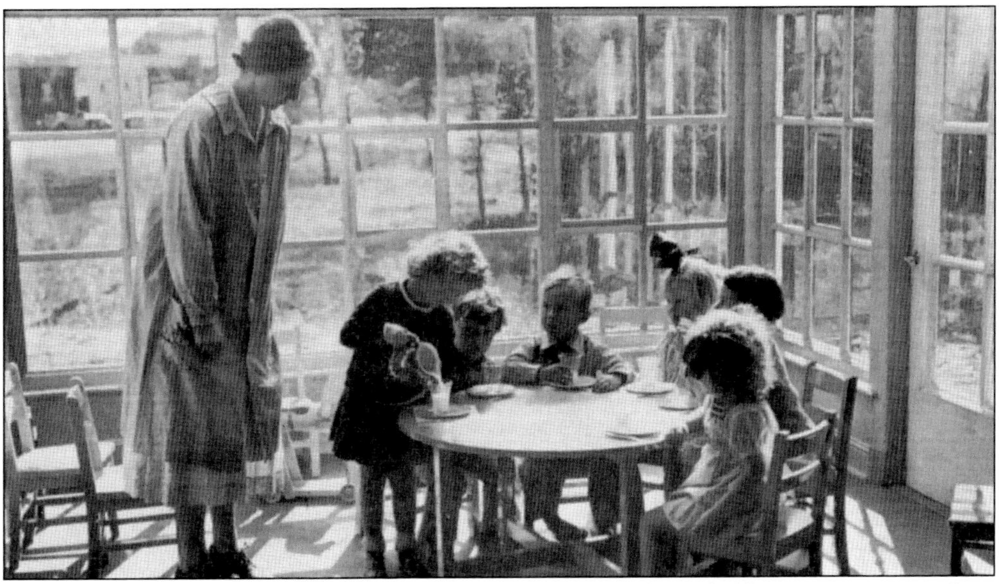

The Wheaton nursery school opened in November 1931, with 24 children ranging in age from 3 to 5. These children came from Norton, Attleboro, and Mansfield. The fee was $1 a month to cover the cost of the crackers and milk served as a mid-morning lunch.

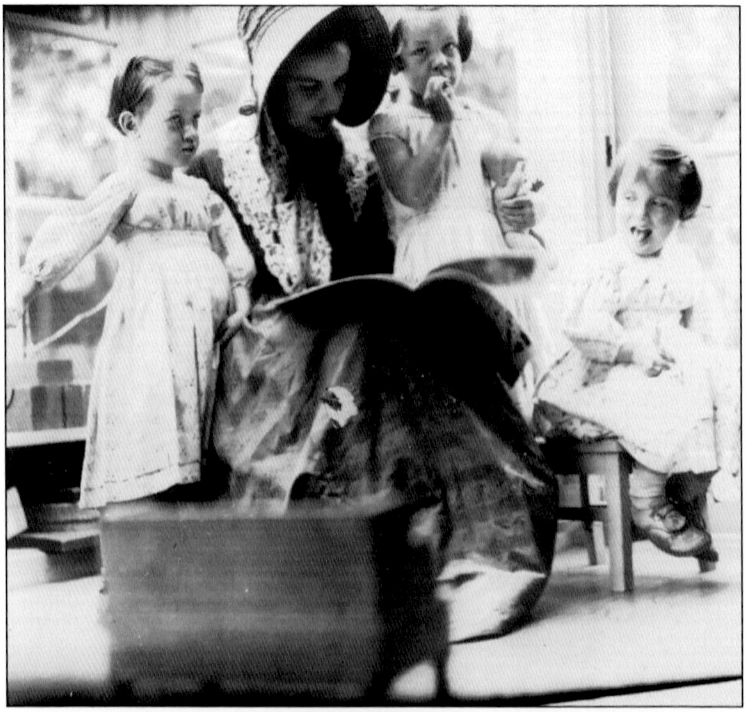

The nursery school children and their teacher participated in Wheaton's 100th anniversary in 1935. The children, dressed in clothing of earlier days, took part in a pageant about the founding of the college. Here, Ruth Goold, Nancy Foster, and Barbara Foster listen to a story being read by a Wheaton student.

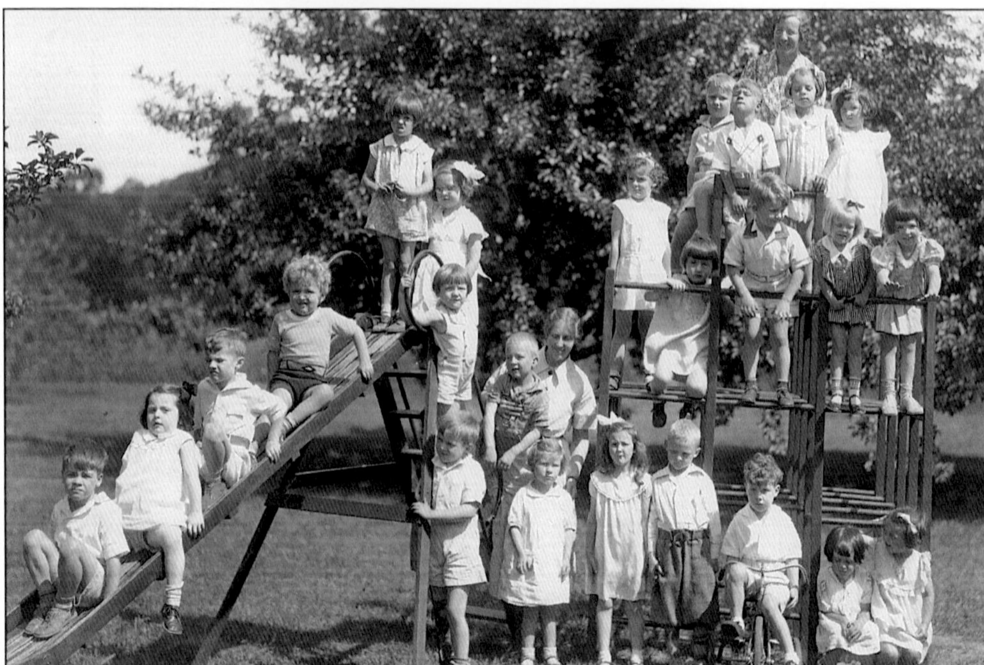

Prof. Elisabeth Amen founded Wheaton's nursery school in 1931. It was built during the summer of 1931 as a laboratory for the Department of Psychology and Education. It was enlarged in 1937, when a one-way vision observation screen was installed. Wheaton students, as part of their practical work in psychology, gave two hours of laboratory work every week to the school.

Some of the town's young ladies furthered their education at Wheaton. Jessie Hunt Foster, the daughter of Frank and Alvira Hunt of South Washington Street, attended Wheaton Seminary. She entered in 1893, at the time when Norton had no high school, at the age of 13. She graduated from Wheaton in 1899.

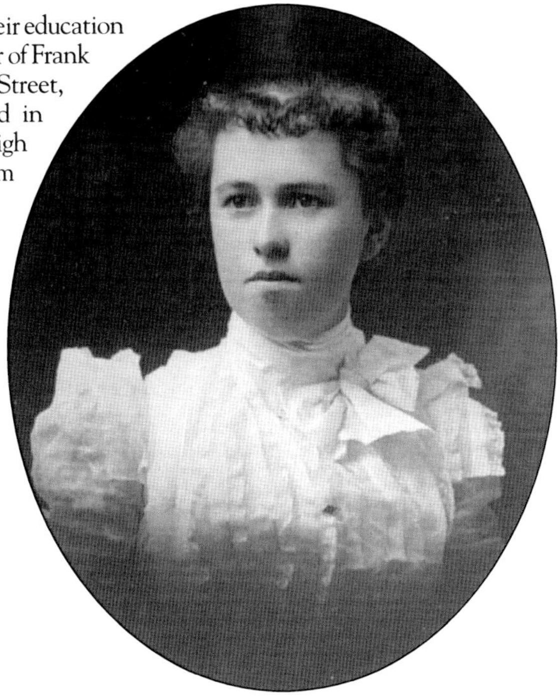

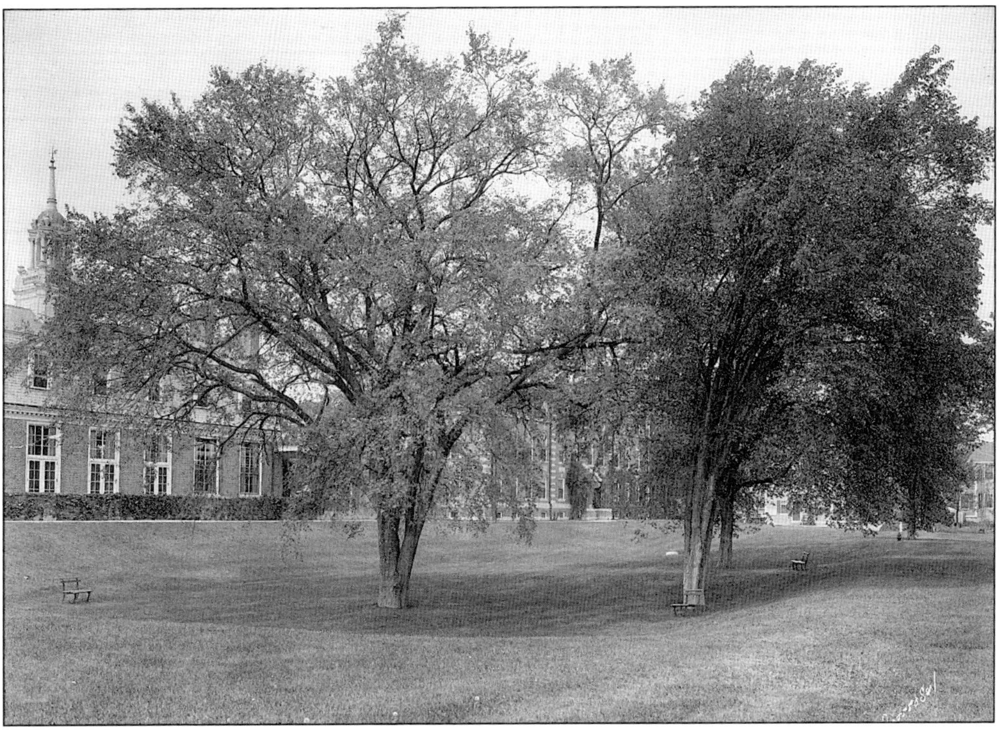

The focus of the college campus is the Dimple. Originally, it was a cellar hole for a barn and was sloped into its present depression when Emerson Dining Hall was constructed in 1908. The Dimple provides a beautiful amphitheater for graduation exercises, May Day celebrations, and other outdoor activities.

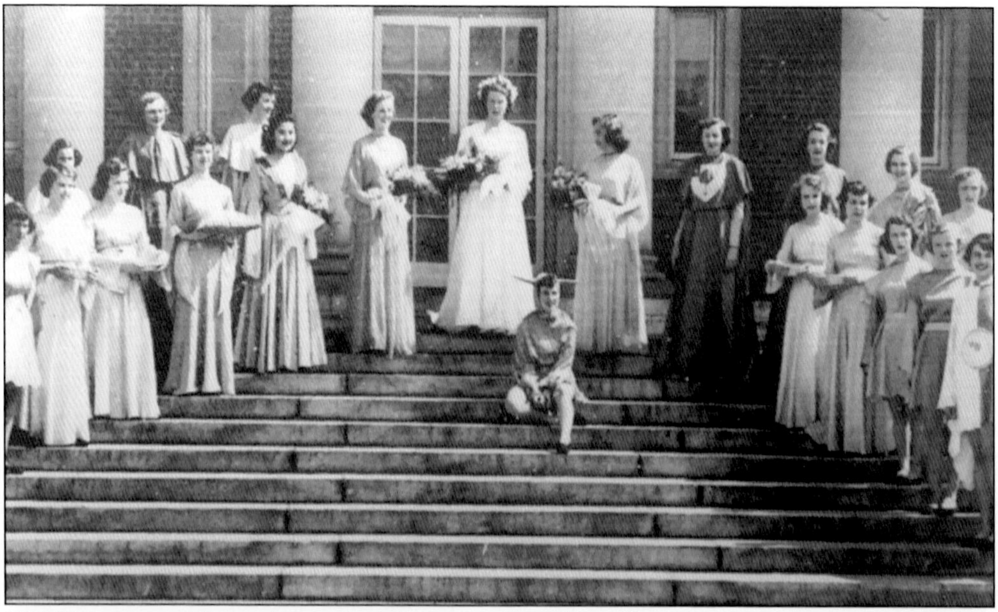

May Day was a traditional spring celebration, which the college began to observe in the 1880s and continued to do until the 1960s. The seniors chose a sophomore to be the May queen. The queen of the May symbolized not only great beauty and character but also new hope and life, which the spring season promised. The winner was not announced until she appeared that day. The immediate attendants of her court were the runners-up.

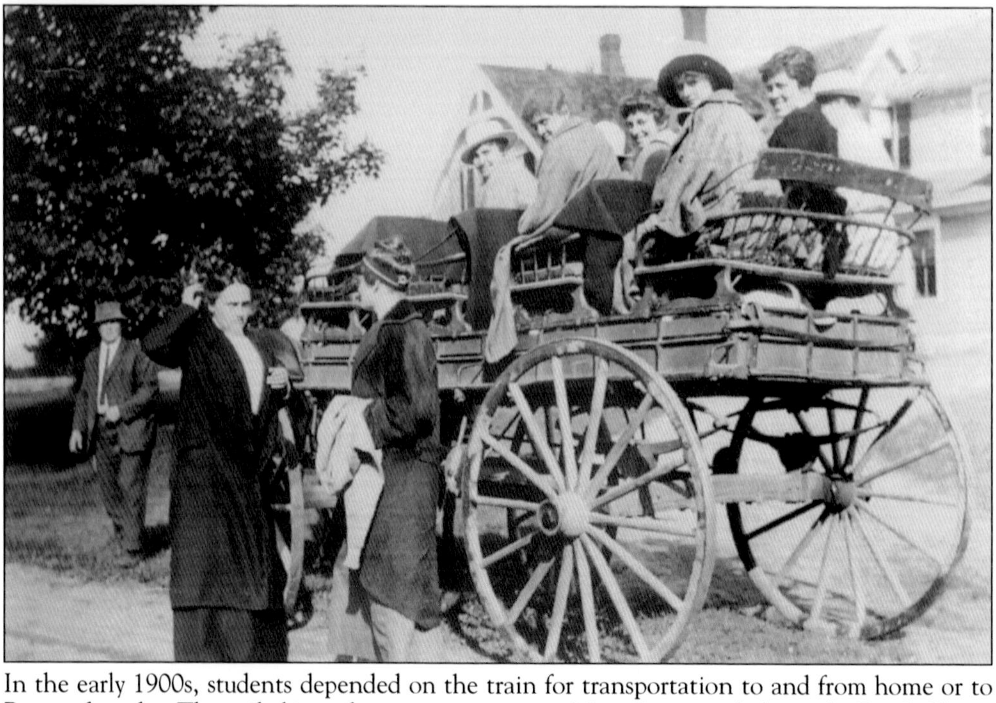

In the early 1900s, students depended on the train for transportation to and from home or to Boston for a day. They piled into the wagon waiting on Main Street and, driven by Frank Clapp, they went a mile down the road to Norton's railroad station. In later years Clapp transported the students in a Ford touring car, which held about eight or ten passengers.

Nine

The House in the Pines

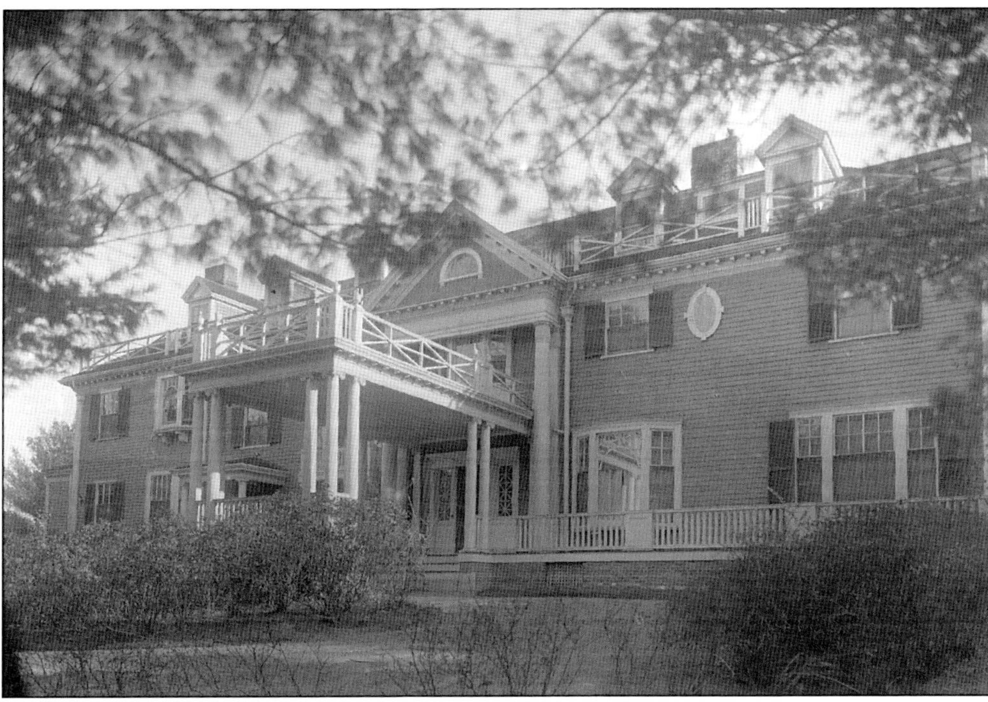

In 1911, the Wheaton Seminary Board of Trustees voted to change the school to a college. This meant the termination of Wheaton's college preparatory program. Pres. Samuel Cole envisioned the establishment of a private secondary school for girls to be situated in the big colonial house in a pine grove on Main Street. Not much is known about this house. It is believed to have been built by two spinsters who found, after a few years, that they could not afford to live in it.

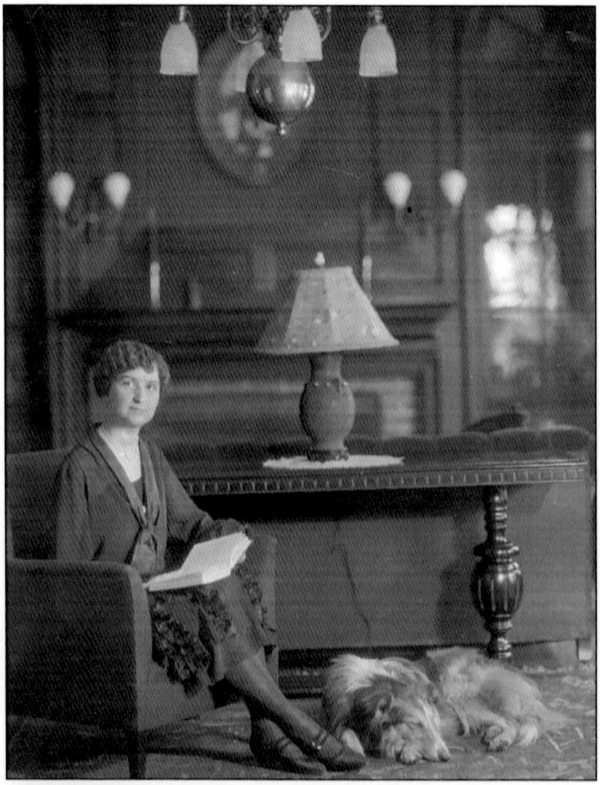

Pres. Samuel Cole contacted Gertrude Cornish, a former teacher at the seminary, suggesting that she establish a preparatory school. In the fall of 1911, Gertrude Cornish and an educational friend, Althea Hyde, opened the House in the Pines. Unlike a finishing school, it was to be a school to prepare young women for college and professions. After a few years, Althea Hyde married and Gertrude Cornish became the sole principal of the school.

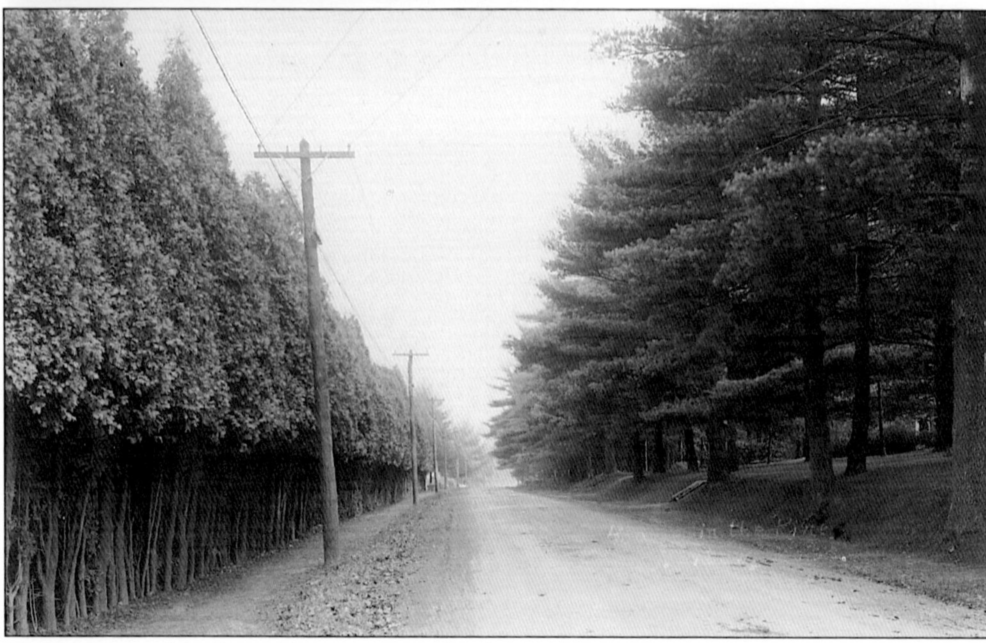

The location of the house for a private school was ideal. The main house was secluded in its extensive surroundings of pine trees along a main dirt road. Across the street was a beautiful row of arborvitae trees. Unfortunately, the Hurricane of 1938, insects, and disease took their toll on these trees.

The main house served as both dormitory and classroom until the school began to acquire surrounding property. The house had beautiful architecture; in the main entrance was a spiral staircase and a grandfather clock. When the school opened in 1911, 16 girls slept in the enclosed porches in long, warm, bunny suits with feet. The girls performed a traditional "bunny dance" down the second-floor front hall with their tin hot-water bottles, which they used to warm their beds.

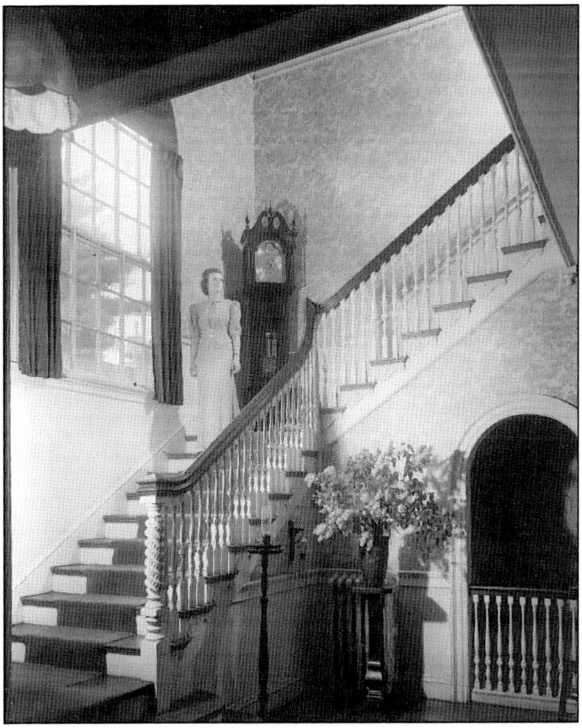

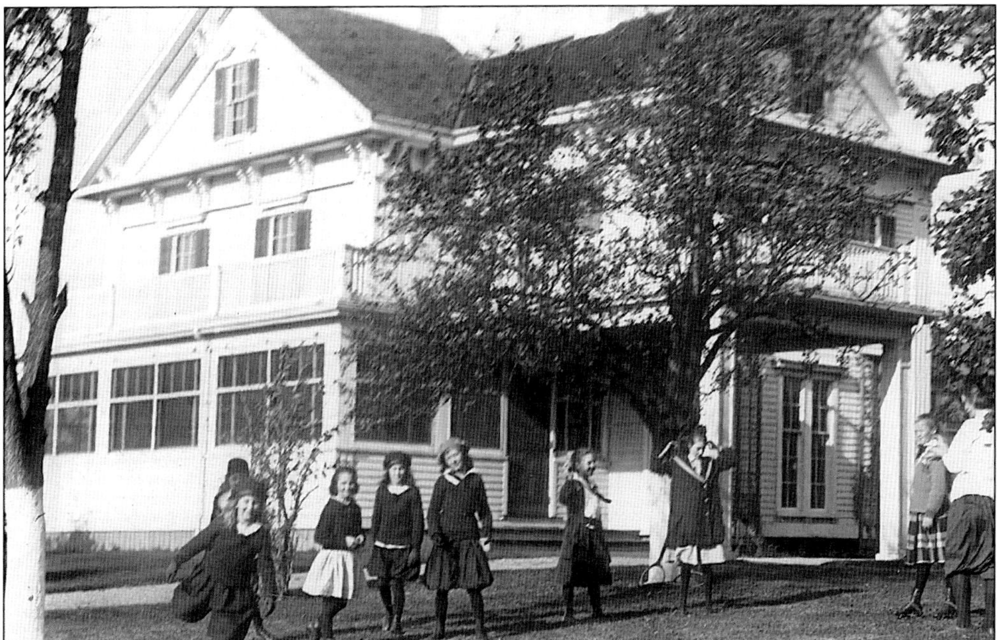

When Gertrude Cornish acquired more neighboring houses, the school developed the cottage system for dormitories. In 1919, the younger girls began living in the Hedges, named not only for the lovely row of arborvitae along the front but also because hedges means "rows of young green things growing side by side." It was hoped fine growth would take place in this new junior school.

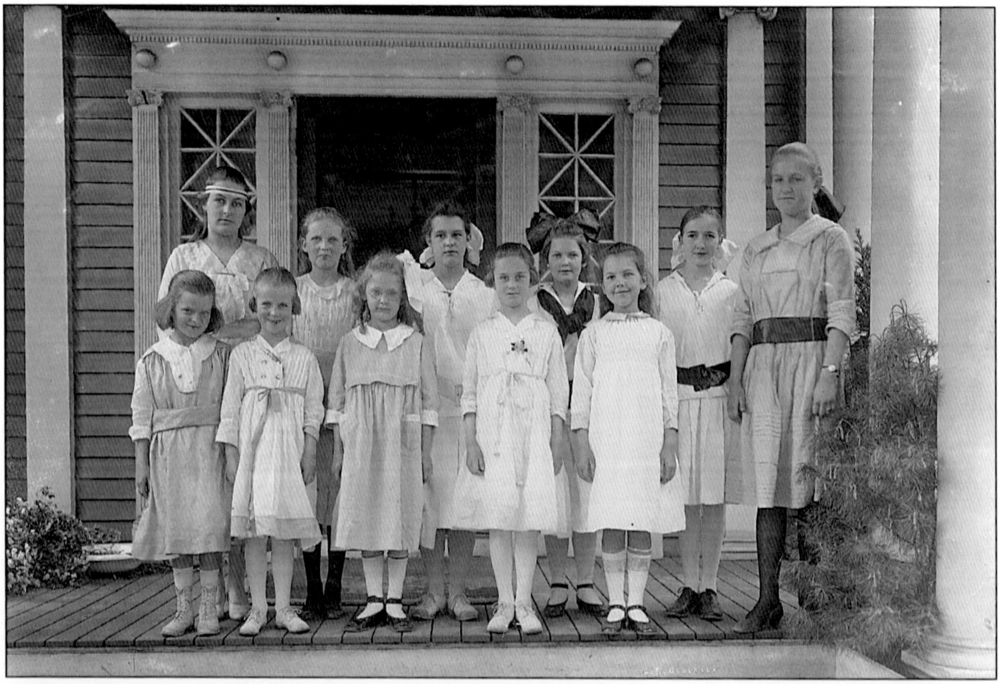

At first, the House in the Pines was a school for younger girls. Its curriculum was established for junior high and high school. In 1935, the school added a junior college program that included semester studies in Europe. This program continued until 1944, when it became more difficult to travel on the continent during World War II.

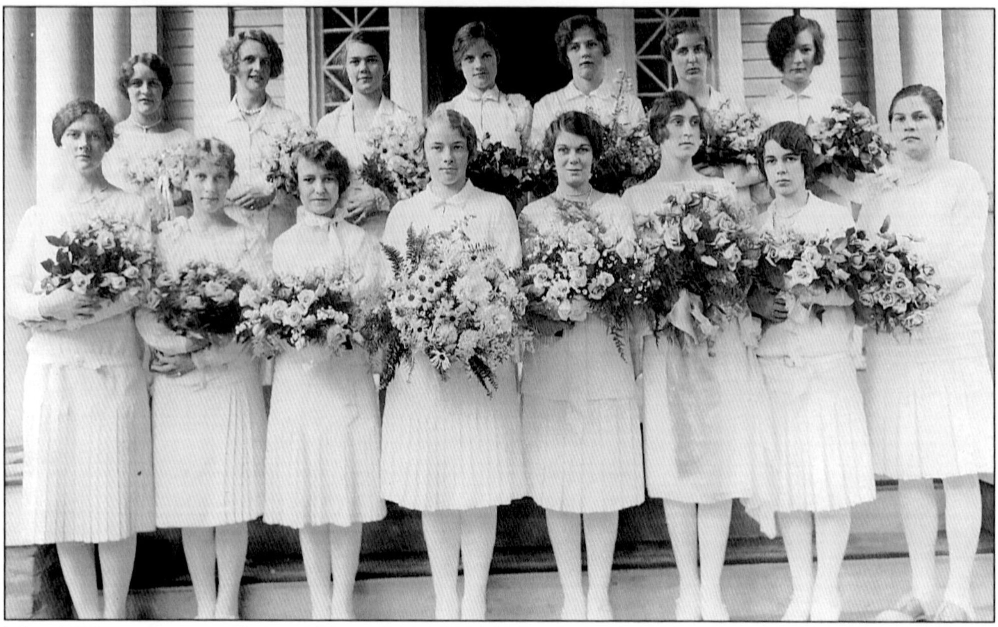

The 1927 graduating class is shown here. Enrollment was kept low enough so that the school could give each student a course of study best adapted to her individual needs. Also, the association with the principal and teachers remained personal. Resident faculty members in each cottage were present for friendly guidance.

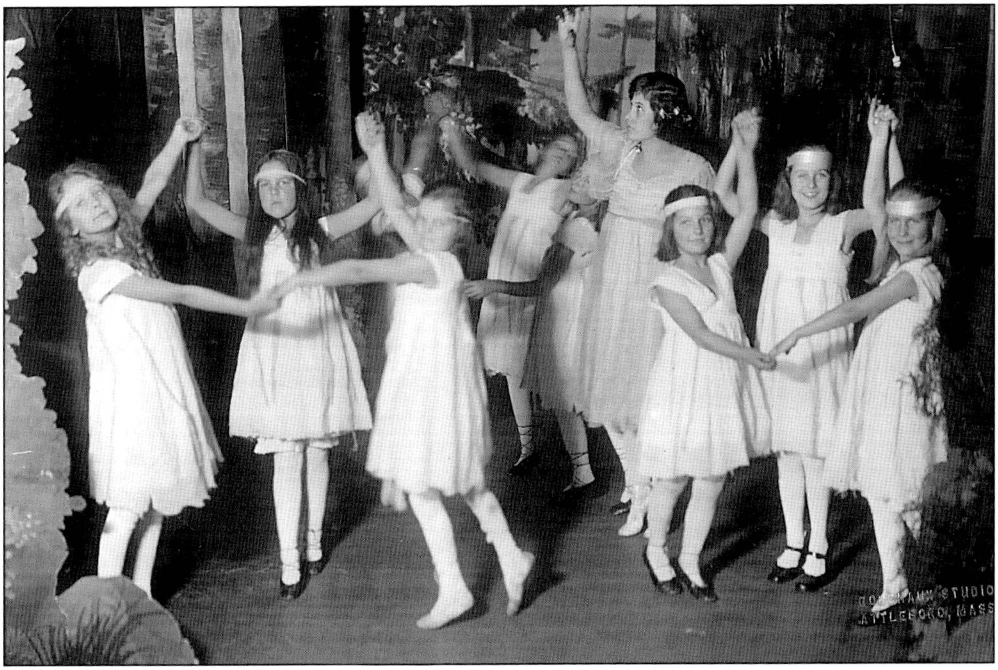

Special attention was given to literature, music, and the arts. Each month there would be pageants, plays, dance and music recitals, operettas, and songfests performed by the girls of the various cottages.

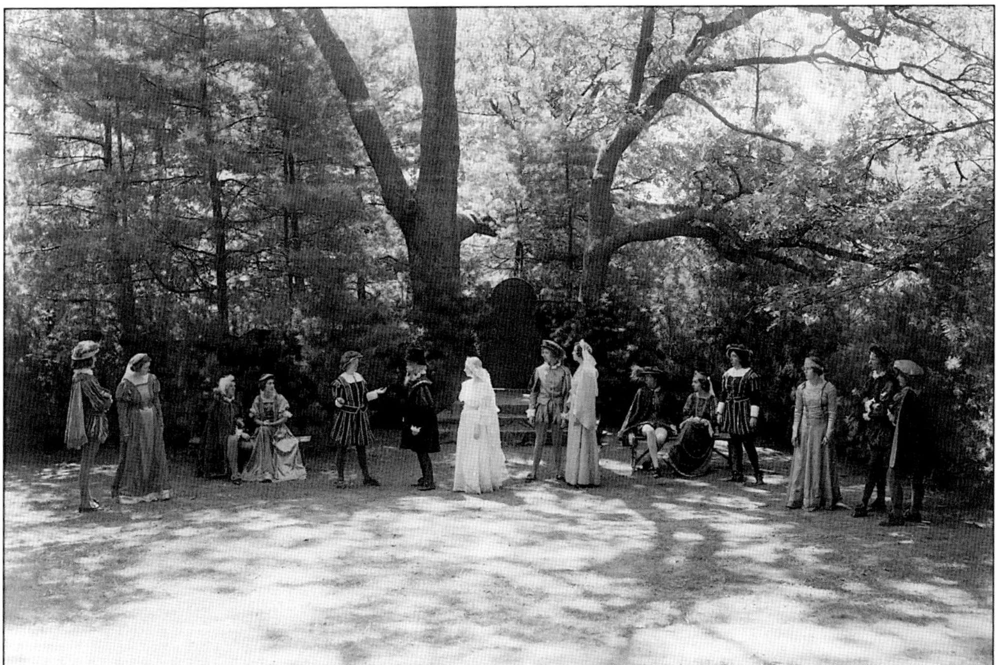

Behind the main house was the amphitheater, where each year the girls performed Shakespearean plays. The school tried to cultivate a love of the truth and beauty in literature through the study of the masters and their masterpieces.

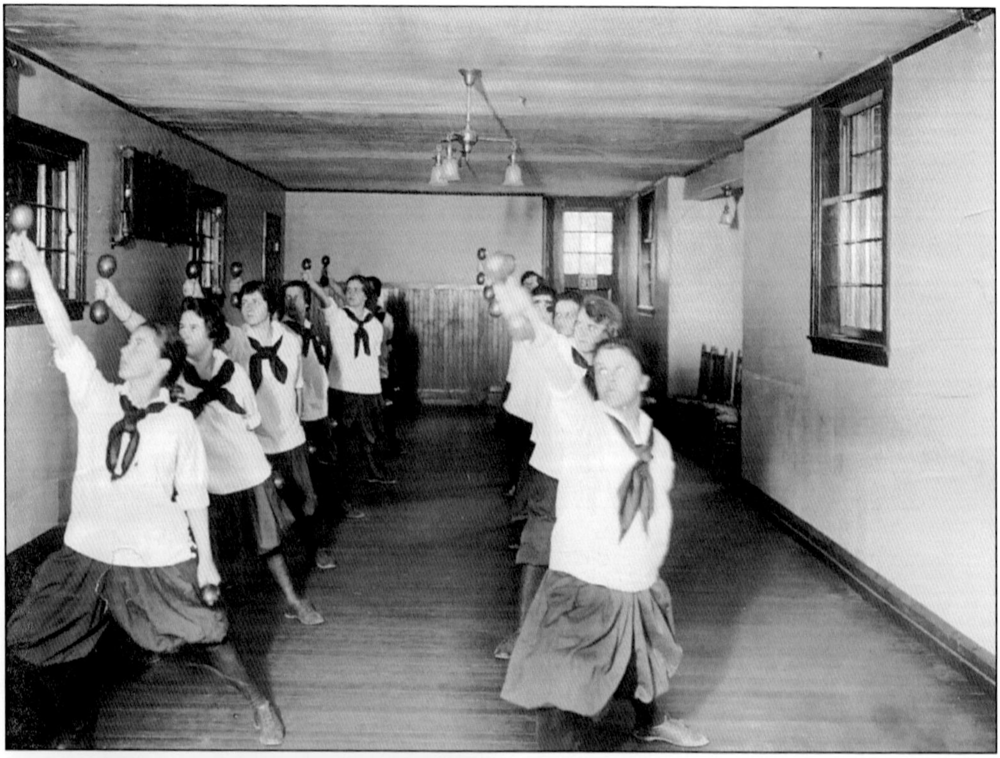

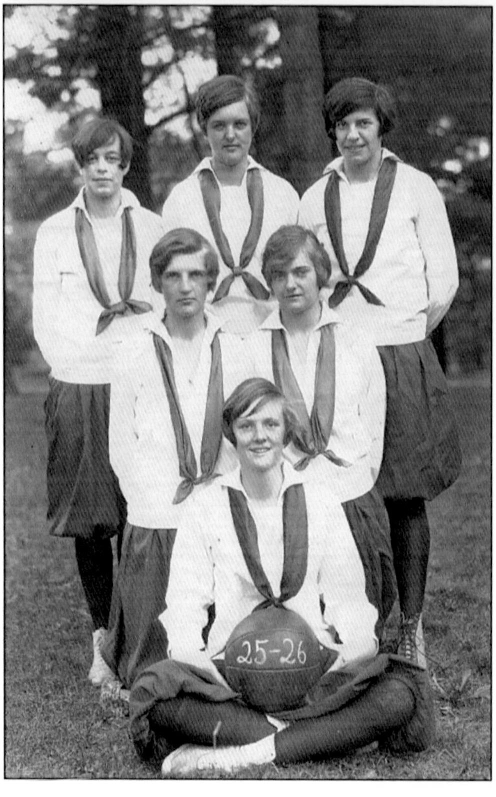

The first gym was part of the dining room of the main house. Miss Floyd taught not only mathematics and chemistry but also gym classes. She taught the girls to handle dumbbells and wands, which were the standard gym equipment of that time. During the winter, the girls used the Wheaton gym for basketball games.

Gertrude Cornish believed that recreation was a very important aspect of the school's curriculum. Two hours each afternoon was set aside for sports. Early on, the school established an athletic organization, choosing captains and teams. Each girl was a member of the Green Team or the Yellow Team. There were many tournaments and games throughout the year, with stiff competition among the teams.

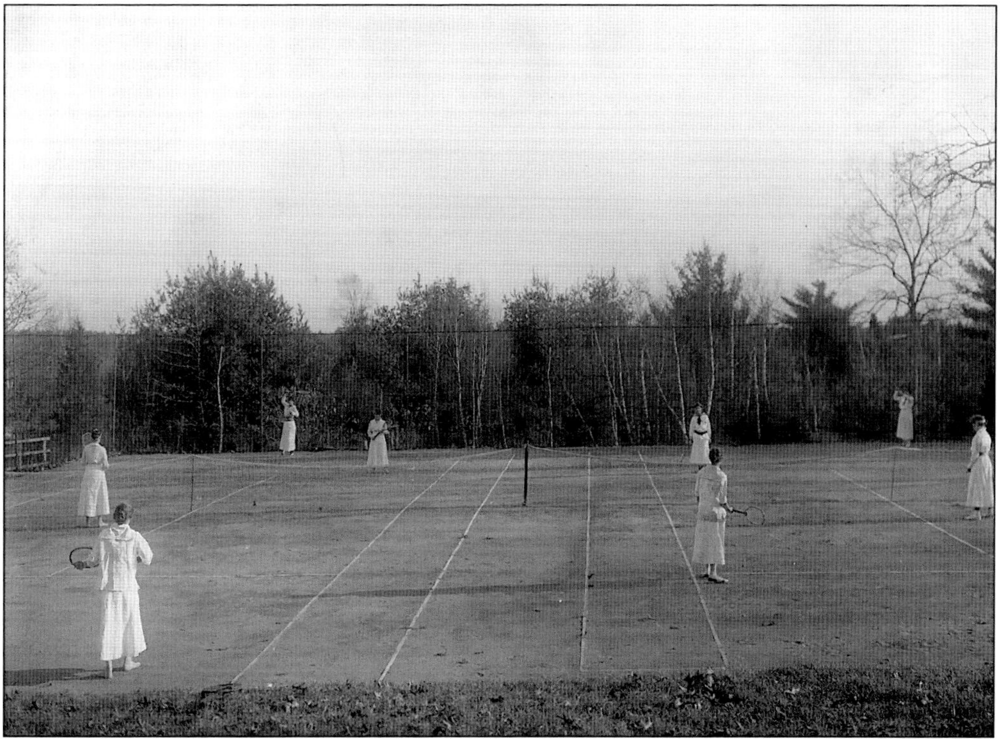

Tennis was a favorite sport at the school. At first there was a grass court; later, new tennis courts were built, and these were flooded during the winter for skating. The area was lighted so that the girls could skate during the evening. The school also had hockey fields, badminton courts, and a softball diamond. The various school teams competed not only against each other but also against the Wheaton College teams.

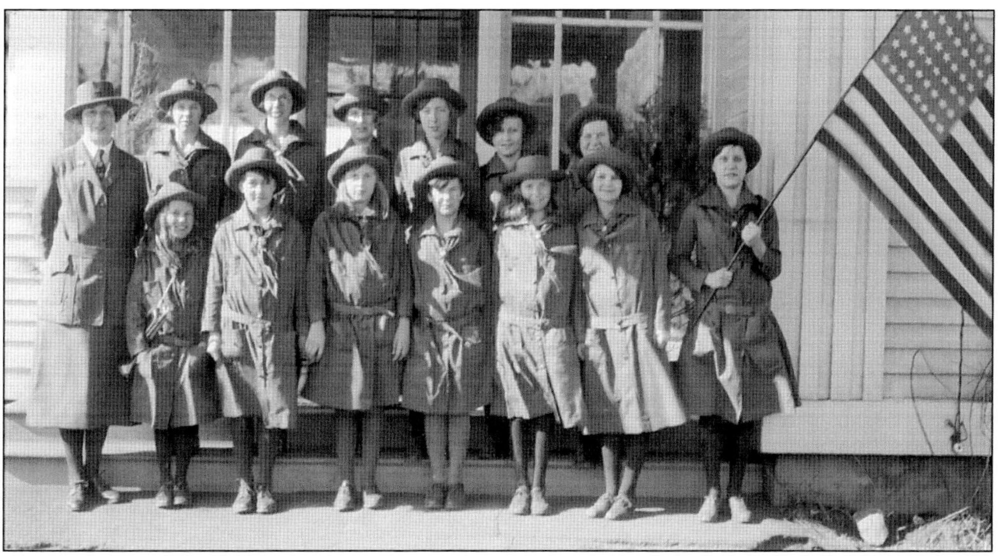

Students often participated in town activities during the holidays and celebrations. Some of them joined the school's Girl Scout troop and marched proudly in the town's Memorial Day parades. Once a year, the troop took the train to Boston to attend the Girl Scout rally.

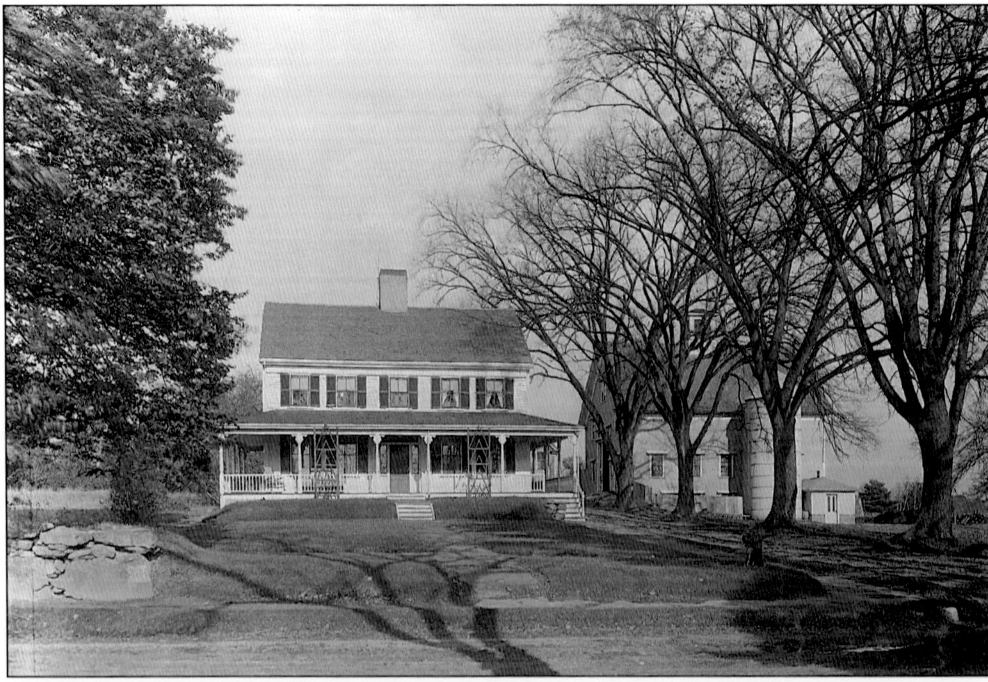

The Briggs Farm was located on Pine Street. The complex around the farmhouse included a dairy barn, a blacksmith shop, poultry houses, and stables for the school's riding horses. Myron Briggs, his wife, and two sons lived in the farmhouse. He was the superintendent of buildings for the school until his retirement in 1965.

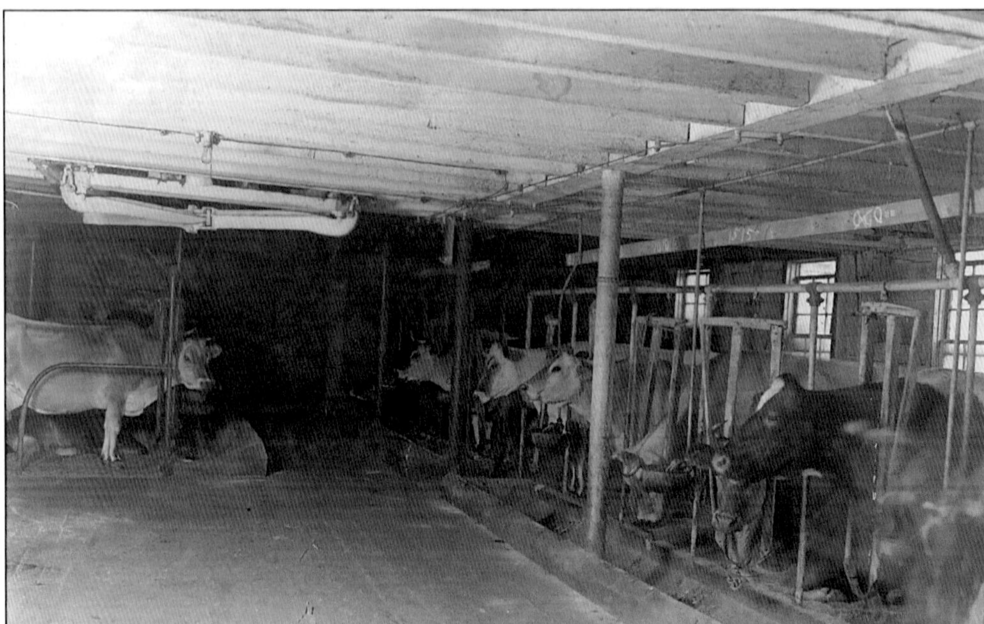

The school's dairy was known for its high-quality milk and cream. While the dairy farm was in operation, Wheaton College purchased all its milk there.

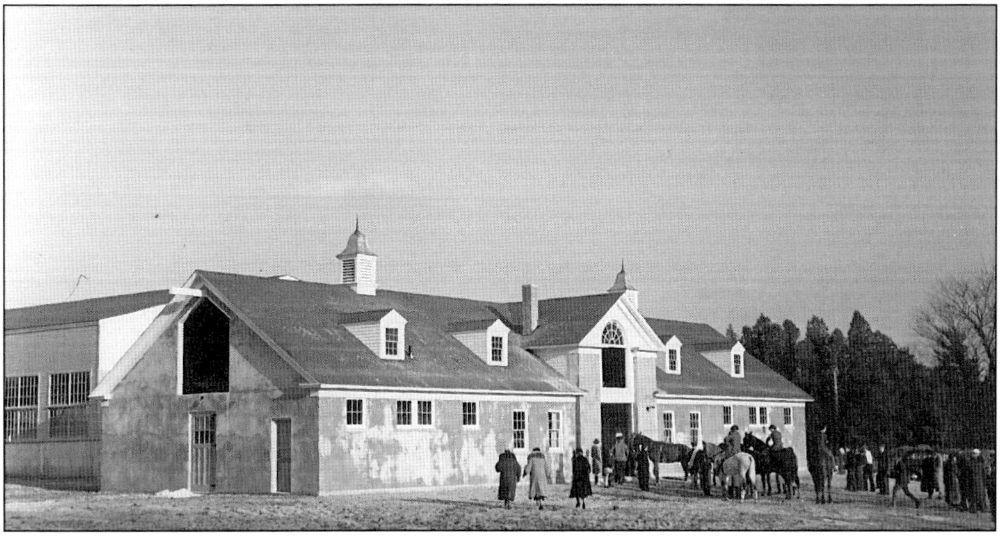

Horseback riding was a popular sport. The school's riding stable was located on Pine Street. It was a well-kept stable with an indoor ring and an outside ring. The first stable was a barn behind the farmhouse. The horse barn and 22 horses were destroyed in a mysterious fire early one morning in 1936. The fire quickly spread to other nearby barns. Remarkably, the Norton firemen were able to save the farmhouse from being destroyed.

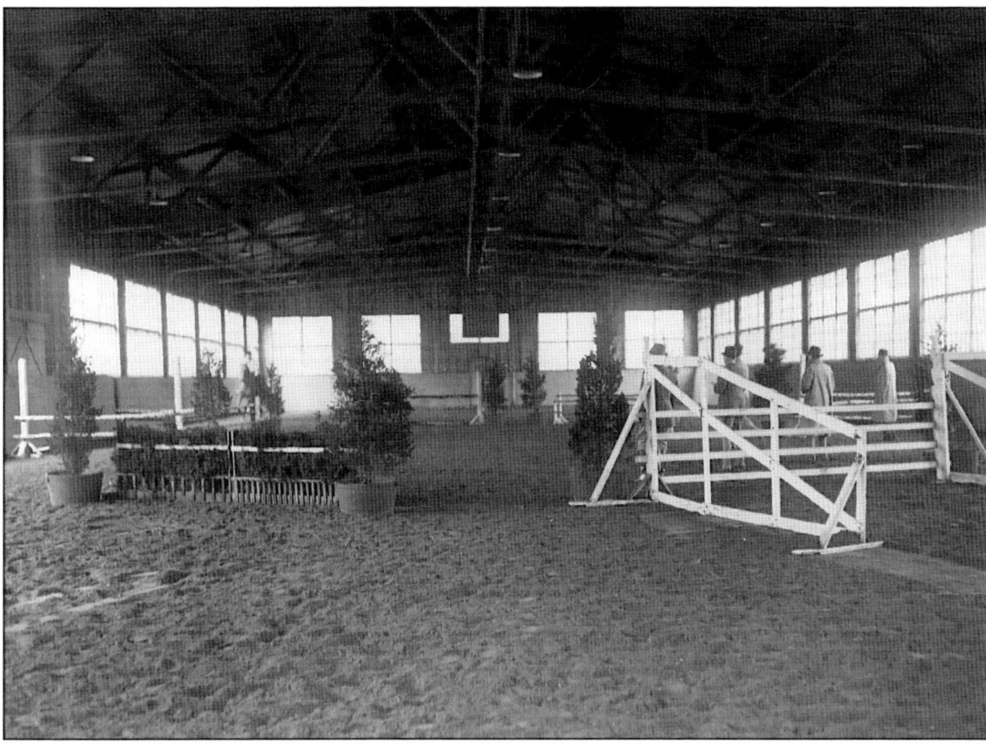

Before the new stable was built, students were unable to ride during the winter months. The indoor ring made it possible for the girls to ride throughout the year. In the winter and during inclement weather, the riders enjoyed jumping, games, and practice in form riding in this spacious indoor facility.

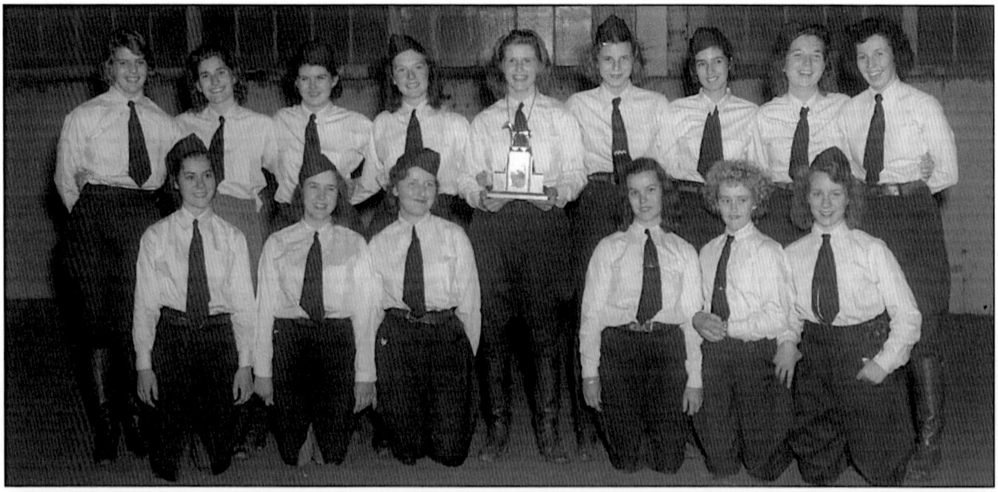

Each fall the House in the Pines riding team staged a riding meet with the Wheaton College team. The meet included form riding of different classes of both schools. The girls were judged on their mounting form, dismounting form, and horsemanship. There was fierce competition between the two schools to see who would win the cup for the Military Drill.

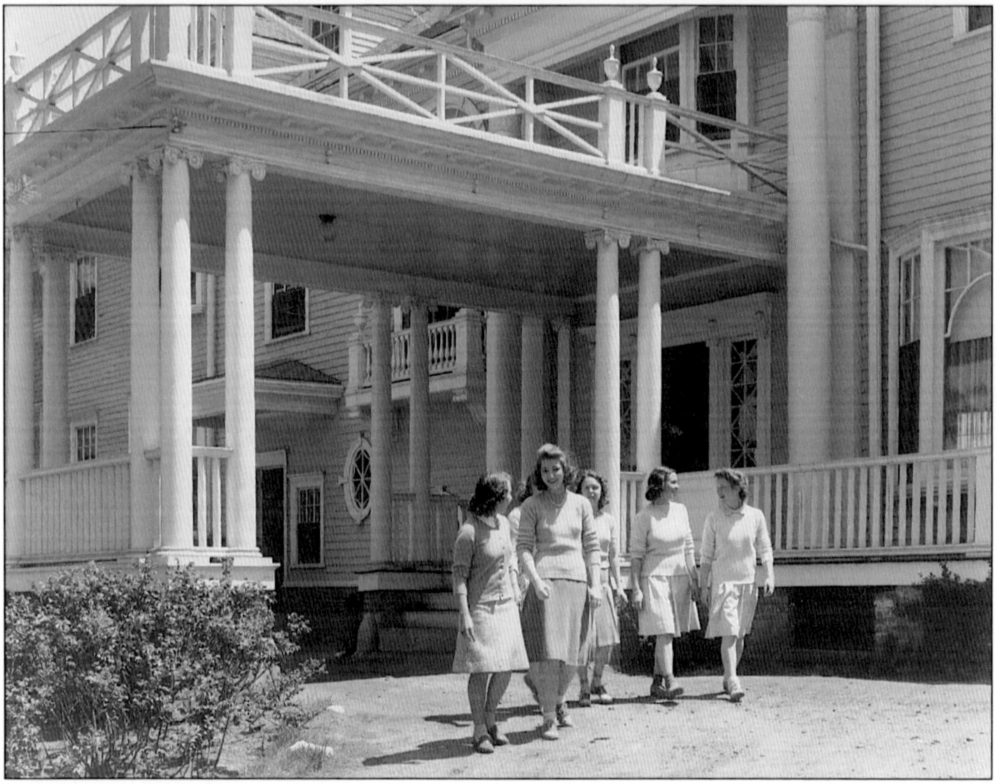

The House in the Pines closed its doors in 1972 after educating young girls for 60 years. Gertrude Cornish, now Milliken, had served as principal from 1911 to 1944. She retired but remained as president of the board of trustees until she died at age 89 in 1969. Miss Johndroe began teaching at the school in 1936 and became its headmistress in 1948. She carried on the school's principles and traditions until it closed.